Global Nation?

Australia and the Politics of Globalisation

John Wiseman

CAMBRIDGE
UNIVERSITY PRESS

PUBLISHED BY THE PRESS SYNDICATE OF THE UNIVERSITY OF CAMBRIDGE
The Pitt Building, Trumpington Street, Cambridge, United Kingdom

CAMBRIDGE UNIVERSITY PRESS
The Edinburgh Building, Cambridge CB2 2RU, UK   http://www.cup.cam.ac.uk
40 West 20th Street, New York, NY 10011–4211, USA   http://www.cup.org
10 Stamford Road, Oakleigh, Melbourne 3166, Australia

First published 1998

Printed in Australia by Brown Prior Anderson

Typeset in Adobe New Aster 9/12pt

A catalogue record for this book is available from the British Library

National Library of Australia Cataloguing in Publication data

Wiseman, John, 1957– .
Global nation?: Australia and the politics of
globalisation.

Bibliography.
Includes index.

1. Internationalism. 2. Australia – Foreign economic
relations – Social aspects. 3. Australia – Civilization –
1990– – Foreign influences. I. Title.

303.48294

ISBN 0 521 59227 5 hardback
ISBN 0 521 59755 2 paperback

For
Fay, Daniel and Jemma

Contents

Abbreviations

ABC	Australian Broadcasting Corporation
ACOSS	Australian Council of Social Service
ATSIC	Aboriginal and Torres Strait Islander Commission
ACTU	Australian Council of Trade Unions
ALP	Australian Labor Party
APEC	Asia Pacific Economic Co-operation forum
CED	Community Economic Development
EPAC	Economic Planning Advisory Commission
EU	European Union
GATT	General Agreement on Tariffs and Trade
GDP	Gross Domestic Product
END	European Nuclear Disarmament
ICJ	International Court of Justice
ILO	International Labour Organisation
ITO	International Trade Organisation
IMF	International Monetary Fund
MAI	Multilateral Agreement on Investment
MIT	Massachusetts Institute of Technology
MTIA	Metal Trades Industry Association
NAFTA	North American Free Trade Association
NATO	North Atlantic Treaty Organisation
OECD	Organisation for Economic Co-operation and Development
OPEC	Oil Producing Economic Community
UN	United Nations
UNESCO	United Nations Educational, Scientific, and Cultural Organisation
UNHCR	United Nations High Commissioner for Refugees
UNRISD	United Nations Research Institute for Social Development
WHO	World Health Organisation
WTO	World Trade Organisation

Acknowledgments

I would like to thank the following friends and colleagues who provided valuable assistance with advice and comments: Joe Camilleri, Fay Chomley, Peter Christoff, Robyn Eckersley, Martin Mowbray, Patricia Moynihan, John Murphy, Rob Watts and an anonymous reader. Phillipa McGuinness from Cambridge University Press was a constant source of encouragement and creative advice. I would also like to thank Anita Seibert and Prue Walker who worked as research assistants at various stages on this project.

Chapter 1

Introduction: Australia and the Politics of Globalisation

An Aboriginal girl in Alice Springs cradles her Pocahontas Barbie while she watches the Winter Olympics on satellite TV. Another factory closes in Newcastle because it can no longer compete with Chinese wages. Another Latrobe Valley power station is sold off to a United States energy corporation. Moody's credit-rating agency warns that Australian governments must keep cutting taxes and services – or else. Australian environmentalists and Aboriginal groups mobilise support from the European Parliament in their opposition to the opening of the Jabiluka uranium mine in the Northern Territory. A public park in Melbourne is taken over for an international car race beamed around the world. A Tasmanian mother frets about her sunburned child and the risk of skin cancer. This is Australia in an age of globalisation.

Globalisation is the most slippery, dangerous and important buzzword of the late twentieth century. It is slippery because it can have many meanings and be used in many ways. It is dangerous because too often it is used as a powerful and simplistic justification for the endless expansion of unregulated capitalist relations into every part of life in every corner of the globe. It is important because debates about globalisation can illuminate a world in which time and space have been so dramatically compressed that distant actions in one corner of the globe have rapid and significant repercussions on people and places far away.[1]

Economic, political, social, cultural and environmental relationships within and beyond Australia have become both more globalised and more fragmented. Daily life is often affected by actions taken in Indonesia, London, New York or the more amorphous world of cyberspace. Many kinds of relationships have also become faster and more complex; more flexible and more insecure. Bank and finance-sector workers find their jobs swept away by automatic tellers and electronic banking. Romances bloom and fade on the Internet without physical or visual contact. There is a pervasive sense of being more closely connected to distant people and places than ever before, yet many people also express a sense of being profoundly isolated and alone.

But globalisation is not a simple, vast, unstoppable thing. As always, there are choices to be made. Governments, corporations, communities and individuals have chosen to make certain decisions that have led us down particular paths. While there are significant differences in power over information, resources and decision making, we all retain the bounded freedom to make our own individual, social, national and transnational histories. The boundaries and conditions of this freedom are changing with ferocious speed, but globalisation is not, as it is often portrayed, an all-powerful Godzilla.

The process of transformation described as 'globalisation' is neither a panacea nor a catastrophe. The term encompasses a range of related and contradictory processes and relationships. These processes need to be demystified so that we can gain a clearer vision of the changing nature of the global arena in which conflicts arising from differences in class, gender, race and ethnicity will be played out in the twenty-first century.

The first aim of *Global Nation?*, therefore, is to provide an accessible, informative and provocative starting point for debates about the implications of globalisation for Australia. The second aim is to explore a range of existing and potential responses to the globalisation process in order to create a sense of possibility and agency in a world that tries to convince us there are no alternatives.

The academic literature on globalisation is vast, but too much of it is narrowly specialist, accessible only to a small circle of initiates. *Global Nation?* attempts to crystallise and synthesise complex debates in a way that hopefully avoids over simplification, but maintains a clear focus on the key themes and arguments. Many relevant references are included in the Bibliography for readers who wish to pursue particular themes further.

One of the central problems of much of the existing globalisation literature is the tendency for arguments to be based on sweeping generalisations and abstract theoretical assertions insufficiently connected to specific historical examples and evidence. There are still too few studies of the implications of globalisation processes grounded in detailed examinations of particular historical and geographical times and places. One further aim of this book is to make a contribution to the grounded exploration of globalisation processes in the way suggested by the United States-based anthropologist, Arjun Appadurai. In the introduction to his recent book *Modernity at Large*, which includes a series of critical reflections on the impact of globalisation on India, he comments that 'this book . . . is a site for the examination of how locality emerges in a globalizing world, of how colonial processes underwrite contemporary politics . . . of how global facts take local form'.[2]

Global Nation? is written with an unashamedly partisan political objective. My intent has been to demystify globalisation so that the implications for both winners and losers are clear and to help recreate a sense of the possibility of emancipation, cooperation and solidarity in globalised localities and nations. Because I also believe it is essential for readers to understand the full range of perspectives on this issue I have endeavoured to provide a fair but critical introduction to diverse perspectives.

While the central focus of *Global Nation?* is on the Australian experience of globalisation, a wide range of current Australian and international examples are used to illustrate and enliven material that by its nature tends to be abstract and complex. Hopefully, this also allows the arguments presented here to be of broad interest and relevance beyond the Australian context. The dilemmas of globalisation are inherently shared across national boundaries and many of the concerns and issues facing Australia are common to individuals and communities in other national settings.

The first section of the book is concerned with explaining the nature of globalisation processes and their implications for Australia. The intent is to provide an accessible introduction to these issues by locating the Australian experience in the broader historical and theoretical context of globalisation processes. In an attempt to facilitate understanding of the abstract forms of analysis and argument involved I have also included, in the second half of this introduction, a short fictional account of the personal experiences of globalisation. This narrative attempts to 'bring to life' the relationships of globalisation through a child's encounter with the webs of globalised relationships that directly and indirectly connect her life with those of distant workers, managers and consumers around the world.

Chapter 2 provides a more systematic critical overview of diverse attempts to understand, define and respond to globalisation processes. If the reader is looking for a brief introduction to key debates about globalisation this might be a good place to start.

In chapters 3 and 4 the economic dimensions of globalisation are explored, first on a global scale and then through a closer examination of changing economic conditions and policy responses in Australia. Chapter 5 focuses on social outcomes and social implications, including debates about the extent to which globalisation has improved or worsened poverty and inequality. Chapter 6 provides an introduction to the relationship between globalisation, media and information technology. Chapter 7 is concerned with the globalisation of environmental relationships and policies, while chapter 8 provides a discussion of the increasingly complex relationships between the role of the state and the transformation of national identities in a globalised world.

The final two chapters explore a range of ideas, suggestions and examples about alternative responses to globalisation at global, regional, national and local levels. After all, as a previous commentator on the political economy of globalising capitalism, Karl Marx, once noted, understanding the world is all very well but the real point is to change it.

Two events with significant long-term implications dominated Australian political debate in the first half of 1998. The waterfront dispute began with a secret attempt by some employers to train potential strike-breaking dock workers in Dubai. In April, 1400 members of the Maritime Union of Australia (MUA) were sacked by Patrick Stevedores. The struggle escalated rapidly, with thousands of citizens joining MUA members on picket lines around the country and unionists from all over the world pledging their support and solidarity. A protracted legal battle ended with the High Court of Australia supporting the interim reinstatement of the union workforce.

In Indonesia another drama unfolded as vast demonstrations threatened the position of President Suharto. This crisis was brought to a head by the actions of the International Monetary Fund (IMF), which forced the Indonesian Government to implement harsh economic and social policies as a precondition of 'rescue' from financial meltdown. In Australia the value of the dollar continued to fall as international money markets judged the Australian currency and economy to be too closely bound up with the economic and political fortunes of Indonesia in particular and Asia in general.

These two unfolding struggles powerfully illustrate the dangers and possibilities of the shifting relationships of globalisation as well as the dilemmas and challenges faced by Australians living in a 'global nation'.

Barbie in Borderless Worlds?
A Case Study

In a train that rattles and swings up out of the underground a little girl stares out the window at the glittering towers and cries to her mother, 'We're here, we're here!'.

Emma is overwhelmed with excitement. She twists her red hair-ribbons between her fingers and leans with fondness and pleasure into the curve of her mother's body. Everything about today is special and wonderful. This is a school day, but she isn't at school. It's not Christmas or her birthday, but she is going to the city to buy a present – a doll – a Barbie doll. And, best of all, she is with her mother. Just the two of them together, for a whole day, in the city, buying a Barbie.

Emma's mother, Tess, feels the warmth and pleasure of her daughter beside her and smiles. It has been so long since she has had time like this. Since David lost his job. Since she started work at DataFlow. Since Grandma came to live with them. There has been so little time and so little money and she has been so tired. She is still tired, but at least this is one small day and she can manage one small treat. If Emma wants a Barbie then a Barbie she shall have.

'What sort of Barbie do you want?' she asks.

Emma hesitates. This is a big decision. 'I think I want Gymnast Barbie,' she says slowly. 'I saw her on TV. On *Cartoon Connection*. You can twist her all different ways. I'd like to be a gymnast. Or a dancer. Like in the Olympics with those long ribbons.'

Tess cuddles her sturdy, red-haired, freckled girl and tries to imagine her as one of the skeletal nymphs pattering along the Olympic balancing beam.

'Or maybe Esmerelda Barbie, like in the *Hunchback* video. Or a wedding Barbie like Suzie's got.' Emma's voice trails off as she wonders how far she can push. 'Mum?'

'Yes, love?'

'You know that new girl at school, from America? She's got a boat for Barbie, and a pink car and a pony. Could I have a pony too?'

Tess explains that a pony is not possible and thinks of her conversation with Suzie's mother at the school picnic. A global soccer mum she called herself. Every year a different country as Suzie's dad moves on from one dazzling promotion to another. Something in banking or insurance. And money, lots of money.

Money. Always the money. If David still worked there would be more money. She remembers the day, hot and unpleasant with the smell of north wind, ash and dust in the air. It was just after Christmas and David came in with the mail, looking lost and confused. He held out the letter.

> We regret to inform you that, due to our need to maintain a
> competitive position in our export markets the company has
> decided to transfer the operations of our Melbourne plant to
> Indonesia.
>
> All employees will receive a generous redundancy package
> of two weeks' pay for each year of service.
>
> As a gesture of goodwill the company has also contracted a
> firm of out-placement consultants to be available should you
> need any advice about your future career options. Please contact
> the Human Resources Division if you would like more details.
>
> The company directors sincerely regret the need for this
> decision, but we do assure you that there was no viable
> alternative course of action.

'Bastards,' he croaked. 'The fucking ferrets couldn't even tell us to our
face before Christmas. Give us a Christmas party and lollies for the kids
and then post us their real present.' He stopped and turned to Tess. 'So how
long will seven years times eight hundred dollars last us?'

Not long. Not long at all.

The train pulls into the station. There seem to be two sorts of people
getting off. There are the suits who stride off with confident purpose,
knowing there is a tower, an office and a job waiting for them. And there
are others who move more slowly. Over there a haggard young woman with
four toddlers struggling to get two pushers out the door. She gratefully
accepts Tess's help.

'They're not all mine you know,' she explains. 'I'm looking after them.
For friends.' Tess nods and the woman battles off up the ramp.

On the platform three teenage boys lounge on the railway-green seats
trying to look arrogant and sullen. Bored and afraid is how they really look
she decides.

'Come on, Mum.' Emma tugs at her sleeve, anxious to get started on the
shopping.

Stupid to come into town thinks Tess. But when they went to their
favourite local toy shop the closing-down sale was almost over. Just a few
old packets of Lego and some jigsaw puzzles with broken boxes. 'Just
couldn't compete,' the man explained. 'Not with the big places. They've
got so much stuff they can always undercut you. They can bury you in
advertising. And then they get these teenagers to work for them. Hardly
older than this little girl. Here you are, love, would you like this?' The man
gives Emma a little stuffed puppy and she looks at her mother to see if it's
alright. Tess nods.

They could have gone to the mall except now they've sold the car it's
easier to get the train into the city than across the suburbs.

'Okay, Emma. Let's see if we can find this Barbie for you.'

It's not much. Probably entirely the wrong thing. But whenever Tess asks Emma what she wants most of all she says she wants a Barbie, so here they are. And Tess wants to do something. Something to make up for all the late nights and weekends working and telling her to go away and find something to do. For the little girl's frightened face as her tired mother yells, 'And stop that noise. I can't think with all this racket.'

Of course, she should be thankful she has the job. Grateful for the endless hours of work. Data entry doesn't pay much and you never know from week to week what the hours will be. And it seems completely meaningless. Keying in an endless stream of figures for some insurance company in Brisbane – or New York or Tokyo, for all she knows. But there seems to be lots of work. Lots and lots. It just keeps increasing. The boss says they have to get the rates up. More productivity: more hours, same money. It's the competition, he says. From the Philippines or Indonesia or somewhere like that. It shits her. But what can you do?

Emma and Tess stand open-mouthed in front of the Barbie shelves. It's as though all the pink plastic and shimmering nylon and fake silver jewels in the world have been brought together in this one place. 'Look! That one's like Supriya's mum,' Emma shouts, pointing at an Indian Barbie in a sari. 'And there's a black one and a Chinese one.' She runs to the other end of the shelves. 'Here's the car like Suzy has and the pony with a little trailer. Mum its *so* cool!'

Tess wanders along the rows, torn between pleasure at her daughter's excitement and suspicion of what this impossible plastic dream-woman suggests to little girls. She remembers her own Barbie. She remembers loving it and dressing it. Marrying it to Ken in an outdoor ceremony behind the garage. Cutting its blonde hair off in revenge when her own hair turned red and curly. And staring into the mirror and deciding her own stocky, thick-wasted figure would never replicate Barbie's pink-lipsticked glamour.

Emma holds up Gymnast Barbie – blonde, spangled and twirling. The doll has the same fixed, perfect smile she has seen on the Olympic gymnasts on TV and on all the Gymnast Barbie advertisements that accompanied them. Gymnast Barbie is definitely her choice.

As she finishes the day's second big treat, chips and Coke at McDonald's, Emma turns the doll over in her hands. 'Mummy,' she asks, 'who makes my toys?'

In another city, far away, a young Chinese woman hunches over a bowl of noodles in the canteen of a vast toy factory. She has only a few minutes left before she must return to her job of twisting white gymnast slippers and dancing shoes onto tiny doll's feet. She shivers at the thought of trying to sleep in her bleak concrete room tonight. She will wake tired and worn and will wash in a trickle of cold water. She will gulp a bowl of grey rice and gather her strength for another long day at the factory. At the end of the week she will stuff a few torn notes into an envelope and send them home to her parents in the village in the mountains. There will not be much.

Across the Pacific on the border between Mexico and California another young woman shivers, but this time from fear as much as cold. She is fleeing the Maquiladoras – the free-trade zone. She huddles in the moonlight shadows of a twisted old pine as she waits to make the dash to the fence. With the others she will chop at the base with the cutters and hurl herself underneath where the truck will be waiting. Or perhaps there will be no truck. Perhaps the Yanquis will be there with the torches and handcuffs to arrest her or send her back.

And the hard men have warned her. You talk about unions in the Maquiladoras; there will be trouble. But how can she not? How can she not when she has seen her friends beaten for taking a piece of bread from the factory canteen; seen their children swollen with dysentery? There is no hope here and there just might be some hope across the border. If she can get there tonight.

Far to the north in Alaska another woman cries out in impatience and annoyance. They have spent so much money moving up here to the far green forests and the clear bright sky. A clean place for the children to grow up, away from the choking air and frightening streets of Los Angeles. And they have spent so much money on a state-of-the-art communication system so that their designs can be faxed and Emailed instantaneously to Mattel or Disney or Fisher Price or any other toy company that wants to contract Elf Inc., the sharpest toy-concept designers on the planet. They have such a tight deadline for the CyberDoll and so much money and status at stake. Now this one storm – taking out all their powerlines and cables – could put them way behind the competition. Shane was right, they should have got that satellite dish. How could she be so stupid?

Over the Atlantic the weather is clear and the air-to-ground phone system in Business Class is working fine. Leo Carlyle, the youngest director of the largest advertising firm in Europe, flicks through sketches for the marketing campaign for the CyberDoll as he waits for his financial adviser in Switzerland to come on the line. The campaign looks great, although there will have to be some changes. He makes a note to tell the design people to come up with some lines that will work as well in India and Turkey as these ones will in New York and Sydney. Won't they ever learn that global marketing means local markets?

'Leo? You there mate?'

Leo can never get used to the idea of a Swiss banker with an Australian accent. Steve's good though. Used to be some sort of Treasury official in Canberra. Even worked for a Labor government, he says. 'About those Brazilian timber futures, Steve. Can we get out of them? My Mum's giving me hell since she saw Sting's show about the Amazon and the rainforests and all that crap. Got anything else going?'

'How about a uranium mine on the Barrier Reef?' Steve suggests. 'Just kidding!' He brays like a donkey at the joke. Leo curses. Maybe the cultural gap is wider than he thought.

Emma is tired when she gets home. She would love to just cuddle up on the couch with her mother and play with her doll. But Tess is working tonight. The price she has to pay for taking the day off. Emma's Dad, Dave, is driving taxis again so Emma is to be picked up by Dave's sister Jessie for the evening. Which is okay, because Jessie's place is FUN. Jessie lives in an old inner-city factory that used to make socks and stockings. Now it's been painted yellow and purple and divided into little apartments with strange angles and weird furniture.

Jessie's apartment is right at the top and has a view of the city lights and the planes coming in to land. Jessie tells Emma that she needs to see the planes, so she can feel that she can escape when she needs to. But more and more Jessie escapes down the wire, through her screens and cables and keyboards and modems. Jessie designs web sites for a living and staying over here usually means chatting with other kids around the world on one of the children's news groups that Jessie has set up for her. There's this one ace kid in Finland who has a reindeer for a pet. Emma promised she would send her a photo of herself with a kangaroo. Next time her mother has time to take her to the zoo.

Jessie makes complimentary noises about the new Barbie, even though Emma suspects she doesn't really mean it.

'Do you know how old Barbie is? Or where she comes from?' asks Jessie. 'Maybe we could find out. Let's see.'

For an hour Emma sits happily on Jessie's knee while they explore the worldwide web of Barbie. They see pictures of little girls with their first Barbie. Collectors with thousands of dolls, each in her own glass case. Pages of information about Barbie and Mattel which describe Barbie's 'birth' in a Californian garage in 1959 and how she was inspired by a German doll and cartoon character. They cruise the Mattel site with its catalogues, price lists, order forms and the information that worldwide Barbie sales generate more than $1 billion. Then they find the Barbie artists. The Barbie icon transformed into thousands of images of playfulness and subversion. Some which Jessie has to censor quickly. Some that have already been censored by corporate legal watchdogs ready to deal with those who would dare to mock their product or undermine Barbie's global good name.

The corporate challenge to free speech in the supposedly democratic world of cyberspace reminds Jessie of McDonald's legal assault on criticism of that company's environmental and labour standards. With Emma asleep on her knee she follows the links through the sites organising protests against McDonald's and other transnational companies. The attempt to build a global boycott against Nike because of the working conditions in its franchise factories in Indonesia. The campaigns against child labour used to make carpets, clothes and soccer balls. The pages linking maritime unions around the world as they attempt to build an alliance to stop Australian soldiers being trained as stevedores in Dubai so they can act as strike breakers in Australian ports.

Jessie convinces herself that her net surfing is really work. After all, only last night she was out celebrating her first big break. A large consultancy setting up an Internet system for environmental organisations all over Asia. Web pages, chat groups, even a specialised search engine. Fantastic. Except for that jerk at the pub who said it was all a waste of money and you couldn't stop real bulldozers with virtual pickets. Well, of course. Obviously you need real people in real local places, too. Why couldn't people see you had to work at all levels if you were to have any chance against the big players with their global ad agencies and their rich-and-famous lifestyles?

Jessie stares out the window. The light from the neon sign across the street flashes and sparkles in the dark rain. She used to love this flat, but now she has to put up with this. A World of Entertainment. Crown Casino. Flash on. Flash off. Flash on.

She turns back to the screen. From Nike to sports and back to games and toys and Barbie and the little girl asleep in her aunt's arms, dreaming of vast flocks of Barbie dolls soaring above the earth, wrapping the planet in ribbons and streamers of red and blue, like the Olympics, on TV, in her head, in her dreams.

Chapter 2

Breaking the Spell?
Understanding Globalisation

Globalisation is a word suitable for a world without illusions, but it is also one that robs us of hope . . . Many over-enthusiastic analysts and politicians have gone beyond the evidence in over stating both the extent of the dominance of world markets and their ungovernability. If this is so, then we should seek to break the spell of this uncomforting myth.
Paul Hirst and Greg Thompson[1]

The argument that globalisation is certainly inevitable and probably desirable has become dominant among many of the most powerful players in Australian political life over the last ten years. In 1995, for example, the conference proceedings of the Commonwealth Government National Strategies Conference argued that,

on globalisation, nowhere was there a 'Little Australia' perspective. The force and inevitability of continued internationalisation was recognised and accepted from all quarters as was the potential for deriving major benefit from pursuing a global orientation for the country's affairs. What is now recognised as unavoidable, has also become a strongly shared objective, that is, for Australia to develop fully as a global nation to achieve its national goals.[2]

In the Cabinet rooms of Australian governments, the boardrooms of Australian corporations or the meeting rooms of Australian trade unions, similar language and assumptions can be heard over and over again. Often the claims made are surprisingly simple. We might hear that globalisation is basically about economic openness and competitiveness. We would certainly be told that it is inevitable and desirable.

But, if we listen carefully we might also hear some important differences. At corporate boardroom tables the emphasis would be on global competition between firms rather than between industries or nations. There would be much talk about lowering costs and maximising global sales. There would also be considerable support for minimising national regulations and maximising opportunities for corporations to shift investments and productions from place to place with as few restrictions as possible. Here can be found the true champions of borderless nations and unfettered globalisation.

In the more cramped offices of many small manufacturers and retailers there might well be much uncertainty. Perhaps some aggressive rhetoric about the need for competitiveness and small government combined with an underlying anxiety about bankruptcies, unemployment and the dangers of removing the last trade barriers with low-wage competitor countries.

Around the Cabinet tables of Liberal governments globalisation and competitiveness would certainly be key words. Australia's Foreign Minister, Alexander Downer, has, for example, informed us that,

> whether we like it or not, we are part of an international com-
> munity which is becoming increasingly global. As the economic
> and social map takes shape for the next century, we all fall into
> one of two camps. You are either a globaphobe or a globaphile.
> This is the great political dichotomy of our age, as fundamental
> as the old conflict between capital and labor [*sic*]. But whether
> people fear globalisation or not they cannot escape it.[3]

Governments, however, are still elected by voters in particular geo-graphical areas. So there is a need to temper the focus on global competitive-ness at all costs with attempts to ensure that the benefits of competition flow to people living in the areas covered by that government. The key question therefore becomes: how can the global game be won at the level of particular nations, sub-national regions, electorates or local government areas?

At the tables of Labor governments or the Australian Council of Trade Unions (ACTU) there might be more concern about the social impact of globalisation and competitiveness. One senior ACTU official recently argued, without apparent irony, that

> [l]ike Don salami globalisation is good. I like pizza and curries
> and all of those things that internationalism brings. The quality
> of life that we have in this country, the range of things that we can
> purchase reflects increased international integration, globalisa-

tion and our shrinking world. Who wants to emulate Albania or North Korea? The ACTU supports an open Australia integrated with our region and the world.[4]

But the constituencies of social democratic parties and trade unions are still supposed to include low-wage workers, the vulnerable and the disadvantaged. Yes, the voices might say, we must compete, but perhaps not at any cost. Is there such a thing as 'globalisation with a human face'?

There are other voices more critical of the dominant language and politics of globalisation and competitiveness. These include many unionists, community activists, small businesspeople, environmentalists, conservatives, socialists and concerned citizens from a wide variety of philosophical starting points who wish to question the prevailing logic of globalisation in a far more fundamental way.

The proliferation of theoretical literature on globalisation has created a vast array of competing understandings about the nature and impact of globalisation. These reflect differing assumptions about the scope, impact and inevitability of global integration and about the extent to which this has undermined the autonomy and sovereignty of national states and civil societies. The purpose of this chapter is to develop a clear picture of the merits of opposing perspectives about the nature of various dimensions of globalised relationships and an overview of the implications of differing political responses. This chapter therefore serves as an introductory overview for the more detailed treatment of key issues and arguments in subsequent chapters.

What is Globalisation?

Globalisation is what happens when you lose your job in Brunswick, Bankstown or Elizabeth because the company for which you work has been bought out by the Australian subsidiary of a Dallas-based transnational company that has decided to relocate its production of T-shirts to Mexico because of cheaper wage costs and lower health and safety standards. It is what happens when you finally get a new job in Brisbane under a new employment contract that lowers your wages and conditions and your boss explains that this is essential to compete with Mexican, or Indonesian, or Chinese, workers. It is what happens when your sister is sacked from her hospital job because of budget cuts by a State Government that defends its actions by saying it must meet the demands of international credit-rating agencies for balanced budgets and lower taxes. And it is what happens when you get skin cancer because of the hole in the ozone layer created by chemicals released by refrigerators and aerosol cans all over the world.

But globalisation is also what happens when you use the computer at your local library to connect to the Internet and find pages of information from unions and community organisations in England, Mexico or Indonesia, which are trying to link up with workers around the world to stop the driving down of wages and the repression of trade-union activists. Globalisation is what happens when young London musicians of English, Caribbean and Indian descent begin to create new cross-rhythms of black reggae, white trance and Hindi rap. Globalisation describes the moment when thousands of women from all over the world come together in Beijing to affirm the solidarity of the women's movement. And globalisation is also what happens when a child sees photographs of this planet taken from space and realises that the Earth is indeed finite.

Social theorists such as Anthony Giddens, Tony McGrew and David Harvey have argued that globalisation is the best word we currently have for describing the many ways in which space and time have been compressed by technology, information flows, trade and power so that distant actions have local effects.[5] This 'action at a distance' varies in its nature and effects in different locales and is subject to challenge from some sections of the state, as well as from non-government organisations and social movements. In this sense the processes of globalisation are helping to create a world of 'nested locales' in which households, neighbourhoods, cities, provinces, nations and regions sit inside the wider global relationships like Russian Babushka dolls.[6]

Other globalisation theorists, such as Roland Robertson and Ajun Appadurai, have also emphasised the ways in which the language of globalisation captures the increasingly widespread *conscious* or 'reflexive' awareness of the interdependence of local ecologies, economies and societies.[7] Globetrotting business executives, international environmental activists, tourists, migrants, refugees and Net surfers have all had to learn different ways of relating across political and cultural borders.

Globalisation is Not All New

Globalisation is far from a completely new process. Exploration, trade, pilgrimage and migration have led individuals and societies to move around the world since the beginning of human history.[8] Information has been carried across distance by word of mouth, talking drums, semaphore or printed pages. The search for new trade routes, resources, markets and sources of cheap labour was the driving force behind the sixteenth-century explosion of European exploration and colonisation. The late nineteenth and early twentieth centuries saw a particularly high level of international trade flows, as well as the initial impact of electronic communication technologies such as the telegraph and telephone.

Invasion and conquest also have a long, inglorious history and the stories of the indigenous and conquered peoples of the world provide ample evidence of the destructive impact of global military ambitions, economic exploitation and cultural genocide. On the other hand, the tenacity shown by many indigenous peoples struggling to sustain their cultural and social relations also provide reminders of the ways in which conquest and domination can and have been resisted.

What is new about the current processes of globalisation is the extent to which time and space have been compressed by new information, communication and transportation technologies.[9] The English political theorist David Held notes that

> [W]hile trade routes and military expeditions can link distant populations together in long loops of cause and effect, contemporary developments in the international order link peoples through multiple networks of transaction and co-ordination, reordering the very notion of distance itself.[10]

The extraordinary speed and spread of global flows, particularly in relation to information and financial transactions, has threatened the capacity of people and governments to regulate, resist or even fully comprehend the local impact of transformations that result from actions and decisions taken on the other side of the globe.

The Dimensions of Globalisation

Much of the literature on globalisation focuses on economic issues. Other writers concentrate on cultural or environmental relationships. However, an adequate understanding of the processes of globalisation requires a more integrated approach, which illuminates the overall landscape of economic, social, cultural, environmental and political relationships. These diverse, related dimensions of globalisation are outlined briefly here and then explored in more detail in later chapters.

One field of globalisation literature and debate is primarily about the increasing interdependence of regional and national economies and the spread of commodified and individualised relationships into every sphere of human activity. While the expansion of global trading relationships is sometimes overstated, the growing significance of regional and global trading agreements, more influential roles for international financial institutions and transnational corporations, and rapid increases in the volume of financial flows have all had a significant impact on national and regional economies.

The champions of globalisation make much of the supposed benefits of free trade and the deregulation of national financial markets. But even the most fervent supporters of deregulation have discovered that the volatility of globalised money markets creates a climate of economic and political instability that can undermine the creation of sustainable long-term investment strategies. Thus, the World Bank notes that deregulated financial markets 'tend towards instability and fraud' and the International Monetary Fund (IMF) belatedly warns that deregulation may 'result in destabilizing and inefficient capital speculation'.[11] Economies such as Australia's, with a small capital base and a high level of dependence on commodity exports, are particularly vulnerable.

While the advocates of global restructuring eulogise its benefits for all, more honest accounts also recognise that 'globalisation does produce losers, serious losers, long term losers, and strategies have to be found to help them'.[12] In fact, the central core of much current social-policy debate is increasingly about how to maximise competitiveness while also managing the problems facing the losers on the global racetrack.

The real danger is that the fierce pressure to attract footloose capital, expand exports and compete on more open world markets generates a process variously described as 'downwards harmonisation', a 'race to the bottom', 'competitive austerity' or 'the low road to restructuring' in which there is constant downward pressure on wages, working conditions, social programs, environmental protection and democratic rights.[13]

While the gap between richer and poorer nations widens there is also a process of polarisation within industrialised nations between a privileged minority with access to well-rewarded jobs and a growing majority banished to the economic and social margins.[14] This polarisation is profoundly gendered, with women in many countries being forced into the bottom end of the labour market at the same time as declining expenditure on health and community services increases demands on women to carry out unpaid caring and domestic work in the home.[15]

Rising inequalities within and between nations also force large numbers of people to move from rural to urban regions and across national borders to avoid poverty and starvation and to find improved living conditions and employment opportunities.[16] The large-scale movement of migrants and refugees is not new. But the tensions are increasing as many nations either close their borders to new arrivals or else accept foreign 'guest workers' without allowing them full citizenship rights. These tensions take many forms. On the Mexican–United States border, United States border guards arrest thousands of Mexican 'wetbacks' as they try to enter the United States to find work. In Rwanda and Bosnia people have made desperate attempts to escape genocide and 'ethnic cleansing'. In Australia new debates continue to erupt about immigration levels, the treatment of 'boat people' and the meaning of multiculturalism.

The spread of global communications technologies and global media empires has helped create a world of globalised culture.[17] Barbie and the Lion King are as well known in Rio as they are in Perth or Hollywood. CNN brings us live coverage of the Superbowl and of missile strikes on Baghdad.

Princess Diana's funeral becomes a globally televised ceremony of planetary grieving. Normally sensible commentators become breathless and uncritical in their excitement about information superhighways and the global cyberspace of the Internet.

Paradoxically, the globalisation of culture has also given rise to heightened localised resistance and the remixing of cultural flows and identities often referred to as 'hybridisation'.[18] From the Balkans to Bougainville, and from Rwanda to Scotland, separatist movements thrive in the context of the fragmentation of old colonial boundaries and national identities. New forms of music and art arise from the cross-fertilisation of cultures producing Bengali rap in England or 'dot' paintings and Aboriginal batik in the deserts of central Australia. Transnational corporations also now recognise that knowledge of local conditions and cultures is an essential part of maintaining a global empire.

How do we explain a world in which the accelerated movement of people and information has made borders more permeable and cultures of all varieties more interrelated and interdependent? How can we describe a world in which relationships are becoming less two-dimensional and hierarchical and more like networks, rhizomes and Internet links?[19] And how are we to understand the significance of new global spaces for cultural flows across new terrains, new 'ethnoscapes, technoscapes, finanscapes, mediascapes, ideoscapes', and the virtual realities of cyberspace?[20]

In exploring these questions it is important to recognise the positive as well as negative sides to the unsettling nature of hybridised cultural relationships. A widespread loss of security, groundedness and coherence also creates the conditions for new ways of challenging oppressive forms of chauvinistic nationalism and racism.

Dramatic developments, such as the nuclear accident at Chernobyl, global warming, and the destruction of the ozone layer have led to an increased awareness of the ways in which distant actions can have environmental consequences for people and places far from the site of the action. Fears of environmental catastrophe combined with anxiety about the global spread of diseases such as AIDS have also led to the creation of 'a risk society' in which many people feel they have little or no control over the environmental actions affecting their lives and those of future generations.[21]

Finally, at the political level the autonomy and sovereignty of national and sub-national decision-making forums in both state and civil society have been constrained by the mobility of capital and the power of international financial institutions, credit-rating agencies, transnational corporations and global institutions such as the IMF, the World Bank and the World Trade Organisation (WTO).

The influence of global financial institutions has been reinforced by the strengthening of global free-trade agreements, such as the Uruguay round of the General Agreement on Tariffs and Trade (GATT) and the development of regional trading blocs, such as the European Union (EU), the North American Free Trade Agreement (NAFTA) and the Asia Pacific Economic Cooperation forum (APEC). Such regional treaties are often far more than trade agreements. Indeed, their real significance often lies in their role as legal guarantees of the rights and freedoms of multinational and transnational corporations to relocate investment and production, unfettered by national or international regulations.

While we are still a long way from the collapse of national sovereignty, national and local economic policy making has become increasingly difficult with interventionist or regulatory policy options made vulnerable to capital flight and the speculative manipulation of national currencies.

Champions, Competitors and Challengers: Strategic Responses to Globalisation

Just as there is a range of interrelated domains and dimensions of globalisation, so too there is a range of political responses that reflect differing assumptions about the desirability and irreversibility of these trends. While the categories outlined below are somewhat arbitrary, it is helpful to see the various strategic responses to globalisation in terms of 'fanatical supporters', 'progressive competitors', 'conservative sceptics' and 'socialist challengers'.

The new fanatics: champions of corporate globalisation

On the cover of the Japanese business commentator Kenichi Ohmae's 1995 bestseller *The End of the Nation State* we are told by the Chair of Nike Inc. that 'Ken Ohmae is the best writer in the world at summarising and forecasting the fast paced changes in international business. *The End of the Nation State* is his finest work to date'.[22] Clearly Ohmae has the ear of major players in the global corporate arena.

His message is very simple. The tyranny of distance has been overcome. We now live in a world where information and money can be moved from place to place with such speed that geographical distances and national borders have become irrelevant, at least to those individuals and corporations with access to the necessary technology. 'Using a telephone, fax machine or personal computer linked to the Internet . . . a Japanese consumer in Sapporo can place an order for clothing with L.L. Bean in Maine have [it] delivered by UPS or Yamato, and charge the purchase to American Express, Visa or Mastercard.'[23] Nation states will therefore collapse and be replaced by regional and city power centres and networks. For Ohmae this development is both exciting and highly desirable.

> The well informed citizens of the global market place will not wait passively until nation states or cultural prophets deliver tangible improvements in lifestyle. They no longer trust them to do so. Instead they want to build their own future now for themselves and by themselves. They want their own means of direct access to what has become a genuinely global marketplace.[24]

This brave new world of global consumerism is the glittering image of the future to be found in business magazine editorials and corporate conference speeches around the world.[25] It is almost always linked to the view that 'an attractive feature of the globalisation phenomenon is the prominent role of the market'.[26]

The central point, repeated again and again like a New Age economic mantra, is that globalisation, competition and the free market are inseparable. For commentators such as Mary O'Hara-Deveraux and Robert Johansen, 'a new landscape is emerging across the business world: the old boundaries of national economies and markets are bowing to globalization even as traditional office walls are giving way to new, borderless vistas'.[27] For Brent Davis, Director of the Australian Chamber of Commerce and Industry, 'the essence of globalisation is competition and competitiveness – that is how business makes locational decisions to enhance its competitive advantage'. [28]

Nor are the implications of the overwhelming of national borders confined to economic relationships. Global media moguls, such as Rupert Murdoch, claim some of the glory for the fall of the Berlin Wall and the opening up of Chinese consumer markets. The Chief Executive of Coca-Cola Australia has provided a particularly colourful illustration of his perception that a global culture dominated by the values of Western capitalism has arrived:

> When the first red and white Coca-Cola truck rolled into Warsaw in the early 90s, some of the locals stood by the side of the highway and applauded. They were not necessarily applauding Coca-Cola per se, but rather what the trademark represented to them–the life, colour and energy of Western commerce that could now be found in their rather drab environment.[29]

For the champions of global capitalism, national boundaries and destinies are simply barriers to be overcome. Enhancing the bargaining power of the corporation and undermining the legal and political regulatory power of national state institutions becomes the primary goal with the construction of regional treaties and agreements protecting the rights of property and capital as key tools in this process. No doubt this is what Walter Writson, former Chair of Citicorp Bank in the United States, was referring to when he enthused that '200 000 monitors in trading rooms all over the world now conduct a kind of global plebiscite on the monetary and fiscal policies of the governments issuing currency . . . There is no way for a nation to opt out.'[30]

For the apologists for corporate globalisation the creation of a global economic order is unstoppable, given the expansion of communication technologies that allow the virtually instantaneous transfer of vast financial flows, making it impossible to reregulate international financial markets. This, in turn, provides a formidable and demobilising weapon for those, such as Margaret Thatcher, who argue that There Is No Alternative to the dominant orthodoxy of extreme neo-liberal, free-market economic policies.

This convenient reworking of the 'end of ideology' thesis and assumptions about the inevitable rise to power of transnational corporations in borderless nations underpin much of the dominant political and economic orthodoxy infecting policy makers at all levels of Australian governance.

Ambivalent supporters and progressive competitors

Not all of those who accept globalisation as inevitable agree that it is unambiguously good. In his 1993 inauguration speech President Bill Clinton told America that 'there is no clear division between what is foreign and what is domestic'.[31] But his Secretary of Labor, Robert Reich, remained deeply pessimistic about the loss of national policy-making sovereignty, deepening inequality and social conflict in a borderless world. In a globalised future, he argued,

> there will be no national products or technologies, no national corporations, no national industries. There will no longer be national economies, at least as we have come to understand that concept . . . Each nation's primary political task will be to cope with the centrifugal forces of the global economy which tear at the ties binding citizens together – bestowing ever greater wealth on the most skilled and insightful, while consigning the less skilled to a declining standard of living.[32]

According to Reich all that can be done is to try to convince the rich to philanthropically redistribute some of their wealth through tax transfers and expenditure on training programs to expand the skills of the ever expanding portion of the population that misses out on the prizes of the global economy.

In a similar vein, eminent British sociologist Ralph Dahrendorf has argued that, because of globalisation, 'it has become hard, and for most impossible, to hide in the world. All economies are interrelated in one competitive market place, and everywhere the entire economy is engaged in the cruel games played on that stage. There is literally no getting away from it, and the effect of globalization is felt in all areas of social life.'[33]

Lester Thurow, Professor of Economics at MIT, also employs a tone of concerned resignation:

> Keynesian counter cyclical policies are . . . blocked by the emerg-
> ence of a global economy that has made one-country national
> Keynesian economics impossible for all but the world's very
> largest countries. The world's financial markets can now move so
> much money around the world so quickly that monetary policies
> have to be adjusted to their dictates – and not to the domestic
> needs of the economy . . . As a consequence recessions can only
> be tolerated – they cannot be fought.[34]

For many national and local governments a completely naked defence of the interests of transnational capital is hard to sell to citizens who are still connected to an older sense of national loyalty, as well as suffering the personal consequences of downsizing, redundancies and reduced public services. For many governments a more or less enthusiastic acceptance of the inevitability of globalisation is often combined with strategies designed to maximise the competitiveness of particular national and regional economies.[35] This commonly involves cost-cutting policies, such as labour shedding, wage reductions and deregulated labour markets, as well as measures designed to boost productivity through technological innovation and improvements in infrastructure, training, production processes, marketing and distribution.

Many trade unions in industrialised economies have accepted the inevit-ability of the competitiveness agenda but have attempted to protect union members through productivity trade-offs supposedly designed to minimise job losses and protect working and living conditions. Similarly, social demo-cratic parties have commonly pursued strategies of 'social market', 'progres-sive competitiveness' or 'globalisation with a human face'. These aim to limit the social dislocation and polarisation of economic restructuring by redistri-buting some of the fruits of export-led growth so as to compensate those who have suffered most.[36]

Progressive competitiveness aptly describes the political strategy pursued for over a decade by the Hawke and Keating Labor governments in Australia, where the social-policy agenda was based on targeting social-wage and income-transfer programs to the groups most disadvantaged by economic restructuring and deregulation. However, the core business of government remained the restructuring and deregulation of the Australian economy so as to increase competitiveness in global markets.

Conservative sceptics

The apparent triumph of free-market capitalism as the dominant economic and social paradigm after the fall of the Berlin Wall has given rise to a deepening split between neo-liberal free-market zealots and more traditional moral and political conservatives. This division is reflected in a growing number of conservative critics of unregulated free-market globalisation. Conservative political commentators, such as Michael Lind, have expressed deep concern about the social impact of the increasingly dominant position of transnational corporations in national political debates and policy-making processes.[37]

Frances Fukuyama, the conservative philosopher who coined the phrase 'the end of history' to describe the post–Cold War triumph of global capitalism, has more recently expressed concern that the capitalist system itself may be threatened by the decay of mutual respect and trust arising from globalised economic relationships built on Thatcherite principles of extreme free-market individualism.[38] These sentiments have received support from some surprising sources, such as the champion global financial speculator George Soros, who has argued that 'the development of a global society has lagged behind the growth of a global economy. Unless the gap is closed the capitalist system will not survive.'[39]

Some conservative Australian political commentators, such as John Carroll and Robert Manne, have consistently challenged the desirability of free trade and financial deregulation. Drawing on an anti-Communist Catholic philosophical tradition, B.A. Santamaria launched a torrent of attacks against Liberal and Labor government support for the rising power of transnational corporations and deregulated global financial markets.[40]

Deepening anxiety about the impact of global restructuring and financial speculation on deregulated global markets has also created fertile ground for right-wing nationalist figures, such as Pat Buchanan and Lyndon La Rouche in the United States, Jaques Le Pen in France, and Pauline Hanson in Australia. In the wake of the Asian financial crisis, the conservative backlash against globalisation has begun to extend into mainstream political debates in the United States, where a renewed isolationist sentiment is being articulated by members of Congress from both the Republican and Democratic parties.[41] Politicians from a range of philosophical starting points wanted to know why it was in the interests of the United States to provide financial assistance to Asian governments. The answer given by the United States Government emphasised the ways in which an ongoing financial and legitimacy crisis in key Asian economies would have adverse consequences for United States investment and trade.

Socialist challengers

At the other end of the political spectrum, critics of globalisation have developed a withering critique of the inequitable and undemocratic consequences of the expansion of global corporate power and transnational markets.

Canadian political economist Robert Cox, for example, argues that the political institutions of the nation state have become mere 'transmission belts' for conveying the interests of transnational corporations into particular national settings.[42] The result is both the undermining of national sovereignty and the creation of what Cox describes as a 'nebuleuse' of intangible, shifting and unaccountable relations of international governance dominated by the financial institutions and money markets. For social theorist Manuel Castells,

> the more the economy becomes interdependent on a global scale, the less can regional and local governments, as they exist today, act upon the basic mechanisms that condition the daily existence of their citizens. The traditional structures of social and political control over development, work and distribution, have been subverted by the placeless logic of an internationalized economy enacted by means of information flows.[43]

These critics have developed a powerful case against the simplistic argument that all forms of globalisation are not only inevitable but desirable. Globalisation is certainly not all good. For the winners there is much that is attractive about the prospect of a world of constant travel and multimedia communication in a networked 'global village' and global marketplace. But for the losers it is also a world of 'global pillage' in which the gap between the powerful and the powerless, the rich and the poor, continues to widen and in which the planet's finite resources are stripped away to feed the escalating consumption of a privileged minority.[44]

A host of critics has convincingly demonstrated the dangers of globalised relationships for productive investment, the distribution of wealth, work, income and power, the integrity of local cultures, environmental sustainability and democratic sovereignty.[45] Many of these concerns, and their implications for Australia, are explored in more depth in later chapters.

However, globalisation is certainly not all bad. A sharp critique of the dangers of exploitative globalisation must be tempered by an awareness of the potential for dramatic improvements in the communication of information and ideas to nurture, as well as overwhelm, understandings of different voices, different ways of seeing and different ways of life.[46]

The facilitation of faster and more effective communication opens up possibilities for solidarities with distant groups and individuals. Indeed, if empowerment is substantially about the recognition and celebration of a creative relationship between diversity and cooperation, then globalisation provides many opportunities for new emancipatory experiments and relationships.

Globalisation is Not All Hopeless

Politics in the age of globalisation should not be seen, as it sometimes is, as a practice of noble hopelessness. These are not good times for starry-eyed optimists, and the pace and complexity of current global transformations does require a degree of intellectual humility to avoid grandiose claims about particular political strategies.[47] However, as the British social theorist and Head of the London School of Economics, Anthony Giddens, has argued, radical engagement in an ongoing process of questioning and contest is surely preferable to pragmatic acceptance or cynical pessimism.[48]

Too often the term 'globalisation' is used as shorthand for the belief that global corporate power has already become an overwhelming juggernaut extinguishing all geographical and historical differences, leading to the irreversible creation of a completely global economy – thus putting an effective end to the sovereignty of nation states and the identity of local cultures.

Increasing global interdependence does not mean that the only path to follow is one that leads towards a completely unregulated free market based on values of rampant individualism and competitiveness at all costs. It may be harder to retain a sense of agency in an age of global power, and the constituencies that will come together to advocate for alternative directions may be more difficult to see at this stage. But similar expressions of despair about the possibility of challenging apparently overwhelming odds were to be heard not so long ago in South Africa and Eastern Europe.

In looking in more detail at the possibility of alternative relationships and institutions at local, global and national levels, we also need to bear in mind the personal contradictions of becoming global citizens while remaining situated in particular spaces and relationships. How do we find new ways of acting on myriad stages with an ever expanding cast of actors while remaining connected to our own place and our own time? These dilemmas are considered in more detail in chapters 10 and 11, but the following points provide some of the key starting points.

The first and most important step is to debunk the myth that there is only one globalisation path to follow. The second step is to develop a repertoire of imaginative, credible and interwoven alternative ideas and practices at a variety of interrelated global, regional, local and national levels.

Global or international strategies often focus on the creation of alternative political, financial and legal global institutions that can form a democratic counterweight to the power of transnational capital.[49] If corporate power has shifted to the global arena, then global trade unions, environmental agencies, community organisations and governmental institutions are part of the remedy.

Such organisations can provide a base for the creation of international corporate codes of conduct, controls over financial transactions, and the construction of new forms of international governance, including the possibility of international corporate taxes.[50] Internationally based government and non-government organisations can also provide the basis for attempts to enshrine trade-union and human-rights principles in international trade agreements and to create multilateral and bilateral social charters specifying minimum standards of living and of social-service provision.

Other critics of globalisation have given greater emphasis to more localist strategies or 'globalisation from below'.[51] This approach has sometimes been described in terms of the 'Lilliputian tactic' of tying down the corporate 'giants' of global corporate power with myriad interconnected local grass-roots movements and struggles. This includes the creation of international alliances between local trade unions, community organisations and social movements, and the opening up of new channels for organising previously unorganised groups within and across national borders.

Paradoxically, too, the globalisation of corporate power is leading to a renewed focus on the fostering of local economic networks and local community relationships as significant arenas within which identity and difference can be protected, solidarity and mutuality nurtured and ecological values sustained.

As the rhetoric of 'think global: act local' becomes more pervasive it is tempting to accept that the room to move at the nation state level has effectively disappeared. It is certainly true that the pressures and transformations of globalisation lead to a need to reconsider the limits and possibilities of action at the national and sub-national levels.

However, while the very idea of national political identity may have been opened to question by the globalisation of capital, it has in fact become more important than ever to reconsider the relationship between social movements, labour movements and nation states and to envisage and create new democratic political entities of both state and civil society at national and regional levels. Without being naive about the autonomy of nation states, it will be a serious error to vacate the arenas of the nation state and of national parliamentary politics. That way lies the hollowed out 'street warfare' politics of Los Angeles and other American cities with no effective focus for contesting the control of transnational capital over decisions in particular societies and locales.

The processes and relationships described by the language of globalisation are not all new. Nor are they all inevitable. The key task is to keep challenging the illusion that globalisation is an unstoppable juggernaut, synonymous with the relentless and exponential growth of free-market capitalism. Demystifying the impacts of globalisation in particular places can then help to clear the ground for resisting exploitation and fostering democratic institutions at a range of geographical levels and in a diversity of cultural contexts.

Chapter 3

Transforming the Global Economy? Trade, Capital and Power in the Late Twentieth Century

At every level, from the personal to the team, corporate, enterprise and far flung joint venture, and in every corner of the globe,
the new economic order is opening worlds of opportunity by
battering down the old barriers and boundaries that divided us
from one another and limited our possibilities for interaction, co-
operation and growth.
O'Hara-Deveraux and Johansen, R. Global Work[1]

The world seems to be a roller coaster with uneven tracks. The
framework is shaking and many of the passengers are falling off.
United Nations Research Institute for Social Development[2]

Views on the desirability of global trade, investment, conquest and exploitation have always depended very much on the point of view of the observer.
European entrepreneurs who benefited directly or indirectly from the
voyages of Marco Polo, Magellan, Columbus, Cortez and Captain Cook no
doubt saw such achievements as both heroic and noble. The indigenous
peoples of Mexico, Cuba and Australia had a very different experience and a
very different understanding of the costs and benefits of global exploration.
Similarly, the low-paid women working twelve-hour days in the free-trade
zones of Mexico and China experience economic globalisation in very
different ways from Bill Gates or Rupert Murdoch.

The aim of this chapter is to provide a critical overview of the major
themes of economic globalisation in the second half of the twentieth century,
as well as to consider various responses to these developments by nation
states and private corporations. The central argument is that while there are

significant globalising trends in relation to trade, investment and financial flows, this process has been uneven and contested, with state and corporate strategies playing a substantial role in determining the current and future directions and outcomes of economic globalisation. This chapter focuses on global economic trends, while the following chapter looks in more detail at developments in Australia.

A common fault in many critical studies of the impact of globalisation is an overestimation of the historical autonomy of national economies and states and an underestimation of the historical scope of global trading relations, particularly in the period prior to the First World War.[3] It is incorrect to suggest that a sudden and overwhelming process of economic globalisation has swept the world since the 1980s.[4] Global economic relationships and colonisation had been expanding steadily since the opening up of trade routes by the European explorers and conquerors of the sixteenth century.

However, the more complex manufacturing processes and resource requirements of the industrial revolution, combined with the creation of the first British and Northern European internationally focussed corporations, led to a dramatic explosion in global trade and investment. By the second half of the nineteenth century Karl Marx was able to describe a pattern of economic relationships that sounds extraordinarily familiar one hundred years on:

> The need of a constantly expanding market for its products chases the bourgeoisie over the whole surface of the globe. It must nestle everywhere, settle everywhere, establish connections everywhere. The bourgeoisie has through its exploitation of the world market given a cosmopolitan character to production and consumption in every country . . .
>
> Constant revolutionising of production, uninterrupted disturbances of all social conditions, everlasting uncertainty and agitation distinguish the bourgeois epoch from all earlier ones . . . All that is solid melts into air . . .[5]

British capital maintained strong control over global financial relations up to the First World War, but this influence declined rapidly afterwards. While United States capital was expanding in the 1920s, the United States Government remained isolationist and unwilling to take over the role of global economic policeman. There was, in fact, a sharp decline in the growth of both international trade and investment as many developed countries pursued more protectionist economic policies during the interwar years.[6]

As the Second World War drew to a close, the ideas of British economist John Maynard Keynes about the desirability of national state economic policy intervention designed to maximise economic growth and full employment through demand management became the dominant view among policy makers in the major Western economies.[7] A logical extension of this view was that support for greater international trade combined with a more managed approach to international finance was necessary to avoid a slide back into the economic conditions that had led to both the 1930s Depression and the Second World War.

In July 1944 representatives of 44 nations met in the town of Bretton Woods in the United States to plan the processes and institutions that would govern the postwar economy. The key principle of the Bretton Woods agreements was that international financial relationships and exchange rates should indeed be managed and that a number of key institutions were required to govern global financial and trading arrangements, as well as to encourage economic development. This led to the establishment of the three key global economic governance institutions of the postwar period: the World Bank, the International Monetary Fund (IMF) and the General Agreement on Tariffs and Trade (GATT).

The World Bank was initially established to help fund the postwar reconstruction of the European economies. However, this task was primarily undertaken under the auspices of the Marshall Plan. This program, named after its designer, the US Secretary of State, George Marshall, involved direct financial assistance to European countries provided by the United States Government. The World Bank's role increasingly became one of encouraging economic development in Third World and less industrialised countries through the provision of loans and the encouragement of free-market economic policies and private-sector investment.

The IMF was established to help maintain the stability of international exchange rates by assisting countries that were having temporary problems with their current account balance (in simple terms, the balance between exports, imports and borrowing). For the first 25 years of its existence this was a fairly non-controversial role. However, as many developing countries began to encounter serious debt problems in the 1980s, the IMF became more involved in 'helping' countries with high levels of international debt. The loans it provided to assist these countries were linked to 'conditionalities'. In other words, the assistance was dependent on the governments of these countries embarking upon a program of 'structural adjustment', often involving drastic reductions in taxes and public-sector services and the privatisation of public enterprises.

At the Bretton Woods conference it was hoped that an International Trade Organisation (ITO) could be established to manage and support the development of free trade. However, agreement on this was not reached in 1944 and the compromise was the GATT, which provided an institutional framework for negotiations about tariffs and trade in the postwar years.

It took until 1995 for a global trade policy institution, the World Trade Organisation (WTO), to be established.

For the first 25 years after the Second World War there was strong economic growth in the industrialised economies, which was associated with a rapid expansion in trade and foreign direct investment (FDI). Economic growth in the immediate postwar years was also fuelled by rapid expansion in demand for a wide range of household consumer goods made more desirable through increasingly sophisticated marketing and advertising strategies and more affordable through the assembly line and other techniques of mass production.[8] Throughout this period the United States Government acted as overseer of the global economic relations within its sphere of influence. The Soviet Union maintained effective control of the economies on the other side of the Cold War 'iron curtain'.

The international financial arrangements established at Bretton Woods assumed a substantial degree of national regulation of financial flows and exchange rates. During the 1950s and 1960s the strength of the United States economy led to the US dollar being treated as the *de facto* international currency. This position was further strengthened by the ongoing assurance by the United States Government that the United States dollar was backed by the 'gold standard', which valued gold at US$35 an ounce.

The 1970s: The End of Managed Capitalism?

By the early 1970s there was increasing international concern about the stability of the United States currency, given the rundown in United States financial reserves due in large part to the costs of financing the war in Vietnam. By 1971 alarm about whether the United States could meet its international financial commitments led the British Government to request that payments be made in gold rather than United States dollars. President Richard Nixon responded by breaking the connection between the United States dollar and the price of gold. By 1974 the United States Administration had also abolished controls on exchange rates and capital flows. These actions had the effect of breaking the Bretton Woods system of a managed approach to international financial relations and created intense pressures for other nations to move to 'floating' international exchange rates. In essence, this meant that, despite some residual government intervention, the relative price of different currencies would normally be set by daily transactions in the financial marketplace.

In 1973 a large number of the major oil-producing countries (collectively known as the Oil Producing Economic Community or OPEC) acted together to raise sharply the price of oil, leading to a vast increase in the funds flowing to these countries. A large proportion of these funds were held as United

States dollars but controlled by European financial institutions, leading to the term 'Eurodollars'. Eurodollar funds had risen in real terms from US$1 billion in 1959 to $80 billion in 1973 to $380 billion in 1977.[9] The European banks and financial institutions chose to lend much of this money to countries with low levels of capital formation and industrialisation, leading to a rapid rise in the indebtedness of many Third World and developing countries.

During the 1970s mass-production technologies and mass-marketing strategies were failing to deliver the rise in profit levels expected by corporate managers and shareholders. Increasing trade-union militancy had delivered some shift from profits to wages and productivity growth was relatively low. The spread of new communication and transport technologies made possible new management strategies referred to by various critics as 'post Fordism', 'lean production' or 'disorganised capitalism'.[10] The emphasis was on increasing profits by expanding markets and cutting costs. This meant exploiting the productivity gains of new information technologies, while achieving greater control over workforce levels, working hours and work practices. Larger sales were to be achieved through a combination of a more flexible, targeted approach to product design, marketing and advertising and the opening up of new regional and global markets.

Free-trade Agreements as New Forms of Corporate Governance

Since the 1970s there have been several periods of strong economic growth (1978 to 1981 and 1986 to 1990) as well as several serious global recessions.[11] The trend towards larger and faster international flows of goods, services and capital has continued, although the variability and unevenness of these processes needs to be recognised. While global trade has continued to grow rapidly, the expansion has not been as fast as in the immediate postwar years.[12] Most of the expansion of global trade is in fact contained within the developed countries, with the increasingly significant addition of the newly industrialising countries (NICs) of Asia, such as South Korea, Taiwan and Hong Kong. The economies of most of Africa, some of Latin America and the Eastern European countries formerly linked to the Soviet Union remain on the margins of expanded global trade.

The most significant developments in global trade in the 1990s have been the formation of the three major regional trading blocs and the creation of the WTO. The oldest of the trading blocs, the European Union (EU), is also the most developed, moving unsteadily towards the full deregulation of trade, a common currency and shared legislative arrangements through the European Parliament. The EU involves a range of political as well as economic relationships and these have provided opportunities for debate and policy development on a variety of human-rights, social and environmental issues. Yet, despite massive pressure from corporate free-trade enthusiasts, resistance to European economic integration continues in many countries, with opinion polls reflecting considerable scepticism about the benefits of the process.[13]

The North American Free Trade Agreement (NAFTA) between the United States, Canada and Mexico was developed in the early 1990s and will incorporate some other Latin American countries in the near future. Many critics have argued that, like most so-called 'free trade' agreements, the more important role for NAFTA is as a 'corporate bill of rights'.[14] In this sense the most significant impact of NAFTA is effectively to prevent governments from carrying out a wide range of economic, environmental and social-policy interventions that might limit the decisions or profits of private corporations investing and trading in North America.

The newest of the three major regional arrangements, the Asia Pacific Economic Co-operation forum (APEC), is still in the early stages of development. APEC arose from what was initially a more limited proposal by the Australian Labor Government of the 1980s. By the end of the 1990s its membership had expanded to include a very broad definition of Pacific rim economies, including the United States, Canada, Russia, Peru and Vietnam. The diversity of interests among the APEC countries has meant that movement towards binding free-trade agreements has been slower than in the EU or NAFTA. However, the 1997 Vancouver meeting of APEC demonstrated that the forum will play an increasingly major role in the promotion of both free trade and neo-liberal economic policy making in the Asia-Pacific region.

The formation of the WTO in 1995 arose from the completion of the Uruguay round of GATT negotiations, which commenced in Montevideo, Uruguay, in 1986.[15] The stated aim of the WTO is to provide a global decision-making structure for setting and enforcing rules in relation to international trade. Its rules are binding on member countries and, given the decision-making arrangements, it will be difficult for small nations to pursue directions or policies that may work against the interests of the most powerful nations and global corporations.

The enormous array of regulations and procedures associated with the formation of the WTO is dense and largely impenetrable to all but the most determined of international diplomats, lawyers and corporate strategists. Yet they will have a profound impact on the lives of everyone on the planet. Again, it is not so much the free-trade provisions themselves that are critical, although these will have a substantial impact on the reduction of tariffs and other direct-protection measures.

The WTO has a range of rules designed to prohibit 'trade-related investment measures' (TRIMs), including many of the ways in which national governments might seek to develop industry and investment policies to assist the development of industries and firms. In addition, these rules can potentially be used to prohibit environmental, health and safety, social, cultural, human- and labour-rights policies that can be seen to infringe the rights of corporations to freedom of international trade and investment. The WTO rules in relation to 'trade-related intellectual property' (TRIPs) provide unprecedented protection for corporations in the areas of copyright and intellectual property rights.

Financial Cowboys on the Frontier of Global Power

While international foreign direct investment continued to expand during the 1980s and 1990s, it has also tended to be confined to the developed nations and the three major trading blocs.[16] The most significant development has been the transformation of global financial transactions as global financial speculators have joined the managers and owners of transnational corporations as key players acting to constrain the economic sovereignty of individual nation states.[17] The combination of floating exchange rates, national deregulation of financial markets and sophisticated information technology has created a new 'world apart' of global financial relationships. Between 1980 and 1992 foreign exchange transactions grew by 30 per cent in real terms – seven times faster than the economic growth rate of the Organisation for Economic Co-operation and Development (OECD). In 1992 daily global turnover in foreign-exchange transactions was worth US$900 billion, almost 50 times the value of global trade.[18] Prominent critic of transnational corporations, David Korten, has argued that

> [t]he financial system increasingly functions as a world apart at a scale that dwarfs by orders of magnitude the productive sector of the global economy, which itself functions increasingly at the mercy of the massive waves of money that the money game players move around the world with split second abandon.[19]

And the money-game players are often playing by some strange and disturbing rules. One senior adviser to the German Bundesbank, Professor Juettnet, has commented that the money-market players

> very often act like a pack of wolves. They have a herd instinct and they are sometimes, under stress, not very rational . . . Global financial markets, unleashed by deregulation, have grown to have unparalleled power over economies . . . But the herd instincts of the markets are driven by perception rather than reality, and governments today have little choice but to toe the line of the new king makers.[20]

Sometimes the private sector itself is vulnerable to maverick operators, as was demonstrated by the 1994 destruction of Barings, the oldest merchant bank in Britain, by the criminal speculative activity of a single Singapore-based employee. Sometimes it is governments who are expected to toe the line, with global credit-rating agencies, such as Moodys and Standard and Poors, playing a key role in setting the electoral and policy directions of governments around the world.[21]

The inference that nation states have become the impotent and blameless victims of global money-market speculators is, however, often overstated and provides a convenient excuse for the common failure of national governments to challenge the dominant ideology of privatised and deregulated free-market capitalism. Australian political economist Rob Watts has noted that 'by treating globalisation as something done to them or to Australia, governments and politicians are failing to recognise that it is their policies which have been integral to, though not exclusively so, the processes to which we now give the name globalisation'.[22]

Often it is the most vulnerable citizens who pay the heaviest price for this failure. The 1994 meltdown of the Mexican economy, when the money-market dealers pulled the plug on the Mexican Government's over-extended borrowing program,[23] provided a powerful example of the implications of deregulated global financial markets. A massive United States assistance package came at the cost of a Draconian structural-adjustment program with severe consequences for unemployment, wages, health and housing.

In 1997 the collapse of the financial systems in Thailand, Indonesia, Malaysia, South Korea and Japan led to the loss of wages, savings and services for millions of families. For some commentators the crashing of the Asian 'tiger' economies showed the danger of interventionist governments opening themselves up to corruption and mismanagement in a forlorn attempt to pick economic winners.[24] Here, they argued, is yet more evidence to support the inevitability of free trade and unfettered globalisation. An alternative perspective is that the Asian financial crisis was partly a result of vulnerability caused by Asian governments' desperate attempts to attract footloose capital in an age of deregulated global financial markets.[25]

During 1997 a new set of draft agreements concerning the deregulation of foreign investment was developed by the major forum of governments of the most industrialised economies: the OECD. The Multilateral Agreement on Investment (MAI) was developed as a 'blueprint' for future investment agreements.[26] The aim was to prohibit governments from taking action to restrict the free flow of all kinds of investment and capital. Severe penalties, including expropriation and compensation, were proposed to prevent governments 'discriminating' against foreign investors, even if this action is taken in the interest of national or local communities.

By early 1998 a powerful international ground swell of opposition to the MAI was developing as the extent of the dangers for democratic governance became apparent. Even relatively conservative governments (including the Howard Liberal Government in Australia) appeared concerned about this attempt to erode control over most remaining areas of national economic decision making.

Corporate Strategies in Global Markets

The initial expansion of global corporate activities in the postwar period was often driven by a desire to reorganise the international division of labour by shifting low-skill and low-technology production to low-wage areas within both developing and industrialised countries. As transport and communication costs fell there was a sharpening of core-periphery differences as corporations in the core economies moved to exploit peripheral resources on the basis of colonial and neo-colonial forms of trade and exploitation. As transport and communication costs fell further there was a new convergence, with many corporations deciding that plant location could be driven purely by the costs of production rather than by physical location.[27]

Approximately 25 per cent of world trade is now intra-firm trade, which reflects the increasingly complex and integrated nature of global production chains.[28] This has helped create a world in which some global corporations have become more and more disengaged from particular local or national loyalties. When the Chair of the giant United States–based corporation National Cash Register (NCR), Gilbert Williamson, was asked what he thought about American competitiveness he answered 'I don't think about it at all. We at NCR think of ourselves as a globally competitive company that happens to be headquartered in the United States'.[29] This kind of logic leads towards the creation of truly transnational corporations (TNCs) with little or no connection to particular national interests.

For some globally focussed corporate executives the aim is to develop a global strategy encompassing customers, product, finance capital, intellectual capital and production processes.[30] The intentions of many transnational corporate strategists are quite clear. One Australian business commentator has, for example, suggested that

> [s]tateless companies can avoid legal and political challenges by shifting their operations from one nation to another . . . global companies can circumvent political problems between nations. Honda exports its USA made cars to Israel although Israel has an embargo on Japanese cars.[31]

Nike shoes, for example, are designed in the United States, prototyped in Taiwan, assembled in over 40 Asian locations and distributed to hundreds of different markets.[32] Asea Brown Boveri (ABB), the seventh largest corporation in the world, has a Swedish Chief Executive and a board made up of Swedes, Swiss, Germans and Australians, carries out most of its business in England, but handles all its accounts in United States dollars.

However, talk of a world dominated by transnational corporations with no national allegiances whatsoever remains premature. Most globally oriented corporations remain based in a small number of countries and domestic operations are still crucial, making it more appropriate to describe them as multinational corporations (MNCs) than TNCs.[33] Many MNCs have recognised that productivity and profitability can actually best be heightened more by maximising design and marketing creativity through strategic alliances than by relying on sheer size or the creation of global empires.

At the simplest level, MNCs can outsource some of their production to areas where labour costs are cheaper or taxes are lower. This becomes a more complex process when it involves integrating production from a range of locations or is on the scale implied by the decision of firms such as IBM and Swiss Air to have all their accounting activities carried out in India.[34] For the firm with global marketing ambitions another attractive possibility is to develop 'multi-domestic' strategies with affiliates of the parent firm being set up in different countries to serve the markets of those countries.

The management of Coca-Cola argues that, while the company is obviously selling a global product, all of its operations are also 'multi local' given that they employ different marketing strategies for different cultural and social contexts.[35] Similarly, McDonald's establishes local franchises that provide the same basic products in thousands of locations, but with small differences in product and marketing to take account of local tastes.

Globalised firms need managers with particular skills. One of the most graphic descriptions of the world of the global corporate manager is provided by the United States management consultant Rosabeth Moss Kanter, who refers to the problems Alice has in playing croquet in Wonderland. In her game Alice must hit the ball with a constantly twisting flamingo. The ball is a hedgehog that keeps moving about. The hoops are card soldiers following the apparently random orders to move to another part of the court made by the Queen of Hearts.

> If technology is the flamingo, employers and customers the hedgehogs, government regulators and corporate raiders the Queen of Hearts, then the reality of a new world begins to emerge. Managers of global corporations deal with constant change in a constantly changing game that cannot be won – but must be continually played in new ways.[35]

In such a world the requisite new management skills include the capacity to manage complex processes of constant organisational change in a range of cultural and political contexts and in an environment where uncertainty and insecurity are the normal state. As the former CEO of Chrysler, Lee Iacocca, noted:

> If a guy wants to be a chief executive 25 or 50 years from now he will have to be well rounded. His education and experience will make him a total entrepreneur in a world that has changed into one huge market . . . He'd better speak Japanese or German and understand history . . . and he'd better know those economies cold.[37]

The management of huge hierarchical structures, often located in one building or one location, is also becoming less relevant. Instead the emphasis is on cross-cultural communication, effective use of information technology and the capacity to facilitate teams that may well be working in very diverse locations.[38] For Doug Elix, Managing Director of International Business Machines (IBM) Australia, the organisational imperative of globalisation is to develop

> a new model where the networks of people who do the job across many functions in many countries is more important than the hierarchy; where people become interdependent and are not at liberty to exercise free will without considering the impact on others; where executives and managers learn to accept shared goals and depend for their success as much on the performance of others outside their function as they do on those within; where empowerment becomes a reality and workers have the knowledge, tools and confidence of management to do the job, and where values and principles hold equal sway with rules and procedures.[39]

Of course, behind this glossy promotion of corporate empowerment lies the reality for many workers of rising workloads, increased stress, falling job security, downsizing and unemployment. From the point of view of the global corporation, 'for workers it [globalisation] simply means that their competition is the world. It will not be good enough to be the best in Melbourne or indeed Australia. Workers will have to be world class, for a global corporation will seek out the most effective place in the world to perform a task.'[40]

The deregulation of labour markets provides a difficult political and industrial context for national labour movements. They have increasingly been forced to choose between defensive attempts to limit free trade and the mobility of capital through regulatory mechanisms and moving into collaborative arrangements with employers that trade productivity improvements (often meaning reduced wages and conditions) for the maintenance of employment. This may also imply support for 'social market' or 'progressive competitiveness' strategies in which political pressure remains focussed on using state institutions to redistribute the fruits of export-led growth in order to compensate those who have suffered most from the processes of economic restructuring.[41]

National Competitiveness in a Globalised World?

Until the mid-1970s most governments in the industrialised West pursued some variation of Keynesian demand-management policies designed to promote high growth, high employment and low inflation. These were often combined with industry-policy strategies aimed at strengthening the import-replacement and export-growth performance of national industries. By the early 1970s the effectiveness of Keynesian strategies was being challenged by structural changes in global capitalism, including the determination of corporate owners and managers to overturn the shift from wages to profits, the emerging influence of new information and transport technologies, the cost of financing the Vietnam conflict, and the OPEC oil price rises.

An increasingly high proportion of global finance was controlled by funds managers and financial speculators with a clear interest in minimising the influence of national governments. Over the same period corporate strategists were beginning to mount a determined assault on the regulatory powers of national governments, attempting to reduce taxation and labour costs and maximise the opportunities for unregulated free trade.[42]

In addition, many governments, particularly those in the English-speaking societies of the United States, the United Kingdom, Australia and New Zealand, became heavily influenced by the promoters of deregulated free-market economic policies, which can be variously described as monetarism, neo-liberalism, public-choice economics or economic rationalism.

Some of these commentators emphasise the significance of new regional arrangements noting the role of the EU, NAFTA and APEC in encouraging deregulated trade and investment within, but not necessarily between, the European, North American and Asia-Pacific regions.[43] Others have pointed to the ways in which global competitiveness has become the dominant force in local decision making, with the Chief Executive of Corning, James Houghton, noting that 'it's not just the United States vs. Japan, but New York vs. North Carolina or Pennsylvania'.[44] In relation to the role of national economic policies, the management literature is full of assertions that

> from now on, any country – but also any business, especially a
> large one – that wants to prosper will have to accept that it is the

world economy that leads, and that domestic economic policies will succeed only if they strengthen, or at least do not impair, the country's international competitive position.[45]

Many academic and bureaucratic supporters of the most extreme forms of *laissez faire* capitalism have argued that the 'end of the nation state' is entirely consistent with the 'the end of history', given that 'no-one except a mere handful of Stalinists believes any more in salvation by society'.[46] They have performed the clever and unpleasant conjuring trick of convincing many people of the 'common sense' reality of this extraordinary claim.

An alternative set of more moderate and interventionist policies has been informed by the view that, despite the increasing mobility of capital, local and national factors can and do still influence some investment decisions. In the real world, transnational and national corporate executives understand very well the value of influencing national governments to maintain a stable and predictable investment environment.

Economists such as Michael Porter and Charles Best remain influential in pointing to the significance of strong local markets, complementary networks of related industries, reductions in bureaucratic regulation and the availability of high-quality, low-cost infrastructure in enhancing the competitiveness of particular firms.[47] The increasing technological and organisational complexity of globalised transactions in fact increase both the importance and the difficulty of government policies designed to provide a competitive environment for the development of national-based firms and industries.[48] John Dunning, Director of the Graduate School of Management at Rutgers University, notes that

> [o]ne of the consequences of globalisation is to underscore the role of national governments as vision setters and institution builders; as ensurers of availability of high quality locationally bound inputs; as smoothers of the course of economic change; and as creators of the right ethos for entrepeneurship, innovation, learning, and high quality standards.[49]

The additional problem facing government policy makers and parliamentarians is that, unlike global corporate executives, they must maintain the support of national and regional electorates with distinct geographical boundaries. They therefore have to pay some attention to the consequences of global restructuring in particular localities and communities and manage the tensions between maximising national competitiveness and minimising social upheaval. There is, therefore, still scope and incentive for national government action to enhance competitiveness and influence employment and living standards in particular places and nations.

More directly interventionist strategies designed to promote a strategic approach to the development of both import replacing and export industries include targeted trade assistance and investment; incentives to particular firms or sectors; incentives for research and development; expansion of transport and communications infrastructure; support for new work processes; and support for a more skilled and qualified workforce.[50] These kinds of strategies, however, are still entirely consistent with and confined by the assumptions of globalised capitalist economic relations. A more detailed discussion of alternative economic policy options is explored in chapters 10 and 11.

The overall pattern of expanded and faster economic flows is complex and it is debatable whether the term 'economic globalisation' overstates the extent of the transformations – and understates the importance of regional economic relationships. It is, however, clear that the speed and scope of international financial transactions, combined with the influence of MNCs and TNCs, has continued to threaten the policy-making sovereignty of nation states, particularly those with small, resource-dependent economies, such as Australia.[51] The next section looks more closely at the implications of this transformation for Australia.

Chapter 4

Onto the Global Racetrack?
Globalising the Australian Economy

When Australia opted for an open economy, the nation committed itself to succeed in an endless race to become, and remain, globally competitive.
Working Nation (Commonwealth Labor Government White Paper on Employment)[1]

That is globalisation; billions of dollars traded across screens, every word of policy makers flashed around the globe to inform buyers and sellers in capital markets operating in different time zones trading a nation's stocks, bonds, or currency, and reacting to economic policy.
Australian Treasurer, Peter Costello[2]

We are in Dandenong to stay, provided Dandenong is efficient and competitive.
Dr. T. O'Reilly, Managing Director, Heinz Australia[3]

At the time of the Hawke Labor Government's 1983 election victory the Australian economy was still a highly protected 'farm and quarry'. It was heavily reliant upon agricultural and mining exports and had a small, uncompetitive manufacturing sector focussed mainly on the domestic market.[4] The Australian welfare state remained a fragile and residual creation based upon assumptions of full employment for men and relatively high wage levels defended by centralised wage fixing.

The story of economic relationships and policies in the 1980s and 1990s in Australia is one of the shattering of the assumptions upon which the settlement between labour and capital was constructed. By the end of the 1990s, Australians were living and working in a deregulated economy in which long-standing principles of security and stability had been overwhelmed by the new mantra of 'competitiveness in a globalised world'.

This chapter provides a critical overview of the main steps in the globalisation of the Australian economy, with an emphasis on the last two decades of the twentieth century. Australian economic relationships have indeed been profoundly altered by a dramatic increase in the speed and scope of flows of capital, goods, services and information made possible by the availability of new transport and communications technologies. But the forms that economic globalisation have taken have not been and are not inevitable. They have been developed as a result of strategic choices by corporations and governments. The supposed inevitability of globalisation has also provided a convenient rationale for the implementation of a radical economic-rationalist program of public-sector cuts, privatisation and labour market deregulation.

From Farm and Quarry to Banana Republic?
Labor Governments and the Globalisation of the
Australian Economy

The uniquely Australian 'labourist' combination of protectionism, centralised wage arbitration and residual welfare provisions began to emerge in the early twentieth century in the context of a neo-colonial economy heavily dependent upon agriculture and mining industries.[5] A strong government role in maintaining high tariff barriers to 'defend' manufacturing industry from foreign competition was combined with an extensive public-sector infrastructure development program. State intervention did not, on the whole, extend to more direct involvement in the development of particular industries or firms.[6]

The Depression of the 1930s demonstrated the vulnerability of the Australian economy to international capital movements and the pressure that could be brought to bear by international investors. Until the Second World War, Britain remained at the centre of Australia's trade and investment relationships and in 1930 the Bank of England sent Sir Otto Niemeyer to tell Australian governments to reduce government spending, cut wages and open up trade. While there was spirited and effective resistance from Australian manufacturing firms to reductions in trade barriers, State and Commonwealth governments duly embarked upon a savage program of deflationary economic policies.

After the Second World War, the views of another Briton, John Maynard Keynes, provided the foundation for the construction of the postwar Australian Keynesian welfare state by the Curtin and Chifley Labor governments.

Although the Chifley Labor Government was defeated when it attempted to nationalise the banking system, Keynesian demand-management policies remained dominant in Australia until the 1970s.

Protectionism also remained a bipartisan article of faith until the election of the Whitlam Labor Government in 1972. As Gough Whitlam has argued, 'the internationalisation of the Australian economy began with my Government's 25 per cent across-the-board tariff cut of July 1973'.[7] The impact of this decision has probably been more significant and longer lasting than Whitlam's abortive efforts to universalise the Australian welfare state and regain national control of mineral and energy resources. Despite a rhetorical shift in the direction of neo-liberal economic policies, the Fraser Liberal Government (1975–83) took only limited steps away from protectionism before it was overtaken by the severe recession and rising unemployment of the early 1980s.

On its election in 1983, the Hawke Labor Government's immediate aim was to generate economic and employment growth through fiscal expansion while simultaneously holding down inflation. This was to be achieved through the Accord, an agreement with the Australian Council of Trade Unions (ACTU) that wages would not rise faster than prices in return for the government's commitment to employment generation and improvements in health and other social programs. Trade union access to key governmental decision-making processes was also a central part of the bargain and led to the establishment of a range of tripartite consultative forums involving government, union and business representatives.[8]

Initial neo-Keynesian optimism was soon overtaken by international pressures. In December 1983 the Treasurer, Paul Keating, overcame spirited opposition within the parliamentary Labor Party to achieve support for the view that the rising speculative activities and power of international financial institutions meant that it was no longer possible to maintain a managed Australian exchange rate. For Keating and his supporters, both within Treasury and the business community, this reform also had the positive effect of ensuring Australia's rapid integration into the harsh realities of global competitiveness.

Throughout the late 1980s and into the 1990s, Australian political, business and trade-union policy agendas were all heavily influenced by the 'globalisation is unstoppable' thesis. For many influential economists, grandiose and simplistic assertions, such as the following example from neo-classical economist Wolfgang Kasper, became commonplace:

> If we want to compete in global markets, Downunder labour and government will only be able to ask for internationally competitive wages and taxes and they must offer productivity support for world-market oriented businesses. If labour and governments failed to make themselves attractive to mobile capital in that way,

the Downunder economy would languish. International competitiveness is therefore the dominant postulate for economic
policy.[9]

The Hawke Government's 1983 decision to float the Australian dollar and
abolish exchange-rate controls was the first step down the path of financial
deregulation, which was completed over the next two years by the removal of
interest-rate ceilings and the entry of foreign banks into Australia. In the
most comprehensive journalistic account of this period, Paul Kelly argued
that

> the float transformed the economics and politics of Australia. It
> harnessed the Australian economy to the international market-
> place – its rigours, excesses and ruthlessness . . . The move to
> financial deregulation was the decisive break made by the
> Hawke-Keating government with Labor dogma and Australian
> practice . . . It was based on the belief that deregulation would
> mean a more efficient financial sector and that market forces, not
> official intervention, could better direct capital to achieve a more
> efficient economy.[10]

By 1986, in a climate of economic recovery, the deregulated Australian
economy faced the problems of rapid currency depreciation and a balance-
of-payments crisis arising from three sources. First, there was ongoing
deterioration in the country's terms of trade (the prices paid for Australia's
exports compared to the price of imports). Second, the volume of imports
was continuing to increase. Third, and most importantly, the cost of servicing
foreign debt was escalating, with the major cause being a sharp rise in
private-sector borrowing.[11] There was serious talk of International Monetary
Fund (IMF) intervention and critical comments from credit-rating agencies,
such as Moodys, about Australia's over-reliance on commodity exports and
'economic and structural weaknesses [which] cloud the nation's flexibility for
servicing long term external debt'.[12]

In May 1986 Keating issued the infamous warning that Australia would
become a 'banana republic' unless economic restructuring was accelerated
to ensure the competitiveness of Australian exports. From then on the policy
agenda of the Hawke and Keating Labor governments was driven by the
imperative of transforming Australia from 'a farm and a quarry' into a
competitive producer and exporter of high-value-added manufactured
products and services. In 1990 Keating summarised the dominant themes of
government economic policy:

> The question at issue is whether we build on our approach of the
> last seven and a half years – of deregulation, of removing the

meddling hands of bureaucracy from the operation of markets, of forcing our businesses and our workers to confront the realities of world markets and international opportunities – or to retreat to the failed policies of the past.[13]

Competitiveness was to become both the diagnosis and the cure for all kinds of economic and social ills, with the choice of remedies underpinned by increasingly dominant 'economic rationalist', neo-liberal economic policies.

The deregulation of financial markets, exchange rates and financial institutions, and the expectation that this would encourage productive investment, was only the first step onto the global racetrack. The second step involved the deregulation of trade through tariff cuts and lobbying in support of free trade on both a bilateral and multilateral basis. The emphasis on energetic and high-profile trade diplomacy was based on the belief that Australia's multipolar trade profile meant that its interests would best be served by the encouragement of multilateral free-trade agreements. To this end Australia was an influential leader of the Cairns Group of commodity exporting nations lobbying for the freeing up of multilateral agricultural trade in the Uruguay round of the GATT negotiations. The possibility of seeking membership of the North American trading bloc was considered and rejected in the mid-1980s, but greater effort began to be focussed on the Asia-Pacific region through the development of Asia Pacific Economic Co-operation forum (APEC) in the early 1990s.[14]

The third step in the global-competitiveness agenda was an extensive program of microeconomic reform designed to improve the productivity and competitiveness of Australia's export industries. Reductions in tariff protection were associated with sectoral strategies for restructuring key industry sectors including the automotive, steel, and textile, clothing and footwear industries.

Despite bitter battles within the Labor Party, the privatisation and commercialisation of public-sector activities, such as banking, transport and telecommunications, was vigorously pursued, as was a contested but continuing process of tax cuts, public-sector expenditure cuts and reductions in grants to the States. The pressure towards radical privatisation and deregulation was further institutionalised by the Review of Competition Policy (the *Hilmer Report*), which laid the foundations for the opening up of private sector competition in all areas of economic activity.[15]

The close connection between the Labor Party and the ACTU meant that full labour-market deregulation did not proceed as quickly or completely as the business community would have liked. None the less, the Accord processes provided a framework for a shift away from arbitration and the award system towards more decentralised enterprise bargaining arrangements.[16] As balance-of-payments problems worsened during the mid-1980s new Accord agreements, which traded off reductions in real wages against tax cuts and improvements in superannuation, were negotiated. By the 1990s the Accord had also become a mechanism for lowering working conditions, boosting productivity and moving rapidly down the path towards enterprise bargaining.

The final component of the Labor Government's strategy was an emphasis on training through the 'Active Society' principle of encouraging (and, some would say, threatening) the unemployed into an expanded range of labour-market programs. This was driven by the belief that the encouragement of skill formation is one of the few ways in which national governments can actively intervene to improve national competitiveness.

The central aim of the competitiveness strategy was to provide a supportive climate within which private-sector investment would surge into productive export industries. Unfortunately, much of this surge went into an orgy of unproductive, in some cases criminal, financial speculation, company takeovers and other 'get-rich-quick' schemes. Such speculative investment worsened balance-of-payments problems as large sums of money were borrowed abroad, leading to a sharp rise in private-sector foreign debt. Australia's net foreign debt rose from $6.9 billion in 1979/80 to $180.5 billion in 1995/96. This represented a seven-fold increase in foreign debt as a percentage of GDP.[17] Importantly, the prime cause of this increase was private-sector rather than public-sector debt.[18]

Throughout the latter part of the 1980s Australia's terms of trade also continued to worsen and imports continued to rise, which led to renewed concern about the current account deficit. The use of high interest rates to slow economic growth accelerated and deepened the recession of the early 1990s. The government argued that this was part of the price Australians had to pay for restructuring the Australian economy, but some clearly had to pay a higher price than others. Official rates of unemployment rose to over 11 per cent in 1993, the highest levels since the Depression of the 1930s. Nearly one million Australians were unable to find employment and many more were forced into low-wage, insecure casual positions.

The government's 1992 *One Nation* economic policy statement signalled a rediscovery of the social costs of unemployment and some expansion of public expenditure in infrastructure development, education and training, and community services.[19] During the 1993 election campaign, wrapping himself in the nationalist cloak of republicanism, Keating managed to engender sufficient fear within the electorate about the divisive impact of the Liberal Party's radical *Fightback!* policy, and its central component of a goods-and-services tax, to win government.

After the election the Keating Government continued Labor's focus on unemployment and commissioned a major inquiry into employment options for Australia, which led to the publication of a White Paper on

Unemployment in May 1994.[20] Yet the heart of this document still defined the answer to unemployment in terms of export growth driven by free trade, deregulated financial markets, reduced business costs, privatisation, enterprise bargaining, and training to improve the 'job readiness' of the unemployed. Trade and industry policies continued to be based on the view that

> Australian and international experience make it clear that protectionism, resistance to structural change and avoidance of competition are inimical to growth . . . An open economy leaves no room for subsidies that prop up uncompetitive firms, nor for detailed prescriptions for industry where government directs the flow of resources.[21]

Between 1983 and 1996, Australia's Labor Government pursued a strategy of 'progressive competitiveness', relying upon the economic benefits of increased competitiveness and improved export performance to minimise the impact of economic restructuring through the generation of employment and resources to enhance physical and social infrastructure.[22] For the most optimistic Labor supporters the goal was the creation of a kind of southern Sweden, combining high-value-added manufacturing exports with relatively humane social policies. This point of view was particularly strong during the mid-1980s with its high point being the joint trade union/government delegation sent to northern European countries in 1987 to investigate policy positions applicable to Australia.[23] One of the key contradictions of Labor's period in government was the notion that a transition to the 'productivist culture' associated with Sweden and other Northern European countries could occur in conjunction with the implementation of a comprehensive program of financial deregulation and free trade.[24]

Labor's strategic mix of financial deregulation, free trade, microeconomic reform, low taxes and the Accord had mixed outcomes. Between 1983 and 1993 Australian economic growth averaged 3.4 per cent compared to the Organisation for Economic Co-operation and Development (OECD) average of 2.8 per cent. Over the same period, Australia's average unemployment rate of 8.4 per cent was similar to the OECD average. An average inflation rate of 5.6 per cent was lower than the OECD average, but higher than many of Australia's major Asian trading partners.[25] Domestic savings rates remained low and the cost of servicing foreign debt was a key factor in the ongoing deterioration of Australia's balance-of-payments position, which was also undermined by poor commodity prices and strong demand for manufactured imports.[26]

Much foreign investment continued to be directed into speculative activities and assets, such as tourist resorts, hotels and office blocks. The performance in relation to investment in manufacturing remained mixed, at best. In the decade to 1993, the real net capital stock per head grew by 24 per cent in mining, fell by 24 per cent in farming, and was virtually flat in manufacturing.[27] Manufacturing exports rose sharply, with a particularly strong increase in high-value-added 'elaborately transformed manufactured' (ETM) products. But manufactured imports rose even faster, leading to a substantial worsening of the manufacturing trade deficit.[28]

Financial deregulation was followed by an explosion of private-sector borrowing, much of it for speculative purposes. Rising debt levels and the volatility of deregulated exchange rates placed tighter limitations on the ability of governments to pursue social and environmental goals. The key architect of Labor's financial deregulation strategy, Fred Argy, notes that

> in the short term markets don't care a tinker's damn about fundamentals: they are mainly driven by charts and a follow the leader mentality. While they do pay attention to fundamentals in the long run, they often view them from a very narrow perspective, focussing almost exclusively on the twin deficits (budget and current account) and inflation.

His ironic strategic conclusion is that 'governments must have the courage to defy financial markets when their policy expectations are clearly unreasonable or threaten vital social concerns. Our national sovereignty and way of life will depend on it.'[29]

The problem for Labor was that it was trying to strike a delicate balance between rapid economic restructuring and the needs and concerns of its traditional electoral constituency. Finally, the balancing act became too difficult. By 1996 it was clear that Labor could no longer satisfy business and academic economic-rationalist critics who argued that the government had failed to follow through on the full range of reforms necessary to deliver maximum competitiveness. Reduced taxes, with the introduction of a consumption tax; reduced public-sector debt and expenditure; greater labour-market flexibility; faster improvements in the productivity of shipping and rail transport; and further privatisation of public utilities, such as Telstra, were all on the shopping list.[31]

For thirteen years Labor rode the tiger of global economic restructuring while trying to prevent the beast from eating too many Australian citizens. In the sport of tiger riding there is a common belief that self-preservation is possible by feeding the tiger what it wants. But the tigers of global financial capital are insatiable. Their appetite for tax cuts, public-expenditure cuts and privatisation is endless. And when there is nothing left to eat they have no hesitation in devouring the riders.

Labor's ride ended abruptly with its defeat at the polls on 2 March 1996. One of the key reasons for that overwhelming defeat was the widespread sense among the casualties of restructuring that their lives were spinning out of control. Keating may well have believed his own rhetoric about building a complementary relationship between competitiveness and social justice. But many Australians had become increasingly fearful about the individual and social costs of competitiveness and begun looking around desperately for an alternative that appeared to offer a more comfortable ride. However, despite its campaign rhetoric, John Howard's Liberal Government quickly demonstrated that it was an even more fierce and less compassionate globaliser than Labor had been.

Neither Relaxed Nor Comfortable: The Australian Economy under the Howard Government

During the 1996 election campaign Howard stated that Australians would feel more 'relaxed and comfortable' following the election of a Liberal Government and no doubt many voters thought they were being offered a reassuring Sunday roast dinner with the ghost of Bob Menzies. The real menu was *Fightback!*, reheated and tough, with new targets for cutting expenditure and reducing services.

The Howard Government came to office with policies based on the pursuit of 'all opportunities for gains in market access for Australian business and to promote Australia's growth through trade and investment'.[32] The government's overall strategic direction involved a deep commitment to free-market, small-government economic policies; a determination to support international corporate competitiveness at all costs, particularly with the economies of the Asia-Pacific region, and the more backward-looking goal of supporting individual and family responsibility wherever possible.[33]

The Liberal Government identified five policy 'tracks' as the basis for promoting competitiveness: a domestic track based on improved productivity (primarily through greater labour market flexibility); a multilateral track supporting free trade through the World Trade Organisation (WTO) and the Cairns Group; a regional track encouraging greater free trade within APEC; a bilateral track encouraging free trade with particular countries; and a trade-promotion track encouraging export industries.

The Treasurer, Peter Costello, argued that the Howard Government's economic policies were informed by the view that the debate about alternative economic policy directions was over and 'the principal focus of economic decision makers around the world' was

- flexible domestic product and labour markets
- trade liberalisation

- reduced government ownership
- sound fiscal and monetary policy
- opening capital markets[34]

The goals of 'sound fiscal and monetary policy' and 'reduced government ownership' were given specificity by the government's stated targets of bringing the underlying budget into surplus within three years, reducing the ratio of budget outlays to Gross Domestic Product (GDP) to 24 per cent, and halving the Commonwealth debt to GDP ratio from 20 to 10 per cent.

The first strategic step was Costello's gleeful 'discovery' of an $8 billion 'black hole' in the deficit figures left by the preceding government. Despite substantial evidence that the size and severity of the 'black hole' was highly contentious, the sense of crisis created by this announcement provided the basis for a 1996 budget designed to cut Commonwealth expenditure by $10 billion.[35]

The budget strategy and the wider goal of reducing the size of government were given further support by the report of the Government's Commission of Audit, which was completed and released a few months after the election.[36] The trick of establishing an 'objective' Audit Commission to review the state of government finances had been piloted by the Kennett Government in Victoria and the Commonwealth Audit team contained some of the same members. The Audit Report argued that the major debt and deficit problems facing the Commonwealth created even stronger arguments for deep budget cuts as well as an extensive privatisation agenda.

The Howard Government began to pursue an aggressive program of privatisation, the most significant component of which was the partial sale of Telstra. It also strongly supported the privatisation of state-government-owned utilities, the further deregulation of the financial sector, and the opening up to competition of government services such as labour-market programs and the Commonwealth Employment Service.

Memories of the 1993 election debacle, in which John Hewson lost a supposedly 'unloseable' election due partly to concern about a goods-and-services tax, meant that progress on tax reform had to proceed slowly and with caution. However, tax reform remained the other pillar of a fiscal strategy designed to reduce corporate and personal income tax in order to increase tax competitiveness, particularly with regional economies.

Despite the need to negotiate some compromises with minor parties in the Senate, the Howard Government also implemented a new *Workplace Relations Act* (1997) that, according to Costello, would

> provide greater choice in the way work place agreements can be negotiated; which reduces the prescribed role of unions in the bargaining process, which simplifies existing labour market

regulations, which has the potential through workplace agreements to free up working hours, rationalise allowances and
include productivity related remuneration arrangements.[37]

According to its many trade union opponents, however, the *Workplace
Relations Act* was in fact an attempt to place the balance of labour-market
power in the hands of employers, thereby undermining the rights and working conditions of workers and threatening to undermine the long-term
viability of the trade union movement.[38]

Trade and industry policy remained areas of greater uncertainty and
ambivalence. The government began by signalling a preference for bilateral
rather than multilateral trade negotiations, but later appeared to adopt a
more enthusiastic approach to regional forums such as APEC. As is discussed in more detail in chapter 7, the Howard Government's approach to
relationships with Asia has been both confused and confusing, with very
mixed signals being sent about the nature of its commitment to regional
economic – and cultural – integration.

The Howard Government also appeared deeply ambivalent about whether
it should simply 'get the fundamentals right' and leave competitiveness to the
marketplace or take more assertive action to promote trade and investment.
This ambivalence has been most clearly demonstrated in the government's
continuing confusion on industry policy.

The hard-line free-market ideology of senior Ministers and bureaucrats
led to rising tensions with some sections of the business community as a
series of reports commissioned by both the government and key industry
groups argued for a more interventionist approach to industry policy. In
August 1997, for example, Howard informed business leaders that his
government would 'strategically intervene in industry to offset distortions
and remove impediments to expansion'. By November 1997, in the wake of
the Asian financial collapse, he was firmly rejecting the key industry policy
recommendations of major government and business reports, arguing that
'one of the take outs from what has occurred in our region is that high
interventionist economic policies do not work'.[39]

The Howard Government at first seemed likely, politely but firmly, to
ignore the key interventionist recommendations of the Mortimer Report into
government business programs, the Goldsworthy Report into support for the
development of information technology industries, and the Metal Trades
Industry Association Report on strategies for increasing the competitiveness
of the Australian economy.[40] Yet the final Industry Policy statement, released
in December 1997, contained over $1 billion in investment incentives
designed to attract foreign investment and encourage export industry.[41]
Despite constantly attacking Labor Opposition leader, Kim Beazley, as
protectionist and isolationist, Howard also actively intervened on several

occasions to cushion the political blow of tariff reductions in the car industry and the textile, clothing and footwear industries.

After two years in office, the overall impact of the Howard Government's approach to Australian economic policy appeared mixed indeed. By early 1998 the inflation rate was close to zero, primarily due to low housing interest rates. For many low-income families unable to enter the housing market, the more crucial indicators were food and clothing prices, which continued to rise. Investment and export growth remained patchy and unemployment remained stubbornly high at around 8 per cent. By the beginning of 1998 the first signs of the implications of the Asian financial crisis for Australia were becoming apparent. In November 1997 the merchandise trade surplus was $509 million. By December of that year the merchandise trade deficit had become $880 million.[42] Much of this turn around was due to rising imports, with the expected reduction in demand for Australian exports yet to have its full impact. During May 1998 the Australian dollar continued to fall as international money markets reacted to the financial crisis in Asia and the riots in Indonesia. Finally, as is argued in the following chapter, the Howard Government's hard-line free-market strategies, combined with a backward-looking nostalgia for a less complex, more family-oriented Australia that had never really existed, were threatening to create deep divisions and social scars.

The champions of free markets and international competitiveness tend to assume that globalisation is solely about economic openness and integration, with little focus on ecological, cultural or social questions. Yet it was precisely the failure to come to terms with broader issues of Australia's cultural identity, environmental responsibilities and relationships with Asia that led the Howard Government to appear increasingly uncertain and incompetent.

The Globalisation of Australian Corporations

Not surprisingly, the catchcry of global competitiveness is as dominant in the boardrooms of large Australian companies as it is in boardrooms around the world.[43] For Ian Salmon, Director of the Business Council of Australia,

> Australian businesses need to be internationally competitive to succeed and for Australia to thrive. International competition is between individual enterprises not between industries or countries. To compete successfully Australian enterprises and their employees need to be innovative, efficient and able to respond rapidly to changing customer demands.[44]

And for the Chief Executive Officer of the large Australian-based company, MIM Mining,

we do live in a global village, where events in America and Papua
New Guinea have echoes in Canada and Australia . . . I am
convinced that there is only one direction for us all, and that is –
increased internationalisation, increased strategic relationships
and increased participation in the market place.[45]

For the corporate advocates of deregulated globalisation the message for
Australian government policy makers has also been very clear. The authors of
an influential report on export industries to the Australian Manufacturing
Council noted that the role of government is 'not to pick winners but rather
create an environment in which (enough) winners pick Australia'.[46] This is
commonly understood to mean reducing taxes, creating more flexible wages
and working conditions, undermining the influence of trade unions, and
providing 'effective and efficient infrastructure at minimum cost'.[47] This
agenda would have been familiar to many employers and boards of directors
in 1880 or 1930. In this sense it is a reminder that globalisation often simply
provides a new set of weapons with which to fight an old battle designed to
maximise profits by wringing as much out of the workforce as possible while
keeping taxes low and expecting public funding to cover as much of the
infrastructure costs as possible.

Corporations themselves have developed a range of strategic responses to
globalisation, depending on their size and ownership structures. The shifts
in focus and fortunes of Australia's biggest company, Broken Hill Proprietary
Company Limited (BHP), provide an illustration of the most common kind
of globalising strategy pursued by large Australian-based firms in the last
twenty years. In the 1950s university students used to sing a song called
'There'll always be a Menzies while there's a BHP'.[48] While BHP has outlasted
Menzies, it is not clear that the 'Big Australian' will survive the pressures of
a fully globalised Australian economy.

Up until the 1960s the primary focus of BHP was on domestic production
and domestic markets.[49] However, corporate strategy was increasingly
influenced by the view that BHP had outgrown the Australian market and
needed to expand international sales if it was to continue to grow. As export
sales expanded it also became clear that international production would need
to expand if international sales were to be competitive.

During the 1970s BHP began to expand its export production with the aim
of establishing a permanent and continuous presence in the export market
for steel.[50] Importantly, it also began to develop its capacity for offshore
production. The first step was the acquisition during the 1970s of John
Lysaght, which owned a number of small steel mills and mines in Asia. In
1984 BHP bought the large United States-based mining firm, Utah, which
had major mining interests in the United States, Canada, Brazil and Chile.
During the 1980s BHP also acquired interests in oil production and

exploration in the North Sea, the Irish Sea, Hawaii and Vietnam, and in 1984 the company opened the Ok Tedi mine in Papua New Guinea.

By 1994 BHP had become a true multinational company and the sixty-sixth largest industrial company in the world. It had mining, oil, steel and engineering operations in 25 countries, including the United States, Canada, Chile, Brazil, New Zealand, Papua New Guinea, Indonesia, Mali, Malaysia, Singapore, Brunei, Thailand, Taiwan, Hong Kong, Vietnam, Fiji, New Caledonia, China, the United Kingdom, Argentina, Bolivia, Russia, and the Philippines.

The nature of BHP's structure and workforce changed dramatically as a result of this globalisation strategy. Between 1981 and 1995 the number of BHP workers employed overseas rose from 1 per cent to 25 per cent. Between 1984 and 1994 the share of BHP production sold in Australia declined from 53 per cent to 35 per cent, while the share of overseas sales rose from 47 per cent to 65 per cent. In other words, two-thirds of BHP sales were now overseas. And between 1984 and 1994 overseas-sourced sales rose from 12 per cent to 33 per cent. The percentage of BHP shares held in foreign ownership doubled to 21 per cent between 1988 and 1994.

BHP's globalisation strategy also included maintaining strong pressure on governments to deal with what it saw as the problem: 'the tax regime, industrial relations, environmental regulations, land access, infrastructure costs, arguments between federal and state jurisdictions and sovereign risk, are all areas that militate against Australia in international comparisons of investment locations'.[51]

By 1997, however, BHP was facing a number of serious problems as its profits disintegrated. Steel-making operations in Newcastle, NSW, were closed, costing thousands of jobs, and there were serious cost overruns in its Pilbara iron works. The company's biggest problem was the Ok Tedi mine in Papua New Guinea. There had been earlier problems with this vast mine due to legal challenges made by local villagers seeking compensation for environmental damage. The problem in 1997, however, was that the severe drought in Papua New Guinea had reduced water levels in the Fly River, which is essential for the mine's operations, to such an extent that no mining could occur. It appeared that BHP itself had become a victim of environmental globalisation, given the connection between the drought, El Niño and the possible wider impact of greenhouse-gas induced climate change. In early 1998, as its share price continued to drop, BHP's Managing Director, John Prescott, resigned and credit-rating agencies began to canvass a further substantial downgrading of the company's credit rating.[52]

As political commentator Judith Brett notes, the fall of BHP has significant implications for the relationship between national politics and globalising corporations:

> As Australian owned companies pursue their economic interests
> on a world rather than a national stage, the circle of mutual
> benefit is decisively broken. The interests of our politicians and
> nationally based companies no longer coincide. Menzies' heirs
> and BHP have parted ways, although it is not clear that Menzies'
> heirs have realised this.[53]

Other large Australian-based firms have also pursued aggressive global-isation strategies. Pacific Dunlop, for example, moved an increasing propor-tion of its production offshore in order to lower costs. Sometimes, as in the case of its Ansell condom-production plant which has relocated to Malaysia, this was done in order to be closer to the relevant raw materials.[54] But Pacific Dunlop's Managing Director made the broader strategy clear when he pointed out that 'we prefer where it's economically efficient to produce in Australia, and we push government policy to provide the necessary frame-work. Failing that we will always go to the best economic source.'[55] In 1998, when Imperial Chemical Industries Australia (ICI) began a major inter-national expansion by taking over ICI International at a cost of $570 million, its Managing Director explained that 'given the globalisation of our customer base and the international position of some of our competitors it is important that we think globally'.[56]

Firms with an existing transnational organisational base, such as Ford, have pursued a slightly different strategy. They have made it clear that, unless government policies are favourable to their interests, they will simply move elsewhere. During the 1980s this meant that efforts by the Labor Government to develop a coherent plan for the car industry in Australia were finally driven by the need to respond to the broader global strategies of Ford (and the other transnational car producers).[57] By the mid-1990s Ford was making it clear that it would pack up and leave the country if it could not achieve further cost reductions through reduced taxes and labour-market deregulation.

An example of the global strategies pursued by smaller companies is provided in a recent article about a real textiles and clothing manufacturer referred to by the author as Corporation X.[58] Corporation X maintains Australian control over entrepreneurial and coordination functions, but relies on international subcontractors for much of its design, production, transportation, wholesale and retail activities.

> Corporation X is simultaneously a global and local corporation.
> However it does not seem to be a national corporation, nor does
> it seem to be a multinational corporation. The company is global
> by virtue of its sources, networks, design and markets. On the
> other hand, it is local by virtue of its continuing dependence on
> the tastes, fashions and revenue of different localities for product
> innovation.

It is not obviously a national corporation because its scope neither reflects national boundaries nor its original national culture. And it is not a multinational corporation because it has not made significant investments or built significant organisational units outside its home base. Instead Corporation X is the quintessential global corporation which is able to treat the globe as a set of discrete opportunities.[59]

Conclusion: Caught at the Apex?

The last fifteen years of economic policy in Australia have demonstrated the problems facing small resource-dependent economies during the transition to globally integrated economic relations. Professor Jane Marceau has correctly noted that Australia continues to face the special problem of being

caught at the apex of an uncomfortable and internally contradictory triangle: socially, politically, organisationally and proprietorially the country looks across to the Eastern Pacific and Europe while in terms of trading partners it must look north. A weak, and increasingly powerless, state combines with a 'foreign' industrial base in a recipe which has been tried nowhere else.[60]

Labor's strategy of globalisation with a human face remains preferable to the Howard Government's more brutal forms of restructuring, but the core problem remains. The struggle for victory at all costs on the global racetrack is fundamentally incompatible with the goals of sustainable production, fair distribution, cooperative citizenship and democratic sovereignty.

Chapter 5

The Price of Competitiveness?
The Social Impact of Globalisation
on Australia

Whether in terms of the quiet immiseration of millions of people who have been pushed to the economic margins or of the shocking scenes of open warfare that are tearing whole countries apart, the world is now paying a heavy price for putting social issues in abeyance.
United Nations Research Institute on Social Development[1]

Ratings agencies and fund managers attach much greater importance to goals such as low inflation, low taxation and small government than to low unemployment and social justice. This means governments are going to find it increasingly difficult to pay for welfare, health, education, labour market programs for disadvantaged workers and social and community infrastructure.
Former Labor Government economic adviser, Fred Argy[2]

The outcome of the 1996 Federal election highlighted two alarming and significant developments in Australian social and cultural relationships. The shift by working- and lower-middle-class voters away from the Labor Party appears to have been driven by an understandable sense that wages and security had both suffered as a result of the restructuring of the Australian economy over the previous thirteen years. At the same time there were the first signs of a resurgence of racially based prejudice and anger directed at migrants and Aborigines. Social polarisation and cultural fragmentation are both dangerous companions of competition in the global marketplace.

This chapter explores the impact of globalisation on Australian social and cultural relationships. The central argument is that the globalisation trends of the last twenty years have contributed to an increasing polarisation of power and resources along with the fragmentation of cultural relationships. These trends have been clearly visible in Australia. However, the Australian experience also demonstrates how political and policy choices affect the ways in which the impacts of globalisation are experienced in particular national and regional contexts.

Global Economy, Local Mayhem?

In January 1997 the cover of the *Economist* featured images of rioting and demonstrating crowds in a range of different countries, with the overall headline 'Global Economy, Local Mayhem?'.[3]

In South Korea, workers and students were protesting against new labour-relations laws designed to make it easier for corporations to dismiss employees and reduce job security and working conditions. The government's response to the demonstrations was tear gas and bulldozers. In Cambodia, women working in the textile industry were seeking wages of $40 a month for a 47-hour week and protesting against beatings by employers, compulsory overtime and the failure to recognise elected representatives. The employers responded by threatening to relocate to countries where workers were more compliant, like Bangladesh or Vietnam. In France, a national transport strike was being organised to protest against privatisation and public-sector cuts. In Peru, the guerilla occupation of the Japanese Embassy continued with demands for action to address the worsening levels of poverty and inequality among working-class and peasant peoples.

The *Economist*'s editorial writers, meanwhile, assured their readers that there was nothing to worry about. From their point of view, concerns about the social impact of globalisation were misguided and paranoid – 'the growing integration of the world economy has in general been an engine of mutual enrichment'.[4]

It is true that, measured in the traditional terms of Gross National Product (GNP), overall economic growth has expanded over the last twenty years and the top 20 per cent of the world's population has indeed prospered.[5] But the experience of those suffering the fiercest effects of globalisation is that it has in fact delivered rising poverty and inequality, as well as increasing fears about the future livelihoods of their communities and their children.

One of the most significant outcomes of globalisation has been the acceleration of the spread of capitalist relations of production and reproduction into every corner of the globe.[6] However, the precise nature of such globalised capitalist economic and social relations vary in particular national contexts depending partly on gender, class and ethnic backgrounds and partly on the policy choices made by political parties and governments.[7]

The Polarisation of Living Standards and Power Between and Within Nations

While the definition of 'northern' developed and 'southern' less-developed societies is increasingly blurred, significant differences in access to resources and power continue to exist between different areas of the globalised economy. The full implications of globalisation have often been most clear in the process of 'structural adjustment' imposed on Third World countries by international financial institutions and the International Monetary Fund (IMF) since the early 1980s. The price for debt rescheduling imposed by the IMF frequently involves 'conditionalities', including financial deregulation, reductions in taxes and public-sector expenditure, restrictions in monetary policy, increased labour-market flexibility, wage reduction and an emphasis on overcoming trade deficits through the expansion of exports.

The iniquitous and polarising outcomes of such policies are hardly surprising. The overall material standard of living in Newly Industrialising Countries (NICs), such as Hong Kong, South Korea and Taiwan, improved during the 1980s and 1990s.[8] The impressive growth rates in other Asian economies, such as Indonesia and Thailand, in the early 1990s encouraged some supporters of the merits of global competitiveness to argue that deregulation and free trade were the fastest route to development. However, there are a number of increasingly obvious problems with this argument.[9]

First, while higher growth rates certainly led to a rising middle class in NICs, many small primary producers, such as farmers and fishermen, were forced out of their industries by the rise of 'agribusiness' and the environmental impact of industrialisation. Second, a strategy of enhanced international competitiveness must, by definition, produce losers as well as winners. Not all countries can be winners on the global racetrack. Third, rapid economic growth often came at a high price in terms of severe limits on democratic and human rights. Fourth, the price of competitiveness often involved massive environmental destruction – the most obvious examples being the choking of cities such as Bangkok and Kuala Lumpur with automobile pollution and the forest-fire smoke haze that enveloped much of South East Asia during 1997. Finally, the Asian financial crisis of 1997 and 1998 illustrates the incapacity of governments in the region to deal with the volatility of deregulated global money markets and speculators.

The overall gap between rich and poor nations has continued to widen.[10] One-third of the world's population is malnourished. Over one billion people live in absolute poverty, without access to safe drinking water and constantly on the knife edge between life and death. Inequalities in relation to health outcomes also continue to rise due to poverty, reductions in health resources and the dumping of medicines of dubious quality by Western pharmaceutical companies.[11]

Some parts of the world are being left further and further behind. In Latin America the proportion of people living in poverty rose from 40 to 48 per cent between 1980 and 1995.[12] The relative and absolute position of people living in Africa has deteriorated dramatically, with more than half the population existing in absolute poverty and more than two-thirds of the labour force living below the poverty line. At the same time, the wealthiest 20 per cent of the world's population controls 80 per cent of the world's wealth.[13] The incomes of the richest people in the richest countries continue to explode. Nowhere is this more starkly illustrated than in executive salaries, with a recent Chief Executive Officer of Disney Corporation receiving a salary package of over $200 million a year.[14]

The impact of structural adjustment conditionalities in the south has been accentuated by the deregulation of international financial markets and trading relations, leading to intensified competition between corporations increasingly disconnected from specific national economies. Such competition has strengthened demands for more flexible labour markets in all societies and has given corporations more credibility in their threats to shift their operations to cheaper locations. These threats have provided formidable ammunition for corporations and politicians in the industrialised countries in their arguments for the implementation of neo-liberal economic policies of labour market and financial deregulation, privatisation, and a minimal public sector in order to compete with the low-tax, low-wage economies of the south.

One of the key outcomes of economic globalisation has been the breaking down of some of the distinctions between rich 'core' economies and poor 'peripheral' economies.[15] As a major report for the 1996 United Nations Social Development Summit argued,

> throughout the world there has been a striking convergence of social problems. Increasing polarisation is evident almost everywhere. Absolute poverty rather than relative poverty, has been emerging in the industrialised countries, so that some people are now forced to take 'third world' jobs and have living standards to match. At the same time, polarisation in the south has been accompanied by increasing crime and social fragmentation to match the levels of these problems in the north.[16]

In most industrialised countries there has been a systematic assault on the Keynesian welfare state, public-sector institutions and the role of trade unions, combined with the rising influence of private-sector corporate ideologies and institutions. Social and economic polarisation within industrialised societies has given rise to the creation of sharp geographical divisions between poor and affluent populations. In the United States, and increasingly in Australia, some wealthy citizens have moved to protect themselves from 'the underclass' through the mechanisms of 'gated' housing estates and private security firms – a process described by commentators such as the conservative United States author Michael Lind as the 'Brazilianisation' of industrial societies.

> Brazilianisation is symbolised by the increasing withdrawal of the White American overclass into its own barricaded nation-within-a-nation, a world of private neighbourhoods, private police, private health care, and even private roads, walled off from the spreading squalor beyond.[17]

Such developments help to explain the extent to which poverty and inequality are rising within the industrialised north as well as in the less industrialised south. At the top end of the scale, the rich elites of the United States or Australia or Pakistan have more in common with each other than with their own national communities. In global cities from Sydney to Los Angeles, and from Kuala Lumpur to Tokyo, concentrations of corporate strategic operations bring together large enclaves of corporate 'symbolic analysts' – highly educated financial and information workers commanding huge salaries and demanding protection from the insecurity and crime in the cities around them.

At the other end of the scale, rising unemployment, casualisation of the workforce, falling wages and cuts to welfare and public services have led to rising poverty and inequality in most industrialised countries. In the United States, for example, relatively high levels of employment have been maintained but the price has been declining wage levels and the undermining of job security and working conditions.[18] As former Singapore Prime Minister, Lee Kuan Yew, recently predicted, 'America's top ten per cent will still enjoy the highest standards of living in the world. But the wages of the less educated citizens will drop to those of workers in developing countries with equal or higher education'.[19] In Europe, wages and working conditions have been maintained to some extent but unemployment continues to soar. Overall, only 30 per cent of the world's workforce is productively employed.[20]

If a wider range of criteria than simply growth in goods and services is included in measures of economic and social wellbeing, the picture of overall glittering global progress becomes even more problematic. One commonly used broader measure is the Genuine Progress Indicator (GPI),[21] which includes factors such as income distribution, the value of housework, costs of unemployment, costs of pollution, the depreciation of natural resources and environmental damage. This indicator continued to rise during the 1950s and 1960s but has declined since the 1970s so that the level in the 1990s is lower than in the 1950s. This helps to explain why many people remain sceptical about economists who tell them that their lives – and those of their children – are continuing to improve, when their own eyes and experiences tell them a very different story.

The underlying relationship between global competitiveness and sexual exploitation was brought into particularly sharp focus by David Mulford, former United States Under Secretary of State for George Bush, when he argued that 'the countries that do not make themselves attractive will not get investors' attention. This is like a girl trying to get a boyfriend. She has to go out, have her hair done up, wear make up.'[22]

Global restructuring occurs on 'a gendered terrain' and many women have borne the heaviest burdens in the process of global economic restructuring.[23] Women have filled the majority of positions in both the unregulated free-trade zones of the developing countries and the expanding low-wage, casualised workforces of the industrialised economies. New, gendered, international divisions and movements of labour have been created by the rapidly expanding demand for domestic workers.[24] In the Middle East the demand for maids has commonly been met by Filipino and Sri Lankan women. In the United States the preferred source of foreign maids is the Caribbean rather than supposedly more assertive local Afro-American women. Such employment is generally poorly paid, insecure and wide open to sexual harassment and exploitation. Many women in Asian countries, such as Thailand and the Philippines, have experienced three additional forms of globalised sexual exploitation: the prostitution industry that developed to serve troops at United States military bases; the thriving sex tourism industry; and the selling of women as mail-order brides to men in Australia, the United States and Europe.

In many societies women have borne the brunt of the cutbacks in social expenditure as more of the caring and domestic responsibilities are transferred back to 'the family'. Ironically, just as the feminist critique of the contradictory gendered nature of welfare state provisions is becoming more widely understood, the welfare state as a whole has come under overwhelming assault. Many traditional areas of women's work are being re-privatised at the same time as there are increased pressures on women to work in insecure and poorly paid sectors of the labour market. The double shift has never looked so bad.

Globalisation also has a special and savage meaning for indigenous peoples, refugees and migrant populations. Migration for both political and economic reasons continues to grow, with over 23 million refugees and over 100 million people living permanently outside the country of which they are citizens.[25] Again, it is permanent and temporary migrants, as well as indigenous peoples, who are most likely to be unemployed or to be in low-paid and precarious forms of employment.

From the Wage Earner's Welfare State to the Competition State: The Social Cost of Globalisation in Australia

For most of this century Australian social policy outcomes were built on a unique mixture of high male employment, protectionism, centralised wages and a weak welfare state operating as a residual safety net. For the twenty years following the Second World War, relatively high standards of living were maintained for households with access to the income of employed, unionised, male workers. These arrangements provided substantially less support to those citizens, predominantly women, who were excluded from the workforce. Despite the struggles and achievements of the Australian women's movement, the gendered division of labour and the assumption that women would normally be dependent on the male breadwinner also remained deeply entrenched.[26]

While there have been both winners and losers as a consequence of the social policies implemented by the Hawke and Keating Labor governments and the Howard Liberal Government, the overall impact has been to accelerate the transformation of Australia from a 'wage earner's welfare state' to a 'competition state' with higher levels of poverty and inequality and a rise in the proportion of the 'working poor'.[27]

As the Hawke Government began to open up the Australian economy, its social-policy agenda was increasingly dominated by the task of ameliorating the most savage impacts of financial deregulation, economic restructuring and rising unemployment. The key components of this strategy were an expansion in the social wage to offset declines in money wages, tighter targeting of income security payments, and a significant emphasis on labour-market programs connected to the goal of creating a more 'Active Society'.

The overall intention of the 'Active Society' strategy, first articulated in the recommendations of the 1987 Social Security Review, was to move away from income-security arrangements designed as a safety net for people who might occasionally be out of work for a few months.[28] The aim instead was to target income support more tightly, and to encourage or force the unemployed into active involvement in education and training programs in an effort to get them back into the workforce.

Working Nation, the 1994 White Paper on Unemployment, argued for a further increase in training places combined with subsidies for employers to take on additional workers and the introduction of a reduced 'training' wage for workers involved in training activities. It also introduced a 'Jobs Compact', which guaranteed people unemployed for more than eighteen months access to at least six months of employment and training in return for an agreement by the long-term unemployed to accept any 'reasonable' job offer.

Perhaps the most significant announcement of all was the statement that the goal of the White Paper policies was to achieve a target of 5 per cent unemployment by the year 2000. In other words, the traditional definition of 'full employment' was officially rejected by the Labor Government. Despite Labor's relatively strong record in promoting employment growth, unemployment rates remained close to 10 per cent and the casualisation of the Australian workforce continued at a fierce pace, with much of the employment growth occurring in the part-time and casual spheres.[29] The part-time share of total employment grew by 40 per cent between 1983 and 1992. This compares with a growth rate of 14 per cent for all countries in the Organisation for Economic Co-operation and Development (OECD).[30] There has also been a significant rise in home-based employment and outsourcing involving a high proportion of women in unregulated and often exploitative employment conditions. The Textile, Clothing and Footwear Union estimates that the number of homeworkers in the Australian clothing industry grew from 30 000 in the mid-1980s to over 300 000 by the mid-1990s.[31]

The second strand of Labor's social-policy agenda was a more targeted approach to income security and tax policies designed to deliver maximum benefits to low-income families and to encourage and support women moving into the workforce.[32] The fundamental contradiction here was the government's broader commitment to reducing taxes and public-sector expenditure, claiming this as a victory for efficient management and tighter targeting of income-security payments. Cuts in areas such as health and education were particularly severe at State and local government levels as difficult decisions were passed down the line by the Commonwealth Government in the form of reduced grants and revenue sharing arrangements.

The Howard Government's first budget in 1996 demonstrated a determination to reduce dramatically Commonwealth involvement in social and community services, ranging across health and dental services, home and community care, migrant support programs, child care, labour-market programs, and university facilities and fees. In the first sign of an ongoing assault on services provided to indigenous communities through the Aboriginal and Torres Strait Islander Commission (ATSIC), $400 million was cut from the ATSIC budget. The winding back and privatisation of education and training was linked to an expectation that employment would be generated by a combination of faster overall economic growth and a more flexible, deregulated labour market.

Importantly, the 1996 budget also signalled a further move towards a privatised, family-based, self-insurance model of welfare provision. This was consistent with the recommendations of the Commission of Audit, which argued that 'action will be necessary to moderate expectations about what support the Commonwealth Government can reasonably be expected to provide in future and to strengthen incentives for self help by those who can afford it'.[33] The Minister for Social Security, Jocelyn Newman, agreed: 'It is important that those who can self provide can be encouraged to do so in parallel with taxpayers funding a scheme for those who are perhaps never going to be able to support themselves'.[34]

Further tightening of means and assets tests, longer waiting periods for newly arrived migrants, up-front fees for entry to nursing homes, and the introduction of work-for-the-dole programs were all driven by this principle of greater individual and family responsibility. So too was the Howard Government's family tax package, which provided the greatest benefits to those families with a single income earner.

In addition to assumptions about the desirability of greater individual and family responsibility, the Treasurer, Peter Costello, has explained why the government's attempt to reduce further social-policy expenditures was also driven by a direct concern about international competitiveness:

> We are becoming more conscious in Australia that we are in tax competition in our immediate region. Although the Australian tax to GDP ratio is not high by the standards of industrialised countries (certainly by European standards) it is high by regional standards. On average tax revenue is around 16 per cent of GDP in our major East Asian trading partners. In Australia Commonwealth tax to GDP is around 24 per cent.[35]

The problem, Costello argued, was that Australia spent about 9 per cent of GDP on social security, while Asian countries spent about 1 per cent. While not actually arguing for the complete reduction of Australian social security to Asian levels, the government was certainly intent on narrowing the gap. Costello maintained that here was 'the vexing question for Australia – how to maintain the social security system of an advanced industrial country whilst being tax competitive in our region.'

The debate about who has won and lost in Australia over the thirteen years of the Labor Government – and during the more recent period of the Howard Government – continues to be hotly contested. Labor Ministers were quick to respond to criticism of rising inequality and unemployment by arguing not only that there were no alternatives but also that 'it could have been worse' and that low-income and disadvantaged groups benefited substantially from income-security reforms, employment growth, and the expansion of the social wage.

No doubt it could have been worse, and it would be foolish to dismiss the significance of social-wage programs, such as Medicare, or the residual sources of protection against the full force of labour-market deregulation. However, an alternative interpretation is that the most lasting legacy of Labor's period in government will be a deregulated economy fully engaged in a race to the bottom with the low-wage, low-tax economies of South East Asia.[36]

The weight of evidence suggests that a significant shift from wages to profits, combined with high levels of unemployment and casualisation, created a more unequal society with rising levels of poverty and insecurity.[37] Between 1983 and 1994 the share of GDP going to wages fell from 63 to 56 per cent, while the profit share rose from 12 to 17 per cent.[38]

A range of studies has demonstrated a pattern of earnings inequality under Labor in which 'the rich got richer but the poor did not get poorer. Instead it was the middle who lost ground'.[39] It is certainly clear that the rich did very well indeed from tax cuts, financial speculation, rising company profits, and massive increases in executive salaries. By the mid-1990s executives in companies such as Nestlé, Coles Myer, Fairfax and the Broken Hill Proprietary Co. Ltd (BHP) were receiving salaries of between $2 million and $5 million a year at a time when the average male wage was $35 000. At the same time, 50 per cent of Australian workers earned less than $25 000 a year and almost 2 million people were living below the poverty line.[40] The 1996 annual survey of world poverty conducted by 'Bread for the World' showed that one in seven Australian children continue to live in poverty.[41] This is the second worst outcome among industrialised countries after the United States.

Between 1982 and 1993–94 the top 10 per cent of income earners in Australia experienced a real increase of $100 a week with the bottom 10 per cent gaining an increase of $11 a week.[42] The middle 80 per cent of income earners experienced real falls in earned income, leading to the average Australian wage earner experiencing a $67 a week decline in real market income during this period. While these changes were offset to some extent by improvements in pension rates and other income-security reforms, such as the Family Income Supplement, many low- and middle-income earners continued to experience a fall in their real after-tax income levels during the 1980s and 1990s.

A major study of geographical inequalities by Bob Gregory and Boyd Hunter also showed a significant 'ghettoisation' of Australian society.[43] Between 1976 and 1991 the average household income in the one thousand poorest neighbourhoods in Australia declined by $8000. In the richest neighbourhoods, average household incomes rose by almost $20 000. Only the top 30 per cent of neighbourhoods had real increases in household incomes between 1976 and 1991. The 70 per cent of the population in middle or poorer areas had declining incomes, with people in the poorest areas showing the steepest declines in income. The study concluded that

> income distribution has become more unequal and the change is extraordinary. There is a significant increase in the geographic polarisation of household income across Australia. The poor are increasingly living together in one set of neighbourhoods and the rich in another set. The economic gap is widening.[44]

The Labor Government's own Economic Planning and Advisory Council agreed that the data showed a widening income gap. In 1995 it noted that, while 'Australia does not yet have unmanageable levels of the homeless and beggars on the streets . . . even a cursory reading [of the available evidence] suggests that measured income inequality, especially that for market-based earnings has been increasing, or at best has been relatively static'.[45]

There is also compelling evidence that in Australia, as elsewhere in the world, it is women, migrants and indigenous populations that have fared worst.[46] Despite gains made by some women through increased employment opportunities and taxation and income security reforms, women were also more likely to be in low-paid, casual and part-time employment. This has often occurred along with an increased burden of caring for elderly and disabled relatives. Women have been worst affected by reductions in public expenditure on health, family support and education services.

It has been many years since most Australian families consisted of a full-time employed male breadwinner and a dependent female outside the paid workforce. Unfortunately, many of the key features of Australian social policy, paid working conditions and domestic labour arrangements have continued to assume that this arrangement still applies. Working hours continue to take no account of family responsibilities, such as the need to collect children from school or kindergarten. Career opportunities and adequate superannuation entitlements still depend on a continuous employment history uninterrupted by the birth and care of children.

Under Labor, the income-security system began slowly adjusting to the idea that women might have a right to an independent income separate from a male partner. This trend has been reversed by the Howard Government, with income-security changes designed to benefit mothers who stay at home with their children accompanied by sharp rises in the cost of child care that place greater financial pressures on mothers seeking to enter the paid workforce.

Initial indications are that inequality and poverty are likely to deteriorate further as a result of the social and economic policies of the Howard Government. As of early 1998, unemployment remained at over 8 per cent, with long-term unemployment continuing to rise. Wage and salary inequality also appeared to be increasing.[47] Despite some progressive reforms in the targeting of tax concessions to low-income families, the overall impact of social-wage cuts and labour-market deregulation had already been sharply regressive. The conclusion drawn by the President of the Australian Council of Social Service (ACOSS), Michael Raper, in January 1998 was that 'the rich are getting richer and the poor, though not getting poorer are getting more numerous'.[48] In February 1988, Dr John Nieuwenhuysen, one of the authors of the largest study of poverty in Australia since the Henderson Poverty Inquiry of 1975, noted that almost one-third of the Australian population was now living below the poverty line. He concluded that

[w]hatever means poverty is measured on and whichever segment
of the population the line of inquiry took, the level, spread and
severity of poverty has deteriorated since the Henderson Report.
Moreover, the prospects for the future are not encouraging.[49]

Inequality, unemployment and casualisation have created a fertile
breeding ground for insecurity, fear and prejudice. As feminist social policy
commentator Eva Cox has recently noted:

You have a huge level of insecurity up and down the line. Middle
class people are becoming very anxious, because they constantly
feel that they are excluded, they are told to pay for their own
health care if they don't want to spend hours on a trolley in
casualty . . .
We have also had nearly 20 years of being told that we should
pay less tax, that government is incompetent, that our economic
system is stuffed, that we are ruined and we are all going to have
to dig deeper. So is it surprising that people are actually starting
to get the disease and ask 'why should I pay more so the poor can
live comfortably?'[50]

It is not surprising, therefore, that there is mounting evidence of a backlash
by middle-class wage earners, not against the wealthy, but against the poor
and the most severely disadvantaged groups, such as Aborigines, migrants
and single mothers.[51]

Perhaps the most disturbing development of all is the extent to which a
climate has been created in which egalitarian and cooperative values have
been swept away by the advocates of economic rationalism and the free
market. In the end, Labor's rhetoric of social justice and citizenship was a
poor defence against the avalanche of claims from business leaders and
right-wing think tanks that an open, competitive economy makes cutting
taxes and public-sector expenditure inevitable.

As Executive Director of the Australian Institute, Clive Hamilton, argues,
Labor helped to bring about a profound shift in the 'rules' by which Australia
is governed and Australian society is organised:

Under [the postwar consensus] citizens agreed to play by the
rules of a civilized and democratic society and their government
agreed to maintain full employment, provide good quality
community services and protect the vulnerable. This contract has
been unilaterally discarded because of the belief by the policy
elite in the imperative of globalisation . . .
The Labor leadership spoke of making Australia an Asian
nation, of the need to appease the credit rating agencies, of the

glitter of the information super highway and of the unceasing
need for 'reform', a euphemistic code word for increasing
exposure to global economic forces.[52]

In this climate it became commonplace for business leaders to call for
ever deeper cuts to the public sector and welfare expenditure, claiming that
there are simply no alternatives in a competitive world. Ivan Deveson, Lord
Mayor of Melbourne and former head of Nissan Australia, made it clear that
'there is no doubt that we cannot afford the "social net" that we have – that
the size of the net must be linked to the economy – that to some degree our
commitment to an efficient economy has been weakened by some excessive
dependency on social support'.[53]

Virginia O'Farrell, director of an Australian firm of 'remuneration
consultants', in a defence of the payment of million-dollar salaries to
business executives captured a common corporate point of view when she
argued that

Australians and Australian companies need to come to terms
with the fact that traditional Australian egalitarianism and views
of fairness are not what is needed today . . . because the race to
prosper in a more competitive world [is] endless.[54]

Economist Fred Argy, the initial architect of the Hawke Government's
financial deregulation strategy, now concludes that 'we are losing control
over our social priorities. Capital markets simply don't like high levels of
government spending on health and social programs.'[55] The same point was
made more colourfully by former Victorian Labor Premier, John Cain, when
he argued that '[The international credit rating agencies] would think social
justice is a horse running at Saratoga [a United States racetrack]'.[56]

All of this leads to some broader questions. Who then is making the
decisions? Who is governing a deregulated Australian economy and society?
And how can national and local democracies survive in an age of global
financial markets that have become contemptuous of national borders and
local populations?

In 1985 the international credit-rating agencies and financial markets
reacted savagely and the value of the Australian dollar plummeted following
the suggestion that the Hawke Government might oppose the testing of MX
missiles by the United States in Australian offshore waters. In 1993 the Labor
Government in Victoria was hurled from office in a climate of mounting
media hysteria about the latest downgrade in credit ratings from Moodys
and Standard and Poors.

In 1995 Ford Australia publicly warned that it would cease its Australian
operations (at a cost of 7000 jobs) unless there were substantial reductions in

the costs of labour and government services. In 1993 Victorian Liberal Premier, Jeff Kennett, sacked all elected local governments and replaced them with appointed commissioners. In 1995, after a show of hands by several hundred businesspeople at a 'power breakfast', he announced that business would be more efficient and competitive if it did not have to deal with an elected Council for the central business district of Melbourne. So perhaps there should be no elections.[57]

In 1997 the Howard Government seemed to have at least tolerated, and perhaps even directly supported, a scheme to train retired and serving military personnel to carry out stevedoring work in an attempt to break the power of the maritime unions on Australia's wharves. The most disturbing aspect of this episode was the degree to which Commonwealth and State politicians appeared to see nothing at all wrong with the use of para-military force to deal with trade unions and defeat industrial action.

The combined impact of low domestic savings, rising levels of private foreign debt and financial deregulation have dramatically increased the influence of international capital markets, financial institutions and credit-rating agencies. In this climate it has become difficult to canvass higher levels of public-sector expenditure or progressive taxation without high-profile media commentators screaming that not only would this make Australian business uncompetitive but, in a deregulated financial system, the international financial markets and credit-rating agencies would never permit such policies to be implemented. This has led in turn to a disturbing trend towards political self censorship, with even progressive politicians and trade unionists refusing to talk about alternatives to current economic policy settings because, it is argued, there is no point discussing policies that would be unacceptable to the financial markets.

In the end this relentless narrowing of alternative policy visions, debates and agendas is the most worrying aspect of the polarising social impacts of the globalisation of corporate power within and beyond Australia. The task of opening up debates about alternative ideas and policy directions is not made any easier by the globalisation of control over the media and new communication technologies. The dangers – and the possibilities – of globalised media are explored in the next chapter.

Chapter 6

Wired to the World?
Australia and the Globalisation of Media and Information Technologies

If you really want to guarantee democracy in a nation, you need three things: you need a vigorous and open parliamentary system; you need an incorruptible judiciary; and you need a vigilant, on occasions cranky and profoundly sceptical media.
John Howard[1]

Mediacracy is not contradictory to democracy because it is as plural and competitive as the political system is. That is not much.
Manuel Castells[2]

The new reality of international media is driven more by market opportunity than by national identity.
Steven Ross, Former head of Time Warner[3]

November 1997. A Telstra executive celebrates the first international stock-market listing of the partly privatised Telstra by ringing the bell to start trading on the New York stock exchange. In Australia, Telstra shareholders laugh and cheer as the price of their shares soar. Government Ministers are delighted. Financial journalists can hardly contain their glee. Foxtel shareholders are grinning too, given the Pay TV partnership between Telstra and Foxtel. Every-one seems to be beaming, even the Australian and Chinese school children chatting to each other on the Internet in Telstra's saturation advertisements. Here is Telstra 'making it easier' by 'bringing the world together'.

This is the happy face of the globalised information economy. The technological wizardry of digitalisation and fibre optics will keep bringing people closer; deregulation, competition and privatisation will ensure falling costs and rising profits; the free flow of information will bring democracy, the free market and Coca-Cola to every corner of the globe.

Or, as the Annual Report of Saatchi and Saatchi, one of the world's most influential advertising companies, enthused:

> We live in an era of global communications. Scientists and technologists have achieved what militarists and statesmen down the ages have attempted to establish but without success – the global empire. There is no doubt that the world is becoming one market place. Capital markets, products and services, management and manufacturing techniques have all become global in nature. As a result companies increasingly find that they must compete all over the world in the global market place. This new development is emerging at the same time as advanced technology is transforming information and communication.[4]

There is, however, another way of understanding the nature of globalised media relationships. We are indeed moving into an 'age of information' in which there are creative possibilities for new modes of communication, new combinations of ideas, new forms of identity and community.[5] But the privatisation of Telstra is just one more example of the ways in which the information economy is being deregulated, privatised and controlled by a small number of vast global corporations. The real price will be a further loss of political sovereignty, economic opportunity and cultural diversity.

This chapter explores the dangers and possibilities of a globalised information society by looking at the technological, political, economic and cultural dimensions of new media relationships, with a particular focus on telephony, television and the Internet. The central argument is that there are indeed enormous dangers in the corporate globalisation of the media. But there are also significant contradictions, ambiguities and possibilities for resistance and creativity.

Imagining New Communities in the Information Age

While Marshall McLuhan's famous assertion that 'the medium is the message' remains slightly over inflated, changing modes of communication have always been at the core of understanding the history of social and economic relationships.[6] The development of speech is one of the defining characteristics in the transition to human civilisation. The use of pictures and writing allowed communication to move beyond the face-to-face requirements of direct speech and facilitated the development of trade and monetary exchange across large distances.

The invention of the printing press played a crucial role in the formation of European nation states.[7] Identification with an 'imagined community' of fellow national citizens was made possible by the capacity to reproduce ideas easily and to distribute them to a large and dispersed population through books and newspapers. Allegiance to national governments and the nation state was overwhelmingly strengthened by the capacity to disseminate rules, laws and proclamations across all territory under a particular state's jurisdiction.

While the introduction of technologies of 'mechanical reproduction', such as the phonograph, photography and cinema, created new opportunities for disseminating images and ideas to wider audiences with increased power and immediacy, the inventions of telephony, radio and television have been even more significant in compressing space and time.[8] Telephony made possible virtually instantaneous two-way communication between any two places on the planet connected by the appropriate wiring and switching devices. Radio and television radically expanded the capacity for broadcasting a single message to a vast audience. The initial reach of these broadcast technologies was limited by the distribution of transmission stations and television sets, but their reach has since been extended by the introduction of satellite and cable technologies.

Some commentators have greeted the introduction of the new communication technologies of the twentieth century with excitement and enthusiasm, seeing them as democratising tools, creating a 'global village' of shared information and international understanding.[9] Others have been far more cautious, even alarmed, particularly about the authoritarian potential of broadcast media. Critical social theorists Theodore Adorno and Max Horkheimer noted that 'the gigantic fact that speech penetrates everywhere replaces its content . . . the inherent tendency of radio is to make the speaker's word, the false commandment absolute. A recommendation becomes an order.'[10] For Marxist philosopher Louis Althusser, 'the communications apparatus [crams] every "citizen" with daily doses of nationalism, chauvinism, liberalism, moralism etc. by means of the press, the radio and television'.[11]

Other commentators have remained more appropriately ambivalent, noting the ambiguous potential for good and evil, democracy and fascism, creativity and passivity inherent, to varying degrees, in different communication technologies, depending on how they are distributed and controlled.[12] For some, the emancipatory potential of new information technologies has been further strengthened by the emergence of the Internet as a decentralised, interactive, inherently democratic network, heralding a 'second media age' of virtual communities and multiple realities.[13] The potential and limitations of Internet technologies in redefining global democracies and communities are discussed in more detail at the end of this chapter.

By the final decade of the twentieth century the reach and influence of communications and information technologies have moved to the centre of the historical stage to such an extent that it is now appropriate to talk of the beginnings of an 'information economy' involving a significant 'shift away from employment in producing raw materials, manufactured goods and tangible economic services towards employment directly related to the collection, processing and dissemination of data/information/knowledge'.[14]

If information processing has become 'the core, fundamental, activity conditioning the effectiveness and productivity of all processes of production, distribution, consumption and management', it is reasonable to begin to understand the world as a network of 'informational cities' and to talk of a transition from an industrial age to an 'information age' characterised by the central importance of flows of information and knowledge.[15]

Most Australians are now living in a world in which the widening reach and startling speed of both broadcast and interactive communications technologies have helped to compress dramatically all kinds of relationships across both time and space. The media in all its forms has become a central influence in the creation of individual, communal and national identities.[16] Before examining the ways in which this process has been played out in Australia, it is important to understand the key features of the technological, political and cultural changes involved.

The Politics of Technological Convergence

For much of the last one hundred years the most striking features of the development of new communications technologies have been the capacity to convey information to an ever-expanding range of audiences with a speed that now makes communication almost instantaneous.

These developments can be overstated. There are still billions of people across the globe without effective access to telephones and televisions, let alone faxes and cabled computers. An Email from Australia to Africa still often takes a day to be transmitted as the messages are placed in queues in order to deal with limited transmission capacity and to minimise expense by using the cheapest calling times. At times the need to ensure common global interconnection standards has created limitations as well as possibilities, given that 'the global telephone network is the world's largest machine. Every telephone in the world must connect to every other telephone. The most modern equipment in the Sydney exchange must communicate with a 100 year old phone box in rural China.'[17]

None the less, the telegraph, telephone, radio, television and fax have all, in different ways, been powerful tools in the compression of time and space that is often characterised as the defining feature of globalisation. The defining feature of new information technology in the last decades of the twentieth century has been the convergence of different technologies into common systems.

Since the mid-1980s the introduction of fibre-optic cables and digital information transmission, and the extensive use of microprocessors in switching equipment has further increased the speed, capacity and flexibility of communications. More debatable is the claim that enhanced storage and transmission capacities have undermined arguments for natural monopolies in telecommunications.

Importantly, the integration of communication technology platforms creates 'a convergent world [in which] all forms of content become digital-ised and can be delivered through a single communication mechanism to a single spot or a single consumer point'.[18] Text, sound, images and video can now be both transmitted and received via the same technological platform. This in turn allows the technologies of the telephone and the television; the radio and the camera; the fax and the word processor; the database and the spreadsheet to be integrated in ways that make the Internet unique in its capacity to support two-way interactions between two or more points across a network expanding to many points on the globe at an exponential speed.

For some commentators, such as director of the MIT Media Lab, Nicholas Negroponte, this is yet one more sign of how 'technology marches on, over you or through you, take your pick'.[19] But the cyborgs of *Bladerunner* and *The Terminator* remain far enough away in reality to caution that it is not yet communications technology that marches. It is still individuals and groups of individuals who determine, use and interpret the information content. And despite the diverse and creative possibilities of interactivity and interconnectivity, the convergence of technology has developed alongside the global convergence of the ownership and control of media content and the means of communicating information.

The Convergence of Media and Telecommunications Ownership and Control

The initial development of telephony and media-infrastructure policies was marked by a high degree of international diversity in relation to both owner-ship and control. Most telephony networks were developed as public mono-polies with the private systems developed in the United States being the most notable exception. Extensive international organisational arrangements were established to ensure interconnectivity through common network standards. Indeed, the International Telecommunications Union and related treaty arrangements represent some of the first attempts to develop effective forms of international governance involving both government and corporate players.

The United States, in line with its approach to telephone technology, also supported a dominant role for the private sector in the development of television. On the other hand, most European governments established public broadcasting companies as the major providers of both transmission technology and programming. As is discussed further below the Australian television network was developed as a hybrid system with substantial involvement from both the public and private sectors.

Since the 1980s governments in all countries have come under increasing pressure to commercialise, privatise and deregulate their telecommunications and media industries. Much of this pressure has come from national and transnational corporations aiming to force down the price of international communications services. The price of international communication has become a vital component of profitability for large corporations, with international telephone traffic doubling between 1988 and 1993 but with only 20 per cent of business customers accounting for 80 per cent of business revenues.[20]

By the late 1990s virtually all national telephone networks have been at least partly privatised and opened up to national and international competition.[21] Corporations with a direct interest in the increasingly strategic and lucrative information and entertainment industries have had an even more direct interest in winding back state regulation and public-sector involvement in production and service provision.[22]

The role of national governments has become limited to promoting competition, encouraging entry for new players, and, in some instances, subsidising low-income groups to maintain broad consumer access. This is certainly the limited regulatory mandate proposed in the United States' 1995 global information infrastructure strategy.[23] At the international level, a powerful network of transnational telecommunications corporations has begun to develop, although many of the most important corporate linkages remain at regional levels.[24]

By 1998 five transnational corporations controlled the vast majority of the media content available to audiences in most nations. The five big global media corporations – Time Warner, News Corp, Bertelsman, Viacom and Disney – have all developed strategies of both vertical and horizontal integration to ensure that their geographical and industry coverage is matched by their control of program content, distribution and delivery systems. They have also developed sophisticated 'multilocal' strategies to ensure effective access to different audiences and markets. Rupert Murdoch, for example, notes:

> I would see us buying world wide sporting events that will go right around the world, great musical events, making programs for a world audience. We will need local programming as well of course, but synergies will exist in special events . . . This is encouraged by the spread of world wide marketing companies, the toy companies, car companies, food and soft drink companies who we can provide a one stop shop for.[25]

Advertising, too, has become globalised in both ownership and content. Again, the initial strategic focus of marketing gurus emphasised the ways in which 'the global corporation looks to the nations of the world not for how they are different but for how they are alike . . . it seeks constantly in every way to standardise everything into a common global mode'.[26] Such strategies have become more sophisticated with the development of multilocal advertising strategies, as suggested by the Global Marketing Director of Coca-Cola, Peter Sealey: 'we still subscribe to global advertising and we think global, act local but we do recognise cultures are different and we need to speak to them using the same language'.[27]

The champions of global communications corporations and cultures often speak in evangelical tones of the enhanced consumer choice and democratic opportunities they are bringing to the peoples of the world. Rupert Murdoch is only one of many media moguls to have argued that it was transborder television and the fax machine that helped bring down the Berlin Wall and that have begun to open up space for political dissidents in China.

But, as the eminent American media researcher George Gerbner has argued, consumer choice is very much at the margins in a world of proliferating channels but narrowing content.[28]

> Mr Murdoch . . . is a master propagandist. He uses these themes, even though he knows very well that he is not interested in democracy. He goes in to any country where he can establish a foothold and a market. When you present a view of the world that by and large his News Corporation, his Fox Network in the United States presents, you may talk about democracy, you may use the slogans and the rhetoric of democracy but you are essentially presenting a world in which power rules and which is powerfully anti-democratic and women and minorities play a relatively negligible and highly vulnerable type of role.[29]

The debate about how the globalisation of media has led to a dramatic narrowing of information sources and a homogenisation of local cultural expressions and industries is explored in the following section.

Wall-to-wall Dallas or the Transglobal Underground: The Relationship Between Homogeneity and Hybridity

French Culture Minister Jack Lang's reputed reference to a globalised culture as a 'wall-to-wall Dallas' is only one of many warnings about the dangers of a homogenised global culture dominated (depending on your perspective) by some combination of the culture of America, 'the West', 'the North', and rich white males.

The increasing concentration of telecommunications networks and media ownership provide grave cause for concern. It would be naive to under-estimate the influence, for example, of Disney's ubiquitous cartoon characters or of News Corp's capacity to reach two-thirds of the world's population through its ownership of BSkyB (Europe), Fox (North America) and Star TV (Asia). In 1998 the dangers of globalised media oligopolies were starkly demonstrated when Rupert Murdoch personally intervened to prevent one of the many companies he controls, HarperCollins, from publishing the memoirs of the former governor of Hong Kong, Chris Patten. Murdoch's concern was allegedly that the memoirs might offend the Chinese Government and therefore jeopardise plans by his News Corp for future expansion in China.[30]

In the communication of news, networks such as CNN and the BBC combine with the five major news agencies to dominate the information that most people receive about the world around them. Not surprisingly, the news programs that most people see, and the advertisements that accompany them, are dominated by the success stories of white, wealthy Westerners and examples of the dangers posed to them by poor, black non-Westerners. Women are still commonly represented in the media by a narrow band of glamorous young actors, supermodels and news presenters.

Despite the excitement about CNN's role in bringing the Gulf War into the living rooms of America, Europe and Australia, more sober assessments have pointed to the ways in which the media coverage of this episode were carefully managed to ensure an impressive demonstration of high-tech United States/Western military power.[31]

In the world of *The Lion King*, *Star Wars* and the Spice Girls, concentrated media production and distribution networks led to the presentation of a disturbingly powerful, narrow and centralised set of symbols and images. It is a world in which 'most of the stories to most of our children most of the time are told no longer by the parent, and no longer by the school or the church or in many places, not even by the native country . . . but essentially by a handful of global conglomerates that have nothing to tell but a great deal to sell'.[32]

Transnational media corporations have also been the driving forces behind the creation of global sporting cultures and events. This process has dramatically undermined more local, 'communal' sporting traditions, as well as providing effective vehicles for the promotion of transnational brands such as Nike and McDonald's.[33]

National sporting associations themselves have developed powerful global marketing ambitions. As the President of *Sports Business Daily* recently noted in relation to the National Basketball Association's (NBA) plans to 'conquer the world', 'this is a league that is a global brand and looking to become an even stronger global brand'.[34] Yet the strength of United States national parochialism ensures that this refers only to the global broadcasting of North American basketball games and to the merchandising of clothing. 'Global basketball' should not yet be taken to mean the inclusion of Brazilian or Australian teams in the NBA.

The persistence of local cultural and language barriers is one of the reasons why cruder theories of American cultural imperialism and global culture need to be treated with some scepticism.[35] It is true, for example, that United States television companies produce over 75 per cent of programs shown on televisions around the world.[36] But it is also true that 80 per cent of those programs are sold into only seven countries. News Corp and CNN have frequently run into trouble through beaming uncensored material into Asia, and European nations fought off a fierce challenge from United States media companies to dismantle cultural trade barriers in the Uruguay round of the GATT.[37]

As social theorist Jan Pieterse suggests, there is something more complicated going on in the world than can be explained in terms of the simple colonisation of the world by the American institutions of MTV and CNN: 'How do we come to terms with phenomena such as Thai boxing by Moroccan girls in Amsterdam, Asian rap in London, Irish bagels, Chinese tacos and Mardi Gras Indians in the United States or Mexican schoolgirls dressed in Greek togas dancing in the style of Isadora Duncan?'[38]

The flows of global culture, ideas and information work in more than one direction.[39] The interactions and flows of global culture have produced much homogenisation. But they have also produced many new cultural connections and relationships.

> Globalisation has increased the range of sources and resources available for identity construction allowing for the production of hybrid identities in the context of a post traditional global society where bounded societies and states, though very much still with us are cut across by the circulation of other global cultural discourses.[40]

The story of technological convergence, concentration of media and telecommunications control and cultural contestation has been played out in particular ways in the Australian context.

After the Tyranny of Distance? Australia and the Globalisation of Communication

November 1997, Teheran. Australian soccer players arrive via Dubai from all over Europe to play Iran for a place in the World Cup. The Head of Soccer Australia, David Hill, expresses anxiety about the transportation, communication and even health problems of playing in what he describes as one of the worst and most inaccessible places on Earth. He makes it sound like Mars, or at least Siberia. Yet within only a few days of the announcement of the game millions of Australians are able to watch a live telecast on the 'ethnic' television station SBS. Around the stadium the hoardings display the brand names of the world's major transnational corporations: Sanyo, Hyundai, Diadora, Motorola, Canon and Snickers. There is even a large advertisement giving the Internet address for the game website.

As *Advance Australia Fair* is beamed out from Teheran into Australian loungerooms, it is difficult not to feel that globalised communications networks have radically changed the relationship between Australia and the rest of the world. As another Soccer Australia Commissioner and ABC journalist, George Negus, has noted, an additional lesson here is that

> soccer is the single greatest universal 'thing' in the world. It's bigger than any religion, it's bigger than any government. It's bigger than any political system. As a world traveller I know wherever I am, whether I'm in Liberia or Tierra Del Fuego, I'm going to see Coca-Cola and I'm going to see soccer. And I suspect at the moment, Pepsi having given Coke the run that they have, that soccer is bigger than Coke.[41]

Isolation and distance have always been central to understanding Australian history. Australian flora and fauna developed down their own evolutionary tracks because of the sea barriers separating the continent from other land masses. While the connections between South East Asia and northern Australia have been underestimated, it is still true that the Aboriginal peoples of Australia developed their own cultures largely independent of influence from other societies and economies.

For the convicts and settlers of Sydney Town, communication with England or even other parts of Australia was extremely slow. One hundred years after Captain James Cook's arrival on this country's shores the first submarine telegraph cable connected Australia first to Indonesia and then to Europe. By the 1930s radio had arrived and a generation of Australians listened in to Donald Bradman's cricketing exploits in England on the crystal set and the wireless.

The vast distances both within Australia and between Australia and the rest of the world played a vital role in strengthening the economic protectionism and cultural isolationism crucial to an understanding of the development of modern Australian society. It has only been since the Second World War, and particularly in the last twenty years, that technological and corporate changes have created an Australian society that is indeed wired to the world. This has solved some old problems. But it has also created many new ones.

The Convergence of Technology and Control in the Globalisation of Australian Telecommunications

Australians heard about the end of the Second World War on public and commercial radio, watched it on cinema newsreels, and read about it in privately owned newspapers. They communicated with far-flung friends and families by mail, telegraph and telephone, each method reliant on technology owned and controlled by the Post Master General's Department of the Commonwealth Government.

By the end of the twentieth century, Australia's print media is in even fewer private hands. Public and private television and radio continue to co-exist, although the private sector has become an even more dominant player with the Australian Broadcasting Corporation (ABC) under constant threat from funding cutbacks. Cinema has survived video to be bigger than ever as an entertainment medium. Postal and telephony services (which no longer include telegrams but do include faxes and cellular phones) have been split, with Telstra partly privatised and competing against its first private-sector rival, Optus. Pressure is also mounting for the deregulation and privatisation of Australia Post.

And then there is the Internet, with the jury still out on how this new technology will interact with television and telephony, as well as on the extent to which it will be either swallowed by transnational corporations or provide an alternative means of democratising two-way communications processes within and beyond Australia.

At the same time as the Hawke Government had begun to race down the path towards financial deregulation and economic rationalism in the mid-1980s, the technological and economic significance of digitilisation and fibre optics was beginning to emerge. Pressure began to mount for radical changes in the ownership and control of both the media and telecommunications industries.[42]

For the large media corporations the last fifteen years have involved a struggle to control the changing mix of media platforms and content in order to maximise profits during a period of convergence between broadcast and interactive technologies. Both developments have been championed and actively supported by Labor and Liberal governments and the implications of technological convergence need to be carefully considered, just as the concentration of control needs to be continually contested.

The following discussion focuses on the key themes underlying major changes in the television and telecommunications industries over this period rather than on the minutiae of entrepreneurial manoeuverings that dominate the mainstream media coverage of these developments.

In 1986 the Labor Government tightened laws preventing cross-ownership of print and electronic media but relaxed rules governing audience reach.

This resulted in Rupert Murdoch gaining effective ownership of The Herald and Weekly Times, as well as a period of takeover fever for the three major television networks, with high-flying, fast-falling entrepreneurs, such as Alan Bond and Christopher Skase appearing and disappearing with the speed, if not the grace, of shooting stars. By the late 1990s, at the end of an extended period of entrepreneurial snakes-and-ladders, ownership of the Australian television industry was split between Murdoch's Seven Network, Kerry Packer's Nine Network and the low-rent Ten Network controlled by Canadian Izzy Aspair.

One of the intriguing features of this process was the way in which the Labor Government appeared to intervene in foreign-ownership decisions without any clear policy rationale other than potential benefits to corporate media supporters and harm to its enemies.[43] Rules on foreign media ownership appeared to vary wildly between United States passport holder Rupert Murdoch, who was allowed substantial access, Canadian Conrad Black, who was limited to minority holdings, and the late British newspaper entrepreneur Robert Maxwell, who was prevented from entering the market at all.

During the early 1990s Labor also struggled to find a sensible response to the introduction of Pay TV into the Australian market. A bizarre and finally ineffective process designed to encourage new media-industry players through a system of Pay TV licence auctions eventually led to a duopoly involving Telstra and Foxtel, on the one hand, and Optus Vision (aligned with Packer), on the other. An attempt to involve the ABC in Pay TV programming was aborted in October 1995 when Pay TV distributors refused to accept the ABC's programs.

The ongoing puzzle of Pay TV was the extreme enthusiasm of the major players, given the clear evidence that Pay TV was highly unprofitable under current Australian market conditions.[44] The answer lay partly in the belief that sufficient pressure could be brought to bear on government policy makers to end the anti-siphoning rules preventing the switching of major sporting events from free-to-air stations to Pay TV. The need to control the broadcasting rights for key sporting events led to a bitter struggle between the Packer-backed Australian Rugby League (ARL) and Murdoch's Super League during 1996. However, the real prize in the overall battle over Pay TV was prime access to the cable network being rolled out across Australia by both Telstra and Optus.

Prior to the 1995 election, Kerry Packer made it clear that he preferred the prospect of a Howard Government to a re-elected Keating Government. Coincidentally, he said he would also be keen to see the cross-media rules reviewed to allow him to take over the Fairfax company, which would give him control of the quality print media in both Melbourne and Sydney. Former Melbourne *Herald* editor, Les Carlyon, wryly noted at the time that Prime Minister John Howard's initial indication that Australia needed another transnational media player like Mr Packer to compete internationally was extremely questionable: 'Steel workers at Newcastle are victims of globalisation . . . On the other hand we all have to rally so that one very rich man down to his last $3 billion can project himself onto the global stage because . . . well we sort of owe it to him.'[45]

Or, as Jock Given, Director of the Communications Law Centre, commented:

> why on earth should we in Australia be looking at liberalising the rules any further when we already have what we would regard as a quite unhealthy concentration of ownership among our major media players. How can we use the opportunities provided by the Internet, Online services, pay TV, digital TV and digital radio to encourage new voices into the Australian media?[46]

In the end John Howard finally gave in to sustained public pressure and the reality of Senate opposition, announcing in September 1997 that the review of the cross-media rules would be 'put on the backburner'.

The Howard Government demonstrated a fierce aversion to the ABC, which appears to have been prompted by direct political hostility and an ongoing ideological agenda of supporting the private sector wherever possible. Cutbacks to ABC funding extended savage reductions in the ABC budget begun under Labor. In this context, the 1997 Mansfield Review of the ABC was surprisingly supportive of the ABC's overall operations.[47] The major casualty was Radio Australia – a truly bizarre outcome given the economic and political significance of strong communication links with the Asian region.

The recent history of the commercialisation, deregulation and privatisation of Telstra needs to be understood in the context of the struggle to control convergent communications media industries. In 1990 a battle between the Treasurer, Paul Keating, and the Minister for Communications, Kim Beazley, led to a victory for Beazley and the supporters of more rapid deregulation of the Australian telecommunications industry.[48] Telstra was corporatised in 1991 and the 1992 *Telecommunications Act* allowed the introduction of a private telecommunications competitor, Optus, in 1992. Full deregulation of competition in the industry was opened up after July 1997. Then, in November 1997, one-third of Telstra was privatised.

There are several competing views of the overall outcomes of the last fifteen years of media and communications policy in Australia. For Terry Cutler, Chair of the Federal Government Information Policy Advisory Council, changing media and information-technology policies and programs can be understood in two ways:

> The growing reliance on telecommunications in business or in households, [means that] we look for more diversity, we look for

more choice of service. Therefore there's been the pressure for competition. But globally with the internationalisation of the economy, telecommunications has been a key part of that, so what we've seen is the breakdown of the old distinctions between domestic communications and international communications. It becomes part of one interlinked global network where you have multiple providers all working together in one shape or another, and all competing with one another.[49]

From this point of view the recent history of media and telecommunications policy in Australia is a story of enhanced choice and competition in the context of technological convergence and globalised access to information and entertainment.

From another perspective the outcome has been less real choice in information and entertainment sources due to further concentration of media and advertising company ownership. Australian content rules continue to be undermined, with Pay TV, in particular, offering a largely foreign diet of news, sport and entertainment. One particularly provocative recent anecdote suggests that Melbourne schoolgirls asked to give the Melbourne general emergency telephone number gave the number used on the United States television soapie, *Baywatch*. The traffic is not entirely one way, as British and European devotees of *Neighbours* and *Home and Away* well understand.[50] But the overall trend is clearly towards greater foreign control and influence of Australia's cultural industries.

Similarly, in relation to telecommunications, Labor and Liberal governments have permitted and encouraged the major media owners to move towards a duopoly in the battle to win control of the increasingly privatised telecommunications network. The privatisation of this network is indeed a serious error, if you believe that

> rather than an expensive Information Super Tollway, part owned and often operated on behalf of a few flashy large entertainment trucking operations, what we need is a national electronic pipeline. Australia needs an infrastructure organisation which provides pipelines for [moving] electrons from one source to another in the most flexible and economical way . . . It [Telstra] should not be in business to make a profit any more than the Main Roads Department is in business for profit.[51]

'Crossing the Rubicon': Real Power in Virtual Societies?

The Keating Government's 1995 *Creative Nation* report on cultural industries waxed lyrical about how new information technologies would provide a bridge to 'cross the Rubicon' to a wonderful future of heightened creativity and emancipation.[52] Since then Australian governments and consumers have taken an enthusiastic interest in the possibilities of the Internet and multi-media technology. A series of major Commonwealth Government inquiries have been held, in an attempt to explore ways of balancing the productivity potential of new media with issues of access and equity.[53] At the State level, the Victorian Government even claims to have appointed the world's first Minister for Multimedia.

The arrival of the Internet has given rise to a host of creative explorations of its potential for enhancing democratic decision making and opening up new kinds of social and political relationships. For the libertarian right, there is the promise of a brave New Frontier of electronic town halls and shopping malls.[54] For communitarians, the virtual community beckons with images of cheery souls in electronic cottages chatting away in the global village.[55] Indigeneous and remote communities have watched with considerable interest as some of the most innovative experiments with new communication technologies have been carried out by Aboriginal communities exploring the potential for satellites and cables to overcome the communication problems of small remote settlements joined by rough, sometimes impassable, roads.[56] Unionists and environmentalists see the possibilities of the virtual picket line and the cyber demonstration – or at least a means of creating global solidarity in an age of global corporations.[57] Some feminists cautiously hope to explore a non-hierarchical virtual world of hidden or shifting gendered identities. Activists and theorists concerned about the anti-democratic and centralising implications of globalisation look hopefully to the capacity of the inherently decentralised spaces of the Internet in creating a more democratic and diverse virtual public sphere.[58]

More sceptical critics note that the reach of the Internet is still extremely limited, extending to no more than 1 per cent of the world's population.[59] Outside of schools, universities and public libraries, Internet access remains an expensive option requiring costly computer equipment and fees. Importantly, the decentralised and democratic nature of Internet access is under imminent threat from commercial interests seeking to gain control of cyberspace in order to maximise its potential for profitable business transactions. The most immediate threat is from Bill Gates's Microsoft Corporation, which is attempting to monopolise software for Internet access, thereby controlling the gateway to any future virtual communities or picket lines. Even such staunch economic conservatives as former United States Republican presidential candidate, Bob Dole, have become so alarmed at the prospect of a Microsoft Internet monopoly that they have actively supported anti-monopolistic legal action to try to prevent it. Nor is at all clear that cyberspace should be seen as a non-hierarchical, gender-neutral forum. The dominance by male users and the pervasive experience of violent, pornographic and harassing forms of communication on the Internet suggest that this space has the capacity to be at least as patriarchal and violent as the more familiar streets and homes.

Ultimately, the Internet is best understood as creating a new set of relationships and places, rather than as a high-technology tool. It is one more global arena in which struggles over the distribution of resources, power and information will be fought out.

Chapter 7

Nowhere to Hide?
Australia in the Global Environment

Globalisation is quite clearly the biggest environmental problem. Globalisation requires that we start to export things that we've never exported before, and start to import things we've never imported before. For instance exporting our biodiversity, our livestock wealth, products of our coastal ecosystem like shrimp, flowers produced through intensive irrigation in low rainfall zones (so that we're exporting our water). Importing things like toxic wastes . . .
Indian environmental activist, Dr Vandanna Shiva, 1997[1]

To call [Australia's position on Greenhouse Gas emissions] irresponsible is too mild. To call it moronic would be to compliment it. Australia could be taking a major role by demonstrating large scale solar power and selling it to China and India. Instead it's behaving like a dumb European country of 1860.
Professor Paul Ehrlich, 1997[2]

On 20 October 1997 a team of Greenpeace activists scaled the walls surrounding Kirribilli House, the Sydney residence of Australian Prime Minister, John Howard. Solar panels were rushed past the security guards and lifted up on to the roof as a 'gift' to the Prime Minister. From the roof the protesters used mobile phones to inform the Australian and international media about their opposition to the Australian Government's refusal to support common and binding greenhouse-gas emission targets.

The Prime Minister's response was that 'noisy groups such as Greenpeace will . . . have absolutely no impact at all on the direction of government policy'.[3] That policy, according to the Prime Minister, was driven by the view that 'economic reform has produced significant reorientation of the Australian economy towards the export sector in general and resource processing sectors in particular. Australia's economy has become both more highly specialised and more emission intensive.'[4]

The greenhouse issue, the Greenpeace action, and John Howard's response to it illustrate three key features of the relationship between globalisation and ecology. First, it is now universally understood that there are many ecological problems that have both global causes and global consequences. Second, this awareness has given rise to a host of government and non-government political organisations aiming to address environmental concerns that cross national boundaries. And third, there is often a fundamental tension between the urgent need to deal with global environmental issues and the logic of unregulated and globalised free-market capitalism.

For many years Australians felt themselves to be far enough away from the rest of the world to be protected from the growing list of environmental concerns and hazards experienced and feared by residents of Europe, Asia or North America. But as skin-cancer rates rise as a consequence of the hole in the ozone layer, as farmers struggle to predict the destructive impact of climate change, and as travellers fly north into the smoky, poisonous hazes over South East Asia it is clear that distance provides only limited protection against ecological risk. How then can Australian governments reconcile the relentless globalisation of Australian economic policy with the consequences of ignoring the impact of global environmental relationships on current and future generations of Australians?

The Globalisation of Ecological Relationships

As the victims of climatic change, downstream pollution, and vermin-spread disease have long understood, human societies have always had to deal with environmental relationships that extend beyond local sources and effects. However, the broader understanding that there are environmental actions that have distant, even global, consequences that require responses extending across local and national boundaries is very new indeed. Even twenty years ago it would have been difficult to imagine the Vice President of the United States declaring, as Al Gore did in 1995, that

> modern industrial civilization, as presently organised, is colliding violently with our planet's ecological system. The ferocity of its assault on the earth is breathtaking, and the horrific consequences are occurring so quickly as to defy our capacity to recognize them, comprehend their global implications and organise an appropriate and timely response.[5]

The symbolic turning point in our awareness of the global environment was the early 1970s, when the first photographic images of Earth taken from space appeared. It was one thing to be told in an abstract and theoretical way that endless population growth was unsustainable and that the planet's resources were finite. The splendour, the limitations and the loneliness of the planet only became fully apparent when it could be seen through the eyes of fellow human astronauts.

This change in perception coincided with increasing awareness of the extent of the environmental impact of escalating pressure on the Earth's renewable and non-renewable resources. The Earth's population grew from 2.5 billion to 5 billion between 1950 and 1987. Global per capita consumption of goods and services grew even faster, doubling between 1950 and 1975, with energy consumption growing by over 400 per cent between 1950 and the mid-1980s.[6]

The combination of rapidly declining resources and an escalating population gave rise to a new growth industry in doomsday predictions about imminent global environmental catastrophe.[7] While some of the wilder predictions about resource depletion underestimated the impact of conservation measures and new discoveries, the fundamental truth remained: there are limits to planetary resources and the breaking point is fast approaching.

During the 1970s and 1980s there was also increasing awareness of the damage caused to the global environment by pollution, toxic wastes and the impact of a wide range of technological processes central to the rise of advanced industrial economies. Particular contributions and events seemed often to crystallise the rising sense of local risk and danger from distant actions.

In 1962 Rachel Carson's *Silent Spring* first articulated the fear about the dangers of the pervasive impact of chemicals and pesticides on wildlife and agriculture.[8] In the 1990s, despite the banning of DDT and similar chemicals in many industrialised countries, the risks continue even if you live far from the places where hazardous chemicals are used. It is the indigenous women of Northern Quebec, for example, who now have the highest concentration of DDT residues in their breast milk, due to the drifting impact of pesticides used in North Africa and the Middle East.[9]

By the 1970s Canada and the Scandinavian communities watched with rising alarm as native forests were killed by sulfuric and nitric acid falling on the trees as acid rain. Yet the source of the chemicals was often factory and car emissions from far away countries and therefore outside the jurisdiction of the government with sovereignty over the area affected.

In 1984, 2500 people died and 200 000 people were injured in the world's worst industrial accident when methyl isocyanate gas leaked from the Union Carbide Plant at Bhopal in India. A new political question was placed on the agenda of relations between industrialised and developing countries: What are the consequences of transnational corporations avoiding protests and regulation in industrialised countries by locating potentially lethal industrial processes in countries with lower levels of environmental regulation?

In 1986 the Chernobyl nuclear power plant explosion destroyed any illusions that the impact of nuclear power-plant disasters could be confined to local areas as threatening clouds of radiation spread out over Northern Europe. Within days Scottish and Swedish dairy farmers found themselves measuring alarming levels of radiation in their cheese and milk as Russian, English, French and Dutch parents all anxiously studied their newborn children, wondering what new risks and dangers they had now been exposed to.

In 1988 the residents of Kassa Island in West Africa found that Norwegian freighters had been dumping highly toxic waste carried from Philadelphia in the United States.[10] No United States community would tolerate having these poisonous cocktails of heavy metals and dioxins dumped in their backyards, so they were sent halfway round the world disguised as 'building materials'.

By the early 1990s doctors in Australia were warning parents of the need to clothe their children in 'neck-to-knee' bathers in order to protect them from the increased likelihood of skin cancer due to the hole in the ozone layer over the South Pole. This, in turn, was the result of a massive rise in the use of chlorofluorocarbons (CFCs) for aerosols and refrigeration between 1950 and the mid-1980s.

By the early 1990s there was also mounting evidence that the climate of the globe was changing as the atmosphere heated up due to the emission of 'greenhouse gases', such as methane and carbon dioxide, into the atmosphere. Predicting the full implications of global warming is a complex task, but its diverse impacts are likely to range from increased desertification and drought in Africa, through the flooding of low-lying areas such as Bangladesh, to the complete disappearance of some island communities in the South Pacific.[11]

In 1994 the salmon stopped running in the rivers of Canada as anglers and scientists puzzled over the connections between over-fishing and climate change that had led to the apparent end of a biennial event which had sustained First Nation peoples for thousands of years.[12] On the other side of Canada the great fishing banks of Newfoundland were empty, fished out as a result of the deregulation of fishing grounds. And in the Southern Ocean Australian authorities continued to struggle to prevent the destruction of maritime species by Japanese and Russian fishing fleets.

In 1997 the societies and economies of Indonesia, Malaysia, Singapore, Thailand and the Philippines were devastated by thick grey smoke emanating from vast forest fires in Indonesia. There is little doubt that these fires were deliberately lit as part of logging and agribusiness operations.

The pressure on finite global resources; the drifting hazards of pesticides, chemicals and radioactivity; the attempts to shift geographically the risks of toxic wastes and hazardous industries; the hole in the ozone layer; the warming of the Earth's atmosphere. These distant and global manifestations of local actions have diverse causes and consequences. Some are examples of the impact of local actions on specific localities across national boundaries or on the other side of the world. Many are examples of attempts to offload environmental costs from industrialised to less industrialised countries. Others demonstrate the ways in which actions in particular places can have consequences for animals, plants, people and environments all over the world. But the common thread is the myriad ways in which local actions have distant and global environmental consequences. No citizen of this planet can completely ignore or escape the damage to the global commons.

The Globalisation of Environmental Politics

The arena of global environmental politics has become densely populated with an array of actors, including nation states, intergovernmental bodies, private-sector corporations and non-government organisations. The abiding problem is that, while the Earth may look both fragile and wholly interconnected from space, there are significant differences between the interests and powers of the various global environmental actors. The consequences of these differences are illustrated by the recent history of attempts to develop global environmental governance processes.

In 1992 the political leadership of the planet's nation states, along with representatives from thousands of non-government organisations, attended the United Nations Conference on Environment and Development (the Earth Summit) in Rio de Janeiro. The conference was the most ambitious attempt in human history to address the full range of global environmental concerns.[13]

There was much fine rhetoric about the dangers of unfettered consumerism and our responsibility to future generations. The final declaration includes many laudable commitments to environmentally sustainable development and reductions in subsidies to unsustainable industries. A non-binding comprehensive global environmental action plan (Agenda 21) was agreed upon, as were two separate non-binding agreements on environment and development and sustainable forestry. International conventions on climate change and biodiversity were negotiated in a parallel procedure, with the signing process begun at the Earth Summit. Significant new negotiating processes were established in relation to concerns such as desertification, fishing stocks, pollution and pesticides. Despite these achievements, the conference was marked by deep conflicts over the relationship between environmental sustainability and economic growth and between the representatives of industrialised and developing countries.

The central argument from the government representatives of many developing countries was that environmental concerns had to be linked to overcoming poverty. Substantial reductions in poverty, it was argued, could only be achieved by rapid economic growth based on exports of natural resources, such as timber, and the expansion of manufacturing industries reliant on fossil-fuel consumption.

Environmental activists from developing countries, such as Vandanna Shiva, often took a different stance, arguing for a more aggressive opposition to globalisation.

> Globalisation is about liberalised imports and exports, which makes India export our best natural wealth and import the junk and wasted pollution of international production, including of Western countries.[14]

Government of most developing countries continued to oppose attempts to regulate or restrict natural-resource trade or energy consumption, while calling for a linkage between environmental action and measures designed to reduce debt in developing countries. And, as the Dutch Environment Minister, Hans Alders, noted:

> [W]e are asking Third World Countries to cooperate in the success of international conferences which we are organising because we are concerned about the environmental problems we have caused. And then we ask them to temper their growth just when they are arriving at the state when gradually they can be granted a measure of economic growth.[15]

The United States President, George Bush, effectively opposed attempts to link debt reduction to the environmental agenda, as well as blocking targets for aid to developing countries. The United States also played a blocking role to prevent the passing of resolutions that advocated reductions in consumption and production levels in industrialised countries.

For some commentators the Earth Summit was an important step in bringing key actors together to promote a range of significant principles and negotiating processes. For others, it was an empty rhetorical exercise in which the hard decisions were either avoided or vetoed.[16]

Understanding of the extent and urgency of environmental problems has both deepened and broadened in the last five years. Public opinion polls consistently show environmental issues to be high on the list of anxieties of citizens, particularly those in industrialised countries. Politicians and corporate moguls all feel compelled to at least appear to recognise the seriousness of ecological issues. Toyota spends millions of dollars to sponsor special environmental issues of *Time* magazine in order to advertise its 'clean, green, cars'.[17] McDonald's assures its customers that it really does care about recycling and the destruction of forests. More concretely, a range of significant agreements and protocols have been negotiated and implemented on issues as diverse as desertification, biodiversity and global fishing resources. Yet the fundamental environmental threats continue to grow and the central conflicts remain unresolved.

For all the mounting evidence about the reality and severity of global warming, the negotiations leading towards the 1997 Kyoto Climate Change Summit provided a stark demonstration of the difficulty of achieving global agreements. Climate change is the most obviously global of all environmental challenges. While cause and effect relationships need to be analysed carefully, there are many indicators that are cause for considerable concern.

The five hottest years in recorded history have been in the 1990s. Sea levels are significantly higher than they were one hundred years ago. In Antarctica the ice sheets are melting and marine mammal populations are declining as the krill, which is the basis of the food chain, disappears. In Alaska and Siberia the perma frost is thawing into swampy bogs. In areas as diverse as southern Africa, Spain, Papua New Guinea and Australia, severe droughts are causing increasing desertification and aridity.[18] The political problem is that there are substantial differences of opinion between countries in relation to the likely consequences of global warming, and these give rise to differing views about appropriate policy responses.

Those most fearful about global warming are the Pacific island states threatened with annihilation by rising sea levels and the African societies facing famine as a result of expanding deserts. The European Union (EU) has argued for a relatively swift reduction in greenhouse-gas emissions, but many developing countries insist on the need to differentiate between the application of restrictions to industrialised and developing countries, given that it is the industrialised economies that have been primarily responsible for rising CO_2 levels. It has been argued that it is unfair to restrict developing countries, thereby preventing them from achieving similar economic growth patterns.

In the United States a ferocious public debate erupted in the lead up to Kyoto as private corporations poured massive resources into a campaign to undermine support for tighter emission controls. As is discussed in more detail below, the Australian Government decided to take up a particularly extreme position by arguing for the right to keep increasing greenhouse-gas emissions because of the economy's dependence on fossil-fuel industries. The conflicts and difficulties encountered in the attempt to develop a global consensus on climate-change policies are indicative of the deeper problem of reliance on the nation state as the primary basis for making global environmental policies. Environmental policy analyst Robin Eckersley points out that

> the modern state did not evolve with complex, transboundary ecological problems in mind. Rather, it evolved to represent the interests of citizens of territorially bounded political communities . . . In an increasingly borderless economic world there appear to be few incentives for states to orchestrate a thorough going greening of the domestic economy in the absence of international regulation or failing that, comparable environmental regulation (and taxation) by relevant trading partners.[19]

The development of effective international governance forums for negotiating environmental regimes and resolving disputes is therefore a matter of considerable urgency – and difficulty.[20] The achievement of international consensus on crucial environmental issues has been made even more difficult by the growing significance of international trade agreements often designed to oppose and prevent international environmental regulation. Agreements such as those negotiated by the World Trade Organisation (WTO) and the North American Free Trade Agreement (NAFTA) contain powerful clauses designed to prevent nation states using 'environmental trade measures (ETMs) to "interfere" with trade'.[21]

Transnational corporations and governments (particularly in developing countries reliant on natural-resource exports) have increasingly turned to the WTO and NAFTA to stop environmental restrictions on trade in products as diverse as tropical timber, tuna fishing and cars with high levels of petrol consumption. Freer trade might have environmental benefits if it leads to higher corporate environmental production standards due to greater demand for 'clean green products'. [22] But it is at least as likely that pressures for greater export growth and competitiveness will lower environmental standards in the context of reduced capacity for national regulation.

There are several ways of reading the story of global environmental politics in the last part of the twentieth century. From one perspective the story is one of increasingly effective activism by environmental movements raising awareness of global environmental threats, challenging the sustainability of unrestricted material consumption, and building alliances capable of pressurising nation states into negotiating effective international environmental agreements.[23] The dominant images here are of the *Rainbow Warrior* and of courageous Greenpeace activists boarding toxic-waste and nuclear-testing vessels on the high seas with the action being broadcast to the world via satellite technology.[24] Enthusiasm for the potential contribution of environmental social movements is also often associated with considerable faith in the capacity of local communities and individual citizens to 'make a difference' by changing lifestyles and reducing consumption. Taking a fairly cynical point of view, environmental policy analysts Pratad Chatterjee and Matt Finger suggest that

> [h]eightened concern about any social ill, erupting at a time of erosion of public confidence in political institutions and (more fundamentally) individual capacities to effect change, will prompt masses of people to act, but in that one area of their lives where they command the most power and feel the most competent: the sphere of consumption.[25]

Many forms of local ecological activism inspire a sense that there are real political, technological and economic alternatives to corporate globalisation.[26] The danger is that local activism can be overwhelmed by the power of global corporations and the potential for global ecological flows to transcend local impacts and places. Too often calls for individual environmental action are understood solely as calls for shorter showers and cleaner soaps.

Another set of images of global environmental politics includes the actions of transnational corporations mobilising vast resources to counter public opinion and government policies that might threaten to regulate or restrict investment and trade in the name of global environmental concerns. It also includes the role of many nation states in attempting to manage the competitive nightmare of globalised economic relations by minimising environmental regulations.

The relationship between these two pictures of the globalised environment were dramatically illustrated in late 1997 by the conjunction of two disastrous events in South East Asia. As the poisonous haze from the Indonesian forest fires choked and blinded millions of people from the Philippines to India and from Indonesia to Thailand, there was mounting political pressure for action to stop the corporate incineration of the region's forests. But the fortunes of the governments of many of these nations were closely tied to the timber companies and agribusinesses responsible for the fires. And then, as the concerns and conflicts intensified, a new catastrophe threatened to overwhelm the region as global financial speculators drove down Asian currencies and sparked a massive sell off on Asian sharemarkets. The global environmental crisis had met global financial power with a sickening crash.

Australian politicians and citizens, as always deeply ambivalent about their cultural, economic and environmental relationship with Asia, watched the twin crises spread with deepening unease. The contradictory relationships between ecological and economic globalisation within Australia itself forms the second part of this chapter.

The Globalisation of Australian Environmental Relationships

The European understanding of the Australian environment has been based on two fundamental misconceptions since at least 1788. The first is that the continent is so vast that it can easily absorb high levels of agricultural and industrial exploitation by millions of immigrants. Many farmers on the marginal arid plains of inland Australia have found, to their bitter cost, that this assumption is very wrong indeed.[27] Stock levels and crop yields that seemed promising in good years proved unsustainable in times of drought when the water disappeared and the thin soil eroded and blew away. Attempts to overcome the lack of water through the use of artesian bores and river irrigation created new disasters of salinity in many areas.

In other areas the initial enthusiasm for slashing and burning the great forests has had to be redressed through a dauntingly large task of reforestation. The vision of cheap hydroelectricity as a source of economic salvation, which looked so hopeful to the postwar engineers of the Snowy Mountains scheme, came into sharp conflict with a different set of environmental visions in the battles over Lake Pedder and the Franklin Dam in Tasmania. And as Australia grew into one of the most urbanised societies in the world, the majority of the population became tightly concentrated in a few congested cities, looking outwards to the sea rather than inland to the arid 'great dead heart'.

The second misconception has been that Australia's geographical remoteness could and would provide a safe barrier against the environmental pollution and degradation occurring in Europe, North America and Asia. As *State of the Environment 1996* argues, it is still true that

> [t]he southern hemisphere is mainly water and is markedly less affected by human activities than the northern. Australia lies in relatively unpolluted air and sea. Its comparative isolation means that transboundary pollution is not as significant an issue as it is for many northern hemisphere countries.[28]

This idea of Australia being protected by its remoteness led to Melbourne being cast as 'the end of the world' in Nevil Shute's novel *On the Beach*, in which the last United States submarine seeks safe haven in Melbourne after a global nuclear holocaust. Unfortunately, as the submariners and the population of Melbourne discover, radiation clouds do not, given time, respect the tyranny of distance or national boundaries.

While it is true that the unique nature of Australian flora and fauna arises from the splendid isolation of the Australian land mass during critical evolutionary periods, the arrival of human beings has had a long and significant ecological impact. Over forty thousand years ago the Australian environment began to be profoundly altered by the arrival of Aboriginal peoples with their companion animals and fire-farming techniques. European colonisation in the eighteenth century led to a rapid increase in population and a sharply accelerated process of environmental exploitation and devastation. The Europeans also brought an array of organisms with devastating consequences for the local ecology.[29] Rabbits, cows and sheep stripped the grasses; foxes and cats exterminated indigenous birds and animals; introduced plants, such as prickly pear and blackberry, swept over the native vegetation. Smallpox and influenza also killed thousands of indigenous people.

The lesson Australian farmers and governments drew from the legacy of damage caused by foreign creatures and diseases was that the nation needed to insulate itself through some of the toughest customs regulations in the world. Behind these walls of distance and quarantine it was hoped that Australian agriculture could thrive on the basis of exporting farm produce cleaner and safer than any in the world. It was also hoped that the country's apparently boundless natural resources would continue to sustain strong export industries and a relatively high level of economic growth and material living standards.

The first wave of environment movement campaigns in the 1970s and 1980s began to illustrate the flaws in this assumption. The struggles over Lake Pedder, the Franklin Dam, the Tasmanian and Queensland rainforests, uranium mining in Kakadu National Park, and the Wesley Vale pulp mill were all battles over the extent to which local communities, provincial states and large corporations could continue to assume that their rights to exploit the country's rivers, minerals, forests and wilderness areas would remain unchallenged.

One striking feature of all these campaigns was the way in which they began to illuminate the relationship between differing levels of local, national and global ecological politics. Thus, for example, the Franklin Dam campaign involved protesters coming to a remote part of Tasmania from all over Australia, often supported by local communities, to block attempts by the Tasmanian Government to build a dam designed to provide power and strengthen Tasmanian national and global competitiveness. The High Court of Australia finally upheld the power of the Commonwealth Labor Government to use globally negotiated World Heritage Treaty obligations to override State opposition.

The conflicts over local resource usage demonstrated both the increasing power and the limitations of the 'think globally; act locally' politics of environmental social movements and Green electoral initiatives. The size and influence of organisations such as the Australian Conservation Foundation, the Wilderness Society and Greenpeace grew rapidly and the Labor

Party seemed to have recognised the advantages of drawing on environmentally concerned voters to win elections.[30] Green representatives were
being elected to parliament and in the late 1980s even entered into a coalition
government with Labor in Tasmania. However, rumours of the decline of
national and global corporate power in relation to resource exploitation were
definitely premature.

The latter period of the Hawke and Keating Labor governments was
marked by the rising influence of resource-exporting corporations and
groupings such as the Australian Mining Industry Council and the National
Association of Forest Industries. In 1991 this led to the launch of a Commonwealth Government Industry Statement that endorsed the principle of
resource-security guarantees. These involved promises that the Commonwealth Government would not intervene in future to prevent State and local
resource-development projects.[31]

The early 1990s also saw an ill-fated attempt to develop a set of ecologically sustainable development principles and policies between governments,
industry and environment groups. Despite protracted consultations and
negotiations, the interests of the various parties remained too disparate for
meaningful agreements and effective targets to be achieved.[32]

By the mid-1990s the independent State of the Environment Advisory
Council's stocktake of the Australian environment could conclude that
Australia continued to benefit from the natural advantage of geographical
isolation, as well as commendable policy initiatives such as the Great Barrier
Reef Marine Park, the Murray Darling Basin Commission, and the Landcare
program designed to improve local land-use practices.[33]

The bad news included an alarming reduction in biological diversity
through habitat loss and species extinction; the degradation of soil and
inland waters; rising urban congestion; and the cross-border problems of
ozone depletion and climate change arising from greenhouse-gas emissions.
In relation to this last concern, it noted that Australia had the dubious
honour of being one of the world's highest per capita contributors to
greenhouse-gas emissions, due to a combination of high car usage, heavy
reliance on fossil fuels for energy and industrial production, and extensive
land clearing.

At the same time there was an emerging debate about sustainable population levels and immigration rates for Australia, which constantly ran the
risk of being divided into parallel debates about the relationship between
immigration and jobs and the most desirable racial composition of the
Australian population.[34]

It was in this context that the newly elected Howard Government began to
implement its 1995 election promises of substantial new action on national
and global environmental issues. Its principal environmental commitment
was the establishment of a $1.25 billion Natural Heritage Trust to fund a

wide range of high-priority environmental programs. The funds for the Trust were to come from the proceeds of the partial privatisation of Telstra. The Howard Government also stated its commitment to balancing the effective management of a limited number of environmental issues identified as being of 'national significance' with the aim of decentralising much environmental policy making back to the States and reducing 'green tape' regulatory requirements on the private sector.

By 1997 the Howard Government had won parliamentary approval for the Telstra sale, but there was substantial evidence that the Natural Heritage Trust funds were likely to be spent on a range of programs that could more accurately be described as rural assistance programs than urgent environmental priorities. Evidence also emerged that the Trust was largely financed by cuts in other environmental and energy conservation programs.[35]

The most controversial and difficult environmental policy issues confronted by the Howard Government were the negotiations leading up to the International Conference on Climate Change held in Kyoto in December 1997.[36] The government's policy was to fiercely oppose common greenhouse-gas emission targets on the grounds that differential standards are required for economies, such as Australia's, that are heavily reliant on fossil-fuel industries, energy-resource exports and agricultural land clearing.

The Prime Minister also argued that common greenhouse-gas targets should be opposed in principle because they were an unnecessary and unfair imposition on private corporations and would distort international trade and investment patterns.[37] The editor of the *Australian*, Paul Kelly, noted at the time that the key issue was that 'the Kyoto meeting is not just about the environment. It is about imposition of restrictions across economies, most notably Australia's.'[38] For the Managing Director of Western Mining Corporation, Hugh Morgan, global emission targets represented nothing less than an anti-democratic attack on Australian sovereignty![39]

The alternative point of view, as expressed by *Age* columnist Kenneth Davidson was that government modelling grossly overstated the impact of reduced emission targets on Australian industry and that

> by claiming special status as a global polluter at the same time as
> it slashes programs designed to reduce that pollution, Australia
> invites international derision now and the threat of future retalia-
> tion and far higher adjustment costs than if a serious program on
> the reduction of greenhouse emission was started now.[40]

Given Australia's poor record as one of the highest per capita contributors to greenhouse-gas emissions, it is not surprising that this position led to substantial protests in Australia, as well as strong opposition from many other national governments.

In October 1997 pressure by the Australian Government at the Common-wealth Heads of Government Meeting in Edinburgh led to a watering down of the position on common greenhouse-gas emission targets. In a remark of questionable wisdom, Howard concluded that he had delivered 'differentia-tion in our time'. This was intended as an ironic reference to the words of former British Prime Minister, Neville Chamberlain, when he announced that he had delivered 'peace in our time' after returning from negotiations with the German Government in 1938. War, of course, followed twelve months later.

The outcome of the Kyoto Climate Change Summit was portrayed as a triumph by the Howard Government. Significant concessions were granted to Australia, including agreement that Australia, along with Iceland and Norway, would be one of only three economies in which emissions could continue to increase.

The Australian Government's determination to defend energy usage and pollution practices opposed by virtually every other nation was particularly disturbing at a time of mounting alarm about the impossibility of national and local communities trying to isolate themselves from either responsibility for or the impact of global ecological relationships. It also provided limited grounds for optimism that Australia will play a positive leadership role in the emerging debates about the nature of ecological political relationships in the Asia-Pacific region and in the forums of Asia-Pacific Economic Co-operation (APEC).[41]

The consequences of ignoring transborder ecological relationships were powerfully demonstrated by the choking smoke that engulfed South East Asia in late 1997. To be in a city like Kuala Lumpur when the haze was thick was to experience a science fiction horror story in a disturbing and personal way. Where there should have been sky and sun there was only grey smoke shot through with a ghostly orange glow. As your throat burned and your eyes watered it became painfully obvious that there was nothing abstract about this environmental problem. The hospitals overflowed with asthmatic children and old people wheezing with bronchitis and emphysema. This environmental danger was as real and invasive as every breath.

Similar, more limited, versions of the forest-fire haze have occurred before, but widespread understanding of its causes only became possible due to global communication technologies. In the past the sources of the smoke have been difficult to identify. Now every citizen could see the satellite photographs of the smoke surging up from Kalimantan and Sarawak. Satellite dishes on shop roofs from Manila to Chang Mai received and distributed the images of American camera crews that showed the deliberate burning of vast forests for timber and agribusiness. 'Ah,' say the timber company bosses on the same broadcasts, 'but we are careful. The problem lies with the villagers. Blame them. And besides, we have no alternative but to exploit our natural resources so as to be profitable and to make our economies competitive in a globalised world.'

The sheer personal and physical immediacy of the choking smoke and the destruction of livelihoods has the potential to help demystify the environmental impact of global competitiveness and challenge the acceptance of globalisation as the unchallengeable triumph of capitalist free-market relations in every place and every community on the planet. An alternative direction will require a reversal of the relationship between ecological and economic globalisation, in which the principles of global and local diversity and balance inform economic decision making and challenge narrow economic paradigms based on short-term self interest.[42]

Chapter 8

Where in the World?
Transforming Australian
Political Relationships
and National Identities

We can only play a part in [the region] if we go to the world as one nation, as a nation united and not a nation in any way divided. That is why Australians need to be clear about their identity and proud of it. That is why you can't go hobbling to the world saying: 'Please put us in the big race, but by the way our indigenes don't have a real part of it and by the way, we are still borrowing the monarchy of another country'.
Paul Keating[1]

National identity develops in an organic way over time. It may be changed by cataclysmic events like Gallipoli. But government and their social engineers should not try to manipulate it or to create a sense of crisis about identity. Constant debate about identity implies that we don't already have one, or worse, that it is somehow inadequate.
John Howard[2]

October 1997. Global speculators begin their attack on the currencies of South East Asia and the headlines in regional newspapers rapidly become apocalyptic. 'Sharemarket Meltdown'; 'IMF Intervenes in Thailand and Indonesia'; 'Malaysian Ringgit falls thirty per cent'.

The Hong Kong stockmarket collapses and there is talk of 'global fallout'. Wall Street and the other northern stockmarkets gyrate wildly. It is clear that Australia will not be immune, but there is widespread confusion about the long-term implications. 'Don't Panic!' advise the financial gurus. 'Don't Panic!'

The high rollers in the global money markets had decided to bet that the South East Asian economies were in serious trouble. This became a self-fulfilling prophecy as their actions helped to drive down the Baht, the Ringgit and the Rupiah. The International Monetary Fund (IMF) came in to assist with its notorious 'rescue package' of financial assistance in return for guarantees of reduced social expenditure, tax cuts, and deregulation.

Suddenly, the 'Asian miracle' mix of high technology export growth, strong state intervention in trade and infrastructure development, and authoritarian labour and human-rights policies was reframed as inflexible, over-regulated and corrupt. Share prices crumbled and the uncertainty spread to the stockmarkets of Hong Kong, New York . . . and Australia.

The response of both the Howard Government and Australian business commentators was confused and extremely revealing of their underlying anxiety about Australia's place in a globalised world. Their first reaction was that it didn't really matter. It was only South East Asia. Then there was the gloating. Just goes to show those Asian Tigers weren't so clever after all. Then, as Hong Kong and South Korea became implicated, the jitters set in. Maybe Australia was in trouble too. Maybe they wouldn't buy our coal and send us their students and tourists. Maybe the whole Asian–Australian strategy was a mistake. Maybe we should go back to being part of Europe. Or the United States. Or somewhere; anywhere; everywhere? Where did Australia belong?

The role and nature of the nation is changing rapidly as globalisation undermines traditional understandings of state sovereignty, international relations and global governance. These pressures are particularly acute for Australia, which faces the unique situation of being a lightly populated former European colony located south of Asia and immediately north of Antarctica; in both the Pacific and Indian oceans. In the more colourful words of Paul Keating, this is a nation 'at the arse end of the world'. Importantly, the colonisers are also having to come to terms with an increasingly assertive indigenous population.

This chapter considers the changing relationships between nation states and national identity in a globalising world. The central argument is that the nexus between nation state and national identity is breaking down under the twin pressures of economic and cultural globalisation. The Hawke and Keating Labor governments attempted to pursue a path of rapid economic globalisation combined with a stronger sense of national identity and belonging linked to an Asian geographical and cultural location. The Howard Government has pursued global competitiveness and deregulation with even greater vigour but has demonstrated considerable confusion about questions of cultural identity and relationships.

Whither the Nation State? Changing Identities and Relationships

The dominant model of the nation state is a European construct with its roots in the transition from feudal political relationships based on personal loyalty to local monarchs and war lords.[3] During the late medieval period of the fourteenth and fifteenth centuries the Christian church, under the leadership of the Pope, provided an overarching moral and political authority. The rise of alternative Christian traditions during the Reformation, and the shifting interests of the emerging groupings of financial and merchant capitalists, led to a situation of chronic political instability and warfare.

By the middle of the seventeenth century a consensus had begun to emerge on the need for new forms of governance that could transcend religious differences and provide a more stable basis for the development of capitalist investment and trade relations. The 1648 Treaty of Westphalia, which ended the Thirty Year War, crystallised the features of this new political settlement: a (European) world of nations with commonly agreed boundaries and sovereign states with final authority for making and enforcing laws.

There was nothing simple or uncontested about this settlement. The ways in which particular communities imagine themselves to be similar or different remains a constant source of doubt and anxiety.[4] The relationship between ethnic difference and national identity – blood and soil – is as difficult and dangerous today as it was three hundred years ago. Fierce debate and conflict continued for centuries about whether sovereign authority should finally lie with an hereditary monarch, male property owners or all adult citizens.

However, a central feature of the Westphalian settlement, which was to hold fast at least until the period following the Second World War, was acceptance of the sovereign authority of other states. There could and would be bitter conflicts between states over territorial boundaries that might be resolved by diplomatic or military means. But the underlying principle of interstate relations was reciprocal respect for political and judicial authority within national boundaries.

The principal roles of the European nation state in the sixteenth and seventeenth centuries were to maintain effective laws for the protection of property, support the exploration and plunder of Africa, Asia and America, and raise the resources required for large standing armies to protect national borders and imperial domains. By the eighteenth and nineteenth centuries, relatively crude practices of imperial expansion and plunder had given way to more sophisticated forms of trading relations based on the carving up of the rest of the world into European colonies. Inequality between coloniser and colonised remained the key feature of such trade, with the profits flowing to the European investors and merchants.

During the nineteenth and early twentieth centuries, nation states in industrialised economies also began to develop significant roles in supporting and regulating private sector economic development, as well as in fostering legitimacy and the reproduction of a more productive workforce through the development of health, education and welfare services.[5] This expanded role for the state often came about as a result of substantial pressure from the political and industrial organisations of the working class.

International trade grew at an exponential rate during the nineteenth century and the interests of expansionist, nationally based corporations became closely aligned with the interests of expansionist, nationalistic politics. By the early part of the twentieth century festering conflicts over colonial boundaries and access to international resources and markets provided the spark for the First World War.[6]

In the period following the First World War there was a brief period of inward turning protectionism as corporate capitalism and the emerging forms of state socialism regrouped behind national boundaries. At the same time, the formation of the League of Nations represented the first abortive attempt to establish a form of supra-national governance. The rapid collapse of the League of Nations in the 1930s was a clear sign that most governments were still deeply suspicious of attempts to limit or override the autonomy of policy making within national borders.

As is discussed in more detail in chapters 3, 4 and 5, the development of the postwar Keynesian welfare state involved an initial expansion in the role of the state in both economic regulation and social redistribution. This expansion has come under sustained political attack since the 1970s and a number of related political, cultural and economic developments have threatened to both overwhelm and fragment the Westphalian nation state system of interstate relationships.[7]

In 1945 a second attempt to establish a supra-national governing body led to the formation of the United Nations Organisation (UN) and the hope that this would provide a more lasting forum for conflict resolution than the ill-fated League of Nations. The Charter of the UN appeared to signal the beginnings of a new world order in which the sovereignty of nation states was partially offset by a common commitment to restrictions on the use of force to resolve international conflicts and a series of universal principles in relation to peace and human rights.

In practice, the UN decision-making structures tended to entrench the dominance of Cold War political relationships and the influence of the most powerful postwar states, with the United States, the Soviet Union, China, England and France retaining veto powers on the Security Council. The UN has remained limited in its authority and vulnerable to pressure from powerful states given its dependence on national governments for its resource base.

Other global inter-governmental organisations, such as the United Nations Educational, Scientific and Cultural Organisation (UNESCO), the World Health Organisation (WHO), the UN High Commissioner on Refugees and the International Court of Justice (ICJ) have all played important roles as forums for exploring new dialogues between nation states. But all are finally dependent upon the consent of members, with the most powerful states retaining effective veto powers.

Some defenders of the potential of the UN as the main foundation for new forms of international governance point to the diplomatic and military roles of the UN in conflicts such as those in Bosnia, Iraq or Cambodia. Yet it is just as easy to see Cambodia as a demonstration of the ultimate limitations of the UN as a peacekeeper. The Gulf War can be seen as an example of the international community fighting a just war against nationalist aggression. But it can also be viewed as the United States and other North Atlantic Treaty Organisation (NATO) powers continuing to use the UN as a convenient cover for maintaining both cultural and military dominance in economically strategic areas, such as the oil-rich deserts of Kuwait.

National governments in the postwar world have chosen to enter into a vast array of international treaties and agreements on matters as diverse as postal services, satellites, the creation of an Antarctic national park, and bans on the use of chlorofluorocarbons (CFCs). Binding international agreements have been far harder to achieve when the interests of particular nation states are threatened – as has been the case, for example, in attempts to achieve global agreements on the banning of whaling, land mines or the proliferation of nuclear weapons.

The emergence of regional trade agreements, such as the North American Free Trade Agreement (NAFTA) and Asia Pacific Economic Co-operation (APEC), has also been a significant factor in the removal of national policy-making power from above. The European Union (EU), with its effective abolition of visa requirements and the move towards a single currency, represents an even more substantial movement towards regional governance, although the extent of the powers of the EU continue to be strenuously challenged by a range of political movements concerned with maintaining more local and national forms of democratic decision making.

The globalisation of economic relationships has been the most powerful factor in reducing the sovereign decision-making powers of nation states. As is discussed in more detail in chapters 3 and 6, global communication technologies have facilitated the creation of transnational financial markets that severely undermine the fiscal and monetary policy autonomy of individual national governments.

The rise of truly transnational corporations (TNCs) pursuing relations of production based on extreme forms of post-Fordist flexibility has meant that the most powerful corporations have become less interested in the outcomes for particular local communities or the interests of national governments.[8] TNCs may choose to play one government off against another for short-term gain. But in the longer term they are more concerned with minimising national controls over trade and investment flows.

The most significant new developments in relation to global and regional economic governance in the last fifty years have been the formation of the World Trade Organisation (WTO), the conclusion of the Uruguay round of the General Agreement on Tariffs and Trade (GATT), regional initiatives such as NAFTA, and the proposed Multilateral Agreement on Investment (MAI).[9] The assumptions underlying these kinds of initiatives are well demonstrated in the following comments in support of the MAI made in late 1997 by Alan Asher, deputy head of the Australian Competition and Consumer Commission.

> I've for a long time had difficulty in believing that there is such a thing as national sovereignty any more . . . If you look at the huge proportion of our lives, that is inherently trans-border, whether it's culture, the economy, the environment, law enforcement, even the weather, even the smoke in Asia knows no boundaries. And so for people who want to cling to a notion of national sover-eignty that's built on lines of geography on a map, it's my percep-tion that that's something that is just no longer a tenable option.[10]

Many of these regional and global trade agreements are best understood as attempts to establish new corporate constitutions – new modes of global and regional governance that override national economic, social and environmental policies and are accountable only to small elites of corporate executives and their representatives. Canadian political economist Leo Panitch correctly notes that

> [t]he internationalisation of the state in the 1990s appears to be taking the form, in the continuing absence of the ideological consensus or capacity to bring about a transnational regulation of capital markets, of formal interstate treaties designed to enforce legally upon future governments general adherence to the discipline of the capital market. This arises out of a growing fear on the part of both domestic and transnational capitalists, as the crisis continues, that *ideology cannot continue to substitute for legal obligation* in the internationalisation of the state.[11]

Thus the trade-related investment measures (TRIMs) provisions of GATT constitute, in effect, an international treaty preventing national governments from intervening to protect national industries through policies such as local-content requirements.[12] Trade-related intellectual property rights (TRIPs) provide transnational corporations with the legally enforceable right to collect seeds from a developing country, patent the genetic code of the seeds, and then sell the intellectual property rights back to the same country from which the seeds originated.

For some commentators, globalisation heralds the emergence of a borderless 'post national' world of transnational producers and consumers.[13] According to others, we are entering an era of fragmented, 'postmodern nations' and decentred, unstable 'postmodern states'.[14] This latter view has often sat uncomfortably with another perspective that stresses the fragmentary nature of globalisation and the rise of ethnically based conflicts between competing cultural tribes.[15]

National fragmentation has a number of sources. From the Islamic militants of Iran to the war lords of Somalia, and from the Zapatista militia of Mexico to the business leaders of Hong Kong, a fierce critique of Western cultural discourses has undermined both the hegemony of colonial political relationships and the universality of assumptions about human rights and the relationship between states and their citizens.

The contradictions between colonial and Cold War territorial boundaries, on the one hand, and much older ethnic, religious and tribal relationships, on the other, have exploded into bitter conflicts in settings as diverse as Bosnia and Rwanda. For some the 'ethnic cleansings' of Bosnia and the bloody massacres of Rwanda demonstrate a massive breakdown in familiar patterns of 'orderly' international relationships and a return to a kind of global medievalism of unstable shifting alliances between competing tribes and ethnic communities.[16]

Aside from overstating the extent of the breakdown of national state power, this interpretation also romanticises the 'normality' and desirability of colonial and neo-colonial power relationships that were always tilted heavily in favour of Western industrialised nations in general and the United States in particular. Social theorist Jan Pieterse captures the ambivalent nature of hybridisation in the following way:

> Structural hybridisation, or the increase in the range of organisational options, and cultural hybridisation, or the doors of erstwhile imagined communities opening up are signs of an age of boundary crossing. Not surely of the erasure of boundaries. Thus state power remains extremely strategic, but it is no longer the only game in town.[17]

While it is true that transborder economic, ecological and communication flows have fundamentally changed the relationship between domestic and foreign policies, and that many policy problems can no longer be solved within state boundaries, rumours of the death of the nation state are definitely premature. Political theorist David Held suggests that

> it is not . . . that national sovereignty . . . has been wholly subverted . . . But political domains clearly exist with criss-crossing loyalties, conflicting interpretations of rights and duties, and interconnected authority structures which displace notions of sovereignty as an illimitable, indivisible and exclusive form of public power.[18]

When this is added to the picture of permeable political boundaries, the pervasive influence of transnational corporations, and a fragile, uneasy sense of national cultural identity the predicament facing the Australian nation state – and the Australian people – becomes readily apparent.

Whither Australis? What is Australia and Where Does It Belong?

The history of the settlement and development of the Australian continent begins over forty thousand years ago with the arrival of small tribes of people who had travelled by island hopping and by sea from what we now call Asia to live in the islands of the Torres Strait and the huge, old, dry land further to the south. The Aboriginal and Torres Strait Islander people's relationship to land and place developed along a very different trajectory to that of European civilisation. Some of the sources of this difference are eloquently captured by the eminent economist and public servant H.C. 'Nugget' Coombs:

> The physical environment which surrounded the Aboriginal hunter gatherer was not only the source of the air, the water, the food and the shelter necessary to survival. It provided also a physical context of which Aborigines were deeply aware, of which their knowledge was profound and with which they experienced an intimate relationship . . .
> In the social environments there was a range of social groups; at the base a small group little more than an extended family among whom complex but precise mutual obligations ensured support for one another . . .
> To the Aborigines both the physical and social environments derived from and were sanctioned by the more fundamental

spiritual environment. Both originated in the Dreamtime, when spirit ancestors travelled through the land creating its physical features and the creatures including people, who were to live within it, and establishing patterns of behaviours governing their relationships with one another, and above all with the spirit ancestors themselves.[19]

The history of the modern Australian nation state begins with the arrival of the First Fleet from England in 1788. A new nation was 'born into a world of ambiguously consolidating nation states and still-vigorous but soon-to-die empires'.[20] The origins of the Australian nation state as a British penal colony under military rule contributed to the development of a relatively interventionist and authoritarian state. Despite rapid economic development based on access to rich agricultural and mineral resources – and despite a growing strain of working-class radicalism and nationalism – the colonial squatters and industrialists chose to remain bound to the political supports and constraints of the British Empire. From the beginning the problem, as historian Humphrey McQueen has argued, was that

> Australia's prosperity, based on wool and minerals, was the prosperity of expanding capitalism. Geographically, Australia was a frontier of European capitalism in Asia. The first of these gave rise to the optimism which illuminated our radicalism; the second produced the fear which tarnishes our nationalism.[21]

Chapters 4 and 5 provide a detailed discussion of the rise and fall of the Australian state's role in economic and social development during the twentieth century. By the 1970s the uniquely 'Australian settlement' of industry protection and centralised wage arbitration had been combined with Keynesian demand-management policies and a residual welfare safety net to produce a social and economic policy regime that could be characterised as a 'wage earner's welfare state shielded behind state sanctioned trade barriers'.[22]

Political commentator Paul Kelly has argued that two further significant features of the 'Australian Settlement' were White Australia and Imperial Benevolence. By the end of the nineteenth century the *Bulletin* had begun to identify an ominously particular national identity.[23]

> By the term Australian we mean not only those who have been merely born in Australia. All white men who come to the shores . . . and who leave behind them the memory of the class distinction of the old world . . . No nigger, no Chinaman, no

lascar, no kanaka, no purveyor of cheap coloured labour is an Australian.[24]

The creation of the Commonwealth of Australia in 1901 federated the States, but the constitution provided for only limited sovereignty, with considerable power remaining with the British monarch and parliament. Symbolic events, such as Gallipoli, the bitter lessons of the Depression, and the influence of artists and writers, such as Frederick McCubbin, Henry Lawson, and Banjo Paterson began to create a stronger sense of a unique Australian national character and culture.

Despite the influx of European migrants and the central military importance of the alliance between Australia, New Zealand and the United States after the Second World War, the 1950s and 1960s governments of Robert Menzies continued to sustain the national self image of a quasi-British nation. While in the early 1970s, Gough Whitlam's Government unleashed a new, more assertive nationalism and diplomacy as the realities of Asian proximity began to be recognised, the Labor Government of Bob Hawke was still elected in the 1980s in the context of considerable uncertainty about the nature of the 'imagined community' known as Australia. As the former head of the Department of Foreign Affairs, Richard Woolcott, noted, Australia was at the crossroads.

> We can stand still and allow ourselves to become regarded as a bucolic, inward looking materialistic, racist, self satisfied, apathetic, pleasure seeking member of the world community, slumbering at the southern end of the globe, a sort of Anglo American step child which never really grew up, a second hand transplanted society which lost its momentum before it decided in which direction it wanted to move. Or we can continue to work to be accepted as a distinctive, tolerant and well regarded nation in the Asia Pacific region.[25]

The overall political strategy of the Hawke and Keating governments was based on holding together several potentially contradictory objectives: economic globalisation, political internationalism (with a special emphasis on Asia) and cultural nationalism. There was also much talk of creating 'one nation' and supporting 'the promotion of individual and collective cultural rights and expressions on the one hand and, on the other, the promotion of common national interests and values'.[26] It was hoped that this attempt to find an appropriate balance between principles of inclusiveness and difference might help to lessen the explosive potential for racist forms of social fragmentation that can easily be triggered by the dangerous combination of rapid economic restructuring and diverse ethnic and racial populations.

The trade and foreign-policy agendas of the Hawke and Keating governments was informed by a determination to overturn the founding assumptions of the Australian nation state.[27] The aim was to transform Australia into an open, deregulated, competitive economy with a reduced level of state intervention and a sharper focus on relationships with Asia, rather than with England or even the United States. For Foreign Minister, Gareth Evans,

> our future prosperity and security rely, to a large extent, on our playing an active and positive role on the international stage. Our contribution to international peace building and the international rule of law, our activism in international forums, and our commitment to establishing and maintaining global standards are what will keep us afloat in a sea of changing power relationships.[28]

This task included the development of a credible role for Australia as a middle power in multilateral forums, such as the UN, in major disarmament negotiations, and as an effective player in the political, economic and cultural forums of Asia.[29] Australia's role in the formation of APEC was a key part of this process, as was its leadership role in the Cairns Group of resource exporting economies in the conclusion of the Uruguay round of GATT.

The second part of the mixture was a resurgent cultural nationalism based on a celebration of the icons of Gallipoli, Kokoda and the Tomb of the Unknown Soldier, combined with the agenda of Aboriginal reconciliation and republicanism. Paul Keating, in particular, began to explore the possibilities of deeper integration between Australian and Asian cultural identities, going so far as to suggest that the Australian icon of mateship itself might be understood as an 'Asian value'.

The Labor Government, under Keating's leadership, was very effective at playing the nationalist card, proposing that Australia should break its last ceremonial ties with the British monarchy by becoming a republic. Broader claims about Labor's defence of Australian cultural sovereignty have a hollow ring, given the extent to which foreign media ownership concentration was permitted and encouraged during its time in office.[30] Certainly the comprehensive deregulation of the Australian economy made something of a mockery of the stated aim of defending democratic decision making and cultural sovereignty.

The contradiction that finally led to the overwhelming defeat of the Keating Government in 1994 was the social dislocation and insecurity being experienced by people and communities who were reeling from the impact of rapid economic deregulation and restructuring. This context of fear and anxiety provided fertile ground for the development of cruder forms of xenophobic and racist nationalism that were to both surround and be sustained by John Howard's Government.

The initial economic policy directions of the Howard Government involved pursuing Labor's privatisation and deregulation agendas with even greater vigour and with a sharper focus on the final dismantling of the central arbitration system. The logic driving the government's foreign affairs agenda, however, was far more ambiguous and was marked by a confusing series of policy shifts, mistakes and mixed messages.

The Liberal Government's overall international relations objective was reflected in the title of its 1997 White Paper on foreign affairs and trade: *The National Interest*.[31] The White Paper reaffirmed the principle that Australia's national economic interests would be best served by an ongoing commitment to globalisation and free trade. The centrality of Asian regional political relationships was emphasised, with bilateral relationships with China, the United States, Japan and Indonesia identified as particularly significant. For Howard, active involvement in foreign affairs issues in general, and APEC in particular, had to be based on a clearly articulated understanding of the benefits in terms of Australian jobs.

> You've got to be able to say to people: Do you know that for the first time we're selling fresh milk into Hong Kong; we're selling cars to Taiwan; we have a financial institutions license with China; even some rice into Japan.[32]

The actual record of the Howard Government's actions and statements in relation to Asia conveyed very mixed messages indeed. Despite constant references to the importance of economic integration with Asia, the Prime Minister also felt compelled to inform an Indonesian audience that 'we do not claim to be Asian . . . neither do I see Australia as a bridge between Asia and the West'.[33]

There were frequent denials that the Howard Government was ambivalent about immigration or multiculturalism. Yet the memories of Howard's 1989 attacks on Asian immigration kept resurfacing as family reunion immigration program levels were slashed and the Office of Multicultural Affairs and the Bureau of Immigration and Population Research were among the first victims of the government's expenditure cuts. At times there were tough statements on human rights abuses in China and Tibet. On other occasions there appeared to be a determination to avoid raising human-rights issues that might offend trading partners in Indonesia and Malaysia.

There was supposed to be an emphasis on supporting Australian exporters, yet programs linking aid and trade (such as the Development Import Finance Facility scheme) were either cut back or abolished. The 1997 Simons Committee Review of foreign-aid policies proposed focussing on poverty alleviation rather than trade, although there were well-founded suspicions that this was also a way of defending overall cuts in foreign aid.[34]

In addition to this sense of policy uncertainty there was a range of unfortunate failures and mistakes. In 1997 a wide range of Asian and Pacific governments supported Portugal rather than Australia in the election for membership of the UN Security Council. Also in 1997 an embarrassing public leak of a briefing paper on Pacific politicians at the South Pacific Forum openly demonstrated the government's contempt for many Pacific leaders. As efforts were being made to rebuild relationships with China, Australia's Defence Minister, Ian McLachlan, tactlessly identified China as a potential military threat. The perception of Australia as a contributor to potential military tensions in the region was further reinforced by the outcomes of the 1997 Defence Review, which advocated a more assertive, forward defence strategy.

The most serious problem, however, has been a growing perception in Asia and the rest of the world that the Australian Government, and perhaps a large section of Australian society, is extremely uneasy about the identity of Australia as a nation. As the *Economist* wryly noted, 'to a world accustomed to images of happy-go-lucky surfers and Crocodile Dundee, the idea that Australians are afflicted by gloomy introspection may seem odd'.[35]

This rising sense of dis-ease was most clearly illustrated by the government's inability to develop a coherent response to the nationalist racism of independent parliamentarian Pauline Hanson and other resurgent 'White Australians'.[36] Despite constant protestations by government Ministers that they opposed her views, Howard's initial refusal to condemn Hanson's anti-Asian and anti-Aboriginal speeches led to abiding and understandable Asian suspicions that the Howard Government's supporters include a strong residual strain of 'White Australians'.

The Howard Government appeared equally ill at ease on questions of national identity and the rights of indigenous Australians. The Prime Minister's personal support for the monarchy did not prevent many senior Liberal politicians and eminent conservatives from joining the republican movement. While Liberal support for the republican cause was limited to the minimalist position of an Australian head of state, it still indicated deep divisions within the government about the nature of both governance and the significance of traditional relationships with England.

The deep and bitter divisions created by the Liberal Government's determination to place the rights of miners and pastoralists above those of indigenous communities in the debate that followed the High Court's decision on Wik was an even more profound indication of its lack of understanding of the connection between reconciliation and the creation of a confident, credible relationship with other societies and economies in the Asia-Pacific region.

By mid-1998 the Howard Government's curious policy recipe of aggressive economic globalisation and an uncertain, backward-looking cultural nationalism was becoming increasingly problematic. The difficult task of managing economic globalisation while holding together some degree of social solidarity and cultural identity is common to all nation states at the end of the twentieth century. Australia, however, faces particular difficulties due to its ongoing economic vulnerability, its uncertain political and cultural relationships with Asia, the renewed unpredictability of East Asian economic fortunes, and a deepening crisis about the nature of Australian history and national identity.

Unity in Diversity: Making Ourself Anew?

How can the contradictions of the nation state and national identity in the context of globalisation be reconciled? Some of the possibilities of new forms of political action and governance at a variety of geographical levels are explored in the next two chapters. But part of the answer for Australians lies in a more honest and mature acceptance of the strengths and errors of the past leading to a genuine reconciliation between new and old Australians.

Part of the answer also lies in the development of a deeper understanding of and respect for the cultures and societies in the surrounding region. This does not imply that Australia is – or is not – an Asian nation. Rather, as in any mature relationship, it implies a thoughtful awareness of the historical baggage and gifts that all partners bring to the meeting, a preparedness to listen and an appropriate mix of self confidence, humility and solidarity.

And, finally, part of the answer lies in listening to and learning from a diversity of stories.[37] The various liberal and conservative traditions of Australian historical narrative developed by W.K. Hancock, Russel Ward, A.D. Hope and Geoffrey Blainey differ markedly from the more radically nationalist perspectives of Henry Lawson, Manning Clark and Humphrey McQueen. Yet they also share some of the same underlying assumptions about the possibility and desirability of finding a 'real' Australian identity. They share – and struggle with – many of the same cultural icons: the *Endeavour*, convict irons, mateship, Merino sheep, the shearer's strike, gold mines, Eureka, Gallipoli, the Kokoda trail, FJ Holdens and, more recently, the Golden Arches of McDonald's.

A different story about Australia's relationship with the rest of the world will need to be respectful of the vast diversity of migrant voices that call Australia home.[38] It will certainly include the stories of Ireland, Scotland and England. But it will also include the stories of the Kanak cane-cutters of the South Pacific; of Chinese miners and merchants; of Greeks and Italians; Chileans and Lebanese; Vietnamese and Ethiopians.

Another story of the country will need to involve respect for the stories of the Currency lasses, as well as the lads; the Drover's Wife as well as the Man from Snowy River. It will remember the suffragettes and the struggles of women such as Muriel Heagney, Irene Longman and Jessie Street to win some measure of economic independence for women in the early years of the Commonwealth.[39] It will mean hearing the voices of women from different cultures and classes in homes and in factories; as colonists, migrants and refugees. And it will mean learning from the keening and the resilience of Aboriginal and Torres Strait Islander women.

Reconciliation means learning as well as saying sorry. There are valuable lessons to be learned from Aboriginal communities about economic relations that value the possibilities of exchange while also respecting the importance of maintaining a sense of place.[40] In cultural and political relations we might also begin to think in terms of the Meriam Island metaphor of the freshwater rivers of the inland meeting the salt seas of the Torres Strait.[41] At the meeting place they are not swallowed up but each retains its integrity as they intermingle. Perhaps our task is to learn to live with more permeable borders in a relationship of unity in diversity.

The gap between older, more one-dimensional understandings of Australian identity and place and these more diverse interpretations helps explain some of the confusion and uncertainty that has marked recent attempts to redefine and reposition Australian identity and relationships. This is a context in which, as the Tasmanian novelist Richard Flanagan notes,

> [w]e are as Australians being presented not only with our past, but with our future. We have, for a short time, that rare opportunity of making ourselves anew. If we wish we can create a state in which morality and politics abide together, a state in which we recognise our individual responsibility to all, other individuals, be it being civil on the street or in the pub, or be it recognising that the denial of legal rights of Aborigines is an offence to us all and diminishes us all.[42]

Chapter 9

Alternative Strategies? Thinking and Acting Globally and Regionally

In the era of globalization it is becoming clearer than ever that the world's problems have the same origins: implementation of a neo-liberal agenda which brings pauperisation and ecological devastation. So the solidarity of the peoples must be built on the following basic principle: 'In helping yourself, you help me'.
Steve Peniche[1]

It is not enough to teach people how to swim better in a tide, a time comes when people have to do more than swim more effectively. They have to get together and say, 'This river seems to be going in the wrong direction and somehow has to be stopped, has to be dammed up and has to be redirected.' That is the role of citizen action.
Stephen Gerbner[2]

This chapter and the next aim to counter the paralysing impact of the belief that there are no longer any political choices in a globalised world by presenting a series of propositions about alternative responses to globalisation. The central argument is that globalisation involves a range of contradictory and contested processes that provide new possibilities, as well as threats, to communities concerned with promoting relationships of diversity, solidarity and sustainability.[3] The central challenge is to recognise the connections between action at different levels of geographical space and political governance and to think and act on a range of levels without losing our grounding in the particularity of our own home place.

In this chapter the focus is on the possibility of alternative responses at political levels above that of the nation state. It begins by looking at debates about global citizenship, alternative global economic and political relationships, and the emergence of new agents of social change through globally connected social movements. The chapter concludes by arguing that the regional level – more than national, but less than global – is a particularly important geopolitical space to explore and contest.

Political Choices in a Globalised World: Global and Regional Responses

In a globalised world we need to begin the process of creating imagined communities of global citizenship.

The sharp imbalance in the distribution of globalised power makes some discussions about global citizenship and cosmopolitan democracy disturbingly naive. There are ways of viewing globalisation in a positive light by seeing it as a series of processes that help to create the preconditions for a 'cosmopolitan democracy' combining the best features of local self-determination with democratic decision making informed by a global perspective.[4] From this point of view the expansion of global trade and communications creates new possibilities for democratic institutions of global governance and the broadening of international alliances between local trade unions, community organisations and social movements.[5]

The more pessimistic view is that the real winners on the global racetrack have been those who have the wealth to enjoy the luxuries of globalised consumption – the emerging transnational overclass of financial speculators, information managers, media operators and other global 'symbolic analysts'.[6] The losers have been the vast majority of people whose livelihoods remain bounded by connections to particular places and whose capacity to resist rising inequality and environmental damage has been significantly undermined as the levers of power have moved away from their sight and influence.

The rights and responsibilities of global citizenship have been key themes in a number of major inquiries into global distribution and development issues in the last thirty years. The Palme Commission on Disarmament, the Brandt Commission on International Development, and the Brundtland Commission on Environment and Development all represent missed opportunities in the search for sets of political values and relationships appropriate for a globalised world.[7] None of them has been able to reconcile the tensions between their admirable focus on the extent and depth of global inequality and environmental concerns and their proposed solutions, which have ultimately assumed and relied on the relentless expansion of private-sector economic growth in a globalised marketplace. Similar tensions affected the debates and outcomes of the major UN summits of the 1990s in relation to the environment, social development, women and the city.

The abiding problem is that 'the citizenship associated with the New World Order is very much a stratified conception based on beneficiaries and victims, inclusion and exclusion . . . and which presupposes the sustainability of high growth capitalism'.[8] Increasingly, the rights of national and global citizenship have become defined in terms of the individualised rights to consume and participate in the marketplace.[9]

The discourse of global citizenship can be a useful starting point for the re-creation of political philosophy and morality if the historical gender blindness of much citizenship discourse can be overcome, leading to a more appropriate balance between autonomy and solidarity, cooperation and difference, rights and responsibilities. As international relations scholar Richard Falk argues, this might entail

> a human rights and democracy orientation toward global citizenship – the world as delightfully heterogeneous, yet inclusive of all creation in an overarching frame of community sentiment, premised on the biological and normative capacity of the human species to organise its collective life on foundations of non violence, equity and sustainability.[10]

The dimension of time also needs to be added to the dimension of space.

> Traditional citizenship operates spatially; global citizenship operates temporally, reaching out to a future to-be and making a person a 'citizen pilgrim', that is, someone on a journey to 'a country' to be established in the future in accordance with more idealistic and normatively rich conceptions of political community.[11]

In the Australian context anecdotal and opinion-poll data suggest that the dominant Australian social mood is one of cynicism and 'sullenness' combined with fears about the effect of rapid change in a fragmented world in which there are few sources of certainty, faith or inspiration.[12] This deepening sense of risk, anxiety and a collapse of trust in religious and political institutions is a pervasive feature of post-industrial, post-Fordist societies and has given rise to a variety of responses by political parties desperately attempting to recapture supporters and a sense of direction.[13]

In claiming victory at the 1993 election, Paul Keating referred to it as a victory for 'the true believers', presumably referring to Labor's traditional working-class constituency, whose way of life had been increasingly threatened due to the very changes in labour-market regulation that the Labor Government had supported so strongly. Unfortunately, it was often unclear what the believers were supposed to believe in beyond a vague commitment to 'the poor', 'the workers' – and 'social justice'.[14]

Fifty years ago, in the heady days of postwar reconstruction, Labor Prime Minister, Ben Chifley, articulated a vision of social justice, security and compassion as Labor's 'light on the hill'.

> It is the duty and responsibility of the community and par-
> ticularly those more fortunately placed, to see that our less
> fortunate fellow citizens are protected from those shafts of fate
> which leave them helpless and without hope. That is the objective
> for which we are striving. It is the beacon, the light on the hill to
> which our eyes are always turned and to which our efforts are
> always directed.[15]

Throughout the 1980s, Labor governments at both Commonwealth and State levels struggled to articulate a renewed sense of direction through the creation of elaborate 'Social Justice Strategies'.[16] Stripped of their rhetorical flourishes about social justice as 'access, equity, participation and rights', the major contribution of these strategies was to provide a justification for the more effective targeting of reduced resources to groups identified as 'disadvantaged', with disadvantage largely defined in terms of exclusion from the mainstream labour market.[17]

As Keating's speech writer, Don Watson, noted, 'so long as you define it as being only for the very needy, the concept of social justice is going to grow increasingly unpopular with the much greater number of people who may not need social justice but reckon they've got an equal right to it'.[18]

A second response has been the technocratic language and politics of economic rationalism, public-choice theory, privatisation, deregulation and 'managerialism'. Some of these ideas are simply reworkings of neo-classical economic ideas about the merits of *laissez faire* capitalism. But they also involve a fundamental distrust of discourses based on morality and ethics.[19] The underlying assumption is that there can no longer be any commonly agreed upon social norms or values – there are only the desires of each individual to maximise his or her sensory pleasure and material gain. The solution is to turn to the market as the arbiter of individual choices and to neo-classical economic 'science' to ensure that the market is protected. The market has finally become God.

A third possibility is simply to accept, and perhaps revel in, the collapse of universal truths and values. After all it was also Don Watson who suggested that Australians should begin to imagine a 'postmodern republic' – a nation which is 'aleatory [dependent on chance], impressionistic, figurative, bebop'.[20] Some strands of postmodern theory have provided a timely antidote to the arrogance of ideological certainty, as well as highlighting the significance of the politics of difference. However, the implications of much postmodernist discourse can also be profoundly nihilistic, leading down a path of moral relativism quite consistent with the reduction of all social relationships to the narrowly contractual and commercial relations of the marketplace. The British social theorist Zygmunt Bauman suggests a way through the impasse of postmodern nihilism by proposing a reconciliation between the principles of solidarity and difference:

> Survival in the world of contingency and diversity is possible only if each difference recognises another difference as the necessary condition of the preservation of its own. Solidarity, unlike tolerance, its weaker version, means a readiness to fight; and joining the battle for the sake of other's difference, not one's own. Tolerance is ego-centered and contemplative; solidarity is socially oriented and militant.[21]

In this arid climate of Australian political discourse about citizenship in a globalising world, one starting point is to oppose the atomistic individualism of competitive 'market citizenship' and to defend and reclaim the significance of interdependence and cooperation.[22] This implies a reaffirmation of the fundamentally social nature of human life and of the ecological interdependence between all forms of life and the natural environment. For political scientist Michael Rustin,

> [i]t is possible to defend the value of social differentiation without abandoning universalistic and egalitarian claims as a foundation for a beneficial diversity of values and lifestyles . . . The central issue is to see that ways of life of . . . complexity and richness depend not just on individuals but on the various kinds of community which make human accomplishment, even the everyday accomplishments of parenthood, craftsmanship, or good citizenship, possible.[23]

Civil, political, social and economic rights and responsibilities can no longer be contained by the borders of the nation state, but neither can they simply be abstracted to the level of global governance. The rights and responsibilities of global citizens need to be constantly renewed through negotiation at a range of spatial levels. The emerging debate about the meaning of global citizenship can also only be given substance through the development of fairer, more accountable and more sustainable relations of production and the creation of new forms of democratic governance at all geographical levels.

The creation of desirable and meaningful forms of global citizenship will require the democratic and ecological transformation of globalised economic relationships.

The astronaut's vision of Earth from space was arguably the symbolic turning point for many people in developing a reflexive sense of themselves as citizens of a planet as well as of a locality or nation. The time has now come for the image of the astronaut managing limited resources in a confined space to replace that of the cowboy exploiting an endless frontier as the dominant role model for citizens of the twenty-first century.[24]

The most urgent global danger is the threat to the global commons of unrestrained exploitation of non-renewable resources and the irreparable damage being done to the biosphere. The challenge of global warming, and the failure of the Kyoto Climate Change Summit to reach effective agreement on greenhouse-gas limits, provides a powerful illustration of the necessity and difficulty of turning the rhetoric of global citizenship into tangible political action. The Australian Government's decision to continue to argue that Australia should be one of the few countries allowed to keep increasing its emission levels provides a particularly dismal example of the ways in which shortsighted corporations and governments are prepared to compromise on long-term global objectives for short-term financial advantage.

In relation to trade an important starting point is to question the assumption that the relentless expansion of global trade is always desirable, particularly in an age where an increasing proportion of world trade is in fact intra-corporate trade. At one end of the spectrum of views on this issue there is the argument put by prominent anti-globalisation critic Paul Ekins that

> the global trading system, far from being a mutually beneficial voluntaristic system of exchange, has become a means of coercion, employed jointly by powerful institutions in the First World and their client elites in the Third, by which to force Third World resources into the global market on terms highly favourable to the vendor.[25]

Criticism of current global trading relationships does not and should not mean a retreat into isolationism and autarchy. There are obvious benefits in being able to draw on resources and skills that are not available in particular localities. However, an alternative trade strategy needs to begin with the recognition that the endless expansion of world trade is not an end in itself.[26] The economic benefits of increased trade must be set against the social and environmental costs of boundless and borderless consumerism.

New accounting systems that provide a more accurate picture of the full environmental as well as financial costs of transport systems required for ongoing expansions in the volume of world trade will be an important step in recognising the real ecological and social benefits in supporting the local circulation of goods and services.

Effective international regulation is necessary to monitor and control the use of intra-corporate trade as a strategy for avoiding environmental, human-rights, health and safety and labour standards. National governments should not be prevented from taking measures to prevent the dumping of products at artificially deflated prices or from using trade barriers to pursue environmental sustainability and biodiversity objectives. Where measures designed to open up international markets are supported there should be clear evidence that the arrangements provide improved access for producers in less-developed economies. More direct trading relationships between producers and consumers at local, national and global levels should also be encouraged.

The decision-making processes in relation to global trade agreements need to be made far more transparent and democratic than is currently the case. Non-government organisations representing a diverse range of groups and concerns require greater access to the documents, debates and decision-making processes of global and regional trade forums such as the World Trade Organisation (WTO), the North American Free Trade Agreement (NAFTA) and the Asia Pacific Economic Co-operation forum (APEC).

In the case of Australia, the opening up of the decision-making processes of APEC is a particular priority, as is the reaffirmation of the connection between principles of human rights, labour rights and economic relations. This is an urgent task given the Howard Government's determination to break the connection between human rights and trade.

The management of global financial flows is arguably the most urgent and difficult task of all in responding to globalisation.[27] This is one challenge that cannot be met through action at the national level alone, a point now recognised by observers from a diverse range of political backgrounds. Former Australian Liberal prime minister, Malcolm Fraser, for example, recently noted, 'at some point, hopefully sooner rather than later, international authorities will decide that much tougher prudential supervision of capital market activities is a global necessity'.[28]

The absence of constraints on the mobility of capital makes it extremely difficult for workers and their unions to maintain bargaining power, given the ease with which the owners of capital can simply run away. Even the threat of capital flight is often enough to prevent effective campaigns in relation to wages and conditions. In the same way, the unregulated mobility of finance capital seriously undermines the capacity of national or local governments to intervene in the market so as to promote objectives – such as full employment or alternative environmental policies – that are not in the interests of the global money markets. This is a key reason why the proposed

Multilateral Agreement on Investment (MAI) needed to be firmly and effectively opposed.

Many commentators from a variety of political perspectives have argued that the capacity for almost instantaneous electronic transfers of vast sums of money has made global financial regulation virtually impossible.[29] There is no doubt that the technical challenges are formidable but, as the Canadian political economist Manfred Bienefeld argues,

> in the final analysis, financial regulation depends on the political will to enforce adequate sanctions, so that, given the risk of discovery, the majority of people will observe the law. The fact that such laws can always be technically evaded (by some, for a time) is not an argument against them or their enforcement, any more than the existence of unsolved murders constitutes an argument against the homicide laws. In fact, the biggest obstacle to the enforcement of financial regulations today, is not the computer or the fax machine, but the poisonous individualism of the eighties which has undermined people's willingness to observe the law by corroding the ethical and ideological foundations on which law enforcement, taxation and the ability to justify social investment ultimately rest.[30]

Implementing policies in the correct order is the key to successful reform of international financial regulation. The first step is to reach agreements between national governments in relation to the monitoring of financial flows and a system of 'stand-by controls' requiring the return of money that crosses borders in violation of national laws. Such controls would need to be complemented by the reintroduction of some degree of exchange-rate regulation and cooperative action on national interest-rate policies to prevent sharp movements in the interest rates of any one country leading to destabilising capital outflows from other national economies. In this context it would be far more possible for national governments to choose to implement effective forms of quantitative and qualitative controls over both incoming and outgoing capital flows.

The next step would be the introduction of a variety of globally levied taxes designed both to limit the attractiveness of globalised financial speculation and to redirect some of the vast profits currently eluding national revenue-collection agencies. The most promising option here is the proposal for a small but universal tax on all international financial transactions. This proposal is often known as the Tobin tax, named after its most eminent advocate, United States economist James Tobin. Other proposals that merit detailed consideration include taxes on international stockmarket and futures-market transactions, arms sales, carbon emissions and air transport.[31]

In the context of international agreements on the regulation of capital mobility, national and international capital-gains taxes on profits gained from assets held for short periods of time could also be introduced in order to encourage productive rather than speculative investment. More effective forms of international cooperation between national taxation offices have begun to be explored in relation to the tax minimisation activities of particular companies. In early 1998, for example, the Australian Taxation Office began discussions with tax investigators from Britain, the United States and Canada in order to establish a multinational strategy for investigating the offshore tax structures of News Corp.[32]

Resources collected through taxation on global financial transactions could be used to help fund a global 'new deal' involving the retirement of debt and substantial investment in employment generating, ecologically sustainable initiatives in the most exploited areas of the world.[33] Some of these resources could also be devoted to the establishment of a Civil Society Development Fund to support a more effective global network of non-government organisations and social movements, providing the first steps towards the creation of a transnational civil society.[34]

In the end, it is important to note the point made by United States economists Jim Crotty and Gerald Epstein that

> enforcing international capital controls need be no harder (and no easier) than imposing taxes. Taxes, like capital controls, are, to some degree, evaded. It costs money and takes effort to collect taxes as it does to control capital mobility. But where there is a will to collect taxes, they are collected; it would simply take a change in the tax law to extend this mechanism to reducing international capital mobility.[35]

The development of democratic and sustainable global economic relationships will require the invention of new forms of transnational governance.

Many critics of oppressive globalisation have focussed on the creation of alternative political, financial and legal global institutions that can form a democratic counterweight to the power of transnational capital.[36] If corporate power has shifted to the global arena, then the United Nations (UN) together with non-government organisations, such as globally organised labour and social movements can provide a base for the creation of international corporate codes of conduct, controls over financial transactions and the construction of more democratic international governance.

It is true that, in the end, the globalisation of economic power can only be adequately dealt with through globalised systems of democratic decision making, regulation and distribution. The problems, however, are obvious. Crotty and Epstein suggest that

> [t]he most effective method for creating global full employment is a cooperative macropolicy expansion, cooperative capital controls, an international central bank in the Keynes mode and an international Social Charter enumerating and enforcing mini-mum wages and working conditions and economic rights and appropriate environmental standards. Unfortunately current prospects for attaining such comprehensive global agreements are dim.[37]

By far the best organised and most influential organisations operat-ing at a global level are transnational corporations, semi-private trans-national agencies such as the International Standards Organisation (ISO), and bodies such as the WTO, which are heavily influenced by corporate interests. It is therefore vital that the control and operation of transnational corporations and other global corporate organisations are the subject of far greater study, public scrutiny and public understanding than is currently the case.[38]

The largest and most significant of democratic global institutions, the UN, continues to suffer from a severe crisis of identity and legitimacy. As Australian international relations scholar and activist Joe Camilleri notes, the role and potential of the UN remains deeply problematic.

> Is the UN an instrument of hegemonic power? Does the UN reflect Western values, and as such is it a continuing symbol of Western dominance? Is it an arena for contending ideologies, for the emerging 'class of civilisations'? Or might it best be described as an embryonic concert of powers, perhaps a meeting point for diverse cultures and traditions? Or, is the UN to be understood as a bureaucratic apparatus devoid of any larger purpose?[39]

The UN is best understood as a fragile set of agreements between national governments with very unequal degrees of influence and power. Its most successful actions remain the codification of global standards of individual human rights.[40] There were few supra-national codes of human rights prior to 1945, and it is impressive that various UN declarations and covenants now guarantee the right to life, recognition as a legal person, due process, peace-ful assembly, freedom of association, security of person, freedom of thought and expression, conscience and religion, freedom of movement and freedom from torture, summary execution, cruel and inhuman punishment, slavery, servitude and forced labour.

Much of the human rights agenda of the UN remains at the level of resolutionary good intentions, with effective enforcement constrained by the ongoing determination of nation states to resist interference in their internal processes. Internationally recognised human-rights indicators and benchmarks are valuable preconditions for democratic and accountable processes of international governance and justice. The International War Crimes trials in relation to Germany, Japan, and, more recently, Bosnia, have demonstrated the possibility of raising the universality of human rights over the defence that those involved were 'only following orders' from their respective nation states. But who was going to take effective action against the United States if it chose to ignore the International Court of Justice's (ICJ) findings in relation to military action against the Sandinista government in Nicaragua?[41]

Cynicism about the ineffectiveness of the UN as a democratic global decision-making forum needs to be tempered with a sober assessment of the alternatives. If we look to individual nation states as potential sources of global regulation and governance, the only candidate in the post–Cold War world is the United States. While its motivations may have been ambiguous, the United States Administration of the early 1990s did explore the possibility of linking trade and labour standards, but this faltered in the face of fierce resistance from major trading partners such as China, Singapore, Malaysia and Indonesia.[42] The experiences of the Gulf War and Somalia led to considerable scepticism about the idea that the United States should be encouraged to play a more active role in relation to either international security or development.

The roles of other major post–Bretton Woods transnational institutions, such as the International Monetary Fund (IMF), the World Bank and the GATT (now the World Trade Organisation), have also been subject to extensive critiques in relation to both the decision-making dominance of Western industrialised nations and their dismal record in relation to financial and development outcomes.[43] One influential critic of the rising power of global corporations, David Korten, summarises the roles of the key institutions of global economic governance in the following way:

> The World Bank has served as an export financing facility for large Northern-based corporations. The IMF has served as the debt collector for Northern based financial institutions. GATT has served to create and enforce a corporate bill of rights protecting the rights of the world's largest corporations against the intrusion of people, communities and democratically elected governments.[44]

Other international organisations and forums, such as the Organisation for Economic Cooperation and Development (OECD) and the G8 grouping (made up of the United States, Germany, Britain, France, Italy, Canada, Japan and, most recently, Russia) have been designed by and for the wealthiest and most powerful of industrialised nations. Some events, such as the regular meetings of corporate moguls in Davos, Switzerland, are explicitly designed as gatherings for the global economic elite. It is therefore essential to begin the long and uncertain process of creating transnational institutions and networks that can provide the basis for the design and implementation of alternative global trading, financial and regulatory relationships.

A reformed set of UN arrangements will provide some of the organisational basis for the establishment of more effective enforcement systems in relation to the regulation of human rights and labour standards. Other global institutions, such as the International Labour Organisation (ILO), can also play a useful role, as can the negotiation of multilateral and bilateral social charters at regional levels.

The limited effectiveness of social charter and trade-union rights agreements in both the NAFTA and European Union (EU) experience suggests that it would be unwise to place too much faith in such strategies alone. The historical evidence in relation to attempts to achieve national and international social reforms through legislated standards and charters leads to the conclusion that such measures are only effective when they are linked to and enforced by vocal and powerful social movements.[45]

Australian government and non-government organisations can and should play a role in supporting a more effective set of UN and globally organised non-government institutions that can provide a framework for reconciling the often paradoxical aims of global citizenship: defending human rights while respecting political and cultural sovereignty and ensuring the fair and sustainable use of the global commons.

Australian non-government organisations should also be actively encouraging the UN to play a role in opening up the space for the effective development of democratically accountable, locally grounded and globally connected trading and financial institutions, which can begin to form a counterweight to the dominance of transnational corporations.

The democratic reform of global governance depends on the successful development of transnational civil society.

The real key to the progressive reform and regulation of global human rights, trade and finance lies in the fostering of stronger global connections between unions, social movements and non-government organisations. This process will not be straightforward.

Labour movements in many countries have a long history of internationalism and there are many examples of successful cross-border organising and solidarity. The success of the Australian Maritime Union in winning international union support to stop potential strike breakers being trained in Dubai during 1997 was a sharp reminder of the power that can be mobilised in key strategic industries. As the conflict between stevedoring companies and the MUA intensified in early 1998, the significance of international trade union action was highlighted by the Secretary of the London-based International Transport Workers' Federation, Kees Marges, who noted that ships that had been unloaded in non-union ports in Australia would be followed around the world and harassed to such an extent that they would end up as 'scrap rather than as a ship'.[46]

Many trade unions are beginning to turn the long-standing rhetoric of labour-movement internationalism into practical strategies. In February 1998 a meeting was held in South Africa to create a global network of trade unions representing workers employed by the giant mining company Rio Tinto. The spread of Rio Tinto's interests was indicated by the number of nations represented at the meeting, including the United States, Britain, Canada, Norway, Portugal, Sweden, Turkey, India, Australia, Papua New Guinea, Brazil, Namibia, Zimbabwe and South Africa. According to the General Secretary of the International Federation of Chemical, Energy, Mine and General Workers Union, Vic Thorpe, the aim of the meeting was to mobilise the 20 million workers represented by the Federation in order to halt Rio Tinto's anti-union campaigns and 'responsibilise' the company by forcing it to adhere, at least, to basic social, health and safety standards.[47]

International trade unionism remains a powerful potential source of global solidarity and the potential of cross-border organising has yet to be fully explored. Trade union influence should not, however, be overstated. Union membership is falling in many (though not all) countries, as workers are increasingly forced to become more flexible and mobile, breaking connections with particular localities and industries – and with other workers.[48]

The situation in relation to political and cultural spheres is even more disturbing, given the loss of connection between local communities, the globalised power of transnational firms, and the capacity of the corporate sector to win the cultural battle for hearts and minds so as to create a dominant culture of extreme consumerism and individualism. 'Pessimism of the head and optimism of the heart' is an appropriate aphorism in relation to the imbalances of globalised power. International relations analyst Robert Cox suggests some of the starting points for tipping the balance in favour of more optimistic scenarios:

> the prospect of turning around the segmenting, socially disintegrating, and polarizing effects of the globalization thrust rests upon the possibility of the emergence of an alternative political culture that would give greater scope to collective action and place a greater value on collective goods . . .

> The condition for a restructuring of society and polity . . .
> would be to build a new historic bloc capable of sustaining a long
> war of position until it is strong enough to become an alternative
> basis of polity . . . If they are ultimately to result in new forms of
> state, these forms will arise from the practice of non state
> popular collective action rather than from the extensions of
> existing types of administrative control.[49]

The embryonic forms of global networks of 'transnational civil society' can be seen in the work of global human-rights, development and environmental organisations such as Amnesty, Oxfam and Greenpeace, and in the non-government forums of the global environmental, women's and social-development summits. They can also be seen in the efforts to build trans-national union alliances and new ways of reaching unorganised workers that can provide some challenge to the power of transnational corporations.[50]

At the regional level, the cross-border trust building and campaigning of the European Nuclear Disarmament movement in Europe in the 1980s, and the difficult – at times dangerous – attempts to build understanding and alliances between trade unions and community organisations in Canada, the United States and Mexico in the 1990s provide important lessons and inspiration.[51]

In the Australian case the challenge is to begin creating far greater understanding and effective links between civil society non-government organisations and social movements in Australia and the Asia-Pacific region. Some of the most useful initiatives might include practical technological and financial assistance aimed at improving regional communications and transport infrastructure systems for NGO representatives, activists and researchers.

Transnational regions will be at least as significant as global spaces in the invention of new economic, political and ecological relationships.

The process of regionalisation is at least as significant as globalisation in understanding the transformation of the context of national decision making. Key decisions and relationships are increasingly contained within the boundaries of the North American, European and Asia-Pacific regions, with the governing structures of the EU, NAFTA and APEC playing very different but increasingly important roles.

The establishment of agreements on human rights and social, economic and environmental benchmarks in the Asia-Pacific region need to be pursued through both the creation of APEC social and human-rights charters and co-operative action between unions and community organisations.[52]

Despite – or perhaps because of – Keating's emphasis on the Asia-Pacific region and APEC as *the* big picture issue, most Australians (outside the business community) remain wary of the idea of Australia as an Asian-focused culture and surprisingly uninterested in the implications of the APEC process. Yet it is at this regional level that many of the most important conflicts affecting the future of the Australian economy and society will be played out. It is therefore vital and urgent that a range of non-government and labour-movement organisational forms be established at the APEC level.[52]

Many activists within the Australian labour movement, and other social movements, have long recognised the importance of defending labour rights and the conditions for the growth of independent trade unions in Asia.[54] Recognising the importance of such networks is a good start. But establishing the understanding and trust to overcome deep cultural differences will require a marked increase in the resources and time devoted to this task.

A concerted effort is required to create a host of stronger direct connections and dialogues between community organisations, trade unions, local governments, schools and universities in the Asia-Pacific region. Such connections and dialogues need to be constructed on an enhanced understanding that this is not a matter of 'rich' Australia helping its 'poor' Asian neighbours, but of people from differing cultural and political contexts coming together to explore common concerns. Some of the ways in which these connections and dialogues can be fostered at local and national levels are explored in the next chapter.

Chapter 10

Alternative Directions?
Thinking and Acting Locally
and Nationally

[The world still] has more depth than a global network of
economic power extending from the centre(s) to the periphery
... To problematise the coherence and durability of national
societies and states, however, does call for new ways of thinking
about the way that social space is organised and reorganised over
time.
Rianne Mahon[1]

While it is increasingly unlikely that a territorial unit can continue
to preserve its distinctiveness on the basis of delinking there is
an increasing probability that distinctive identities may be formed
as a unique crossroad in the flow of people, goods and ideas.
Z. Mlinar[2]

This chapter addresses the possibilities and limitations of local and national
responses to globalisation. It begins by arguing that the re-imagining and re-
creation of local community identities and relationships has become more
important than ever. The processes of globalisation have brought about and
been affected by changing forms of localisation and the reshaping of
relationships between the individual, the family, the household and the
community.[3]

Localism is a politically ambiguous principle with sectarianism and
prejudice often on the other side of the coin to self-determination and
diversity. New forms of aggressive tribalism, prejudice and intolerance are
readily visible, but so too are many struggles to sustain the economic viability
of local communities and respect the diversity of local cultures.

Struggles to maintain a diversity of social and economic relations are vital if empowerment is understood as a process of 'promoting, preserving and engaging the diversity of expertise; it means promoting innovation through localised, poly vocal activity, and the active use and solicitation of indigenous lore'.[4] Caution is required, however, to avoid naive and confused understandings of the nature of local political and economic relationships.

In looking closely at the possibility of alternative relationships and institutions at local, global and national levels, the personal contradictions of becoming global citizens and remaining situated in particular spaces and relationships should also be borne in mind. How do we find new ways of acting on myriad stages with an ever-expanding cast of actors while remaining connected to our own place and time?

The chapter concludes by arguing that national governments are still major players in the governance of economic, social, cultural and environmental relationships in particular localities and that it is too soon to write off the nation state as a significant arena of political creativity and contest.

Political Choices in a Globalised World: Local and National Responses

Re-imagining communities in a globalised world requires re-imagining the meaning and nature of local relationships.

For many community activists the answer to the globalisation of power is 'grassroots action' and 'globalisation from below'.[5] Advocates of localist strategies draw on a diversity of political traditions including community development, international development, 'small is beautiful' economics, localist socialism, communitarian anarchism, and the environmental and women's movements.[6] The common thread is a belief in the fostering of local economic networks and community relationships as arenas within which identity and difference can be protected, solidarity and mutuality nurtured, and ecological values sustained.

The possibilities of progressive localist politics have been subject to a sustained critique based on the concern that, for all their good intentions, many local activists remain naive about the extent to which oppressive political and economic relationships can be effectively challenged by focussing only on the local level.[7] From this point of view constraints on local resistance and self reliance have become even greater as the key relationships of corporate power have moved further upwards from the national to the global level.[8]

Other critics of grassroots panaceas have pointed out that there is nothing intrinsically progressive about locality- and community-based politics. There are any number of examples of sectarian, narrow-minded and oppressive grassroots campaigns and organisations.[9] Much of the pressure for decentralisation is driven openly or covertly by agendas more concerned with cost cutting and stripping away regulatory systems than with principles of local democracy and participation.[10] Finally, an uncritical emphasis on the merits of localism and 'community care' can readily become a justification for loading increased responsibilities onto women in the realm of the family and the private sphere.[11]

There is often considerable confusion about exactly what is meant by 'the local'. In different contexts and settings the local can refer to levels as diverse as the household, neighbourhood, municipality, city, sub-national, or even sub-global, region. This is related to the changing nature of 'localism' with a shift from older, inward-looking and unreflective forms of localism to more reflexive and outward-looking local understandings and action.[12]

As the economic, technological and cultural pressures towards con-sumerist individualism rise, the meaning of 'the local' is changing as many 'consumer citizens' retreat below the level of the local community into family fortresses, while attempting to 'stay in touch' globally through Fly Buys holidays, Email and cyberspace. In this context it is unrealistic to imagine or sustain self-contained and self-sufficient local communities in the image of the Athenian polis. Yet, globalisation also has the potential to connect local groups and institutions in new ways with discussions and negotiations often bypassing the nation state. Without being naive about a romanticised vision of localism, one paradox of globalisation is that the creation of more effective local social movements, more democratic local institutions and more co-operative local relationships is more important than ever.[13]

The re-imagination and reinvention of local communities requires the democratisation of local economic relationships.

There are many champions of the view that small is indeed beautiful and that the most effective response to globalisation is to act locally to create more truly democratic and accountable social, political, economic and environ-mental relationships.[14] While the focus here is primarily on the possibilities and limitations of alternative local economic relationships, the same tensions between autonomy and solidarity, and state, market and civil society, also apply to other social, environmental and political institutions.

The key variables in local, regional and community economic development are the extent to which private-sector control and free-market principles are accepted or challenged and whether policies and practices are linked to broader goals of social transformation.[15] Thus, from the more extreme end of the neo-liberal economic spectrum, inequalities between localities are the inevitable and often desirable result of changing geographical patterns of demand and supply. Underpinning much current Australian economic policy is the view that if particular rural, regional or urban communities go into decline, then so be it. The inhabitants will just have to move if they want to improve their employment prospects.

There are limits to the local political acceptability of such extreme forms of *laissez faire* regional policies, and local economic responses to global restructuring more commonly involve measures designed to retain and attract private business in particular localities through improving the competitiveness of local taxation levels, labour markets and infrastructure.[16]

The re-creation of local economic democracy begins with research and advocacy demonstrating the local impact of restructuring and the need for action to assist those who are paying the heaviest price. At best the 'high road' to local competitiveness means investing in a more skilled work-force, high-quality transport and communications technology, and an attractive living and working environment. An emphasis on improving networks between firms to provide a 'virtuous circle' and create a positive climate for local and regional growth is also a frequent component of such strategies.[17]

At worst, the 'low road' to competitiveness becomes a 'race to the bottom' between localities desperate to attract jobs at any price, with fully deregulated, low-wage free-trade zones such as the Maquiladoras (the northern part of Mexico on the United States border) the most extreme outcome. The Director of the Washington-based Institute for Policy Studies, Michael Schuman, captures the challenges facing local communities and governments:

> The rapid globalization of once local corporations has placed communities in a terrible dilemma: either cut wages, gut environmental standards and offer tax breaks to induce corporations to build new factories or offices, or prepare to become an economic ghost town. Even 'progressive' mayors and city officials find themselves hobnobbing with the captains of industry to pony up the best bribes for corporations to stay in or relocate to their locales. Yet this is a competition with no winners, as communities everywhere bid down the quality of life.[18]

More interventionist strategies by government and non-government organisations can involve research and advocacy designed to demonstrate the local impact of restructuring and the need for financial assistance, regulatory initiatives designed to protect local jobs, support for local job creation and labour-market programs, and more direct roles in investing in employment-generating enterprises, including a wide variety of community economic development initiatives.[19] As Schuman argues, the local impact of global and national restructuring should be formally and regularly monitored and publicised through a system of annual studies and public hearings in all localities.

A number of local authorities in the United States have passed legislation requiring corporations to take some responsibility for relocating their activities through measures such as mandatory economic and social impact statements, assistance to workers in finding alternative employment, and the provision of opportunities for workers, communities and local governments to explore the possibility of buying and operating the plant.[20]

Such attempts to regulate the mobility of capital have generally been successfully challenged in the courts and do not adequately address the fundamental problem of the increasing capacity of globally organised corporations to play one locality off against another and simply move away from areas that are seen as being over-regulated. For this reason some policy makers have argued for a system of locally connected charters covering key employment practices (such as child labour, minimum wages, the right to organise, and health and safety standards).[21]

Local-government charters can be developed covering the employment, consumer and environmental standards of firms within the locality and firms exporting into the locality. These are only likely to be successful if they are linked to national and international networks of local government and community organisations buying from and investing in corporations that meet agreed-upon standards.

Ironically, the globalisation of markets and interdependence of many large firms has also made them more vulnerable to large-scale, concerted action by consumers.[22] To take only one example, the Seikatsu Club Consumers Co-operative was begun in 1965 by a Tokyo woman who organised two hundred women into a buying collective designed to lower the price of milk.[23] Over thirty years Seikatsu has developed into a computer-assisted, collective-buying organisation with over 170 000 members. The collective uses its buying power not only to lower prices but also to create pressure on corporations in relation to working conditions, environmental and social issues. If the collective finds that there are no satisfactory products or firms, then a new enterprise is created based on direct links between consumers and producers. At the same time, the buying club has focussed on the consumption patterns of its members and has also begun to pursue more traditional forms of political action including contesting parliamentary elections. More broadly, 'the objective of Seikatsu Club is to learn how to self govern society through self management of our lives. Our visions for rebuilding local societies derive from this principle.'[24]

It is possible to imagine an extension of this model that might involve the establishment of an international network or bloc of local authorities and non-government organisations that could monitor indicators of corporate behaviour and agree to buy from and invest in only those corporations that meet agreed-upon standards in relation to employment, environmental and marketing practices.

The creation of such a bloc would clearly conflict with the anti-protectionist rules contained in so-called 'free-trade' agreements, such as the North American Free Trade Agreement (NAFTA) and the Uruguay round of the General Agreement on Tariffs and Trade (GATT). The legitimacy and enforceability of those provisions might well be tested by a sufficiently strong network of local community groups, consumer organisations, and national and local governments.[25]

The facilitation of networking and information sharing has been a key feature of many initiatives, with an explicit focus on local community economic development (CED).[26] A wide range of intermediary and support organisations have been created to assist community-based enterprises in sharing information and providing mutual support through newsletters, seminars, conferences, electronic clearing houses, training programs, combined marketing strategies and personal support services, such as child care.[27]

During the 1980s the Esperance Local Enterprise Initiatives Committee in Western Australia developed an impressive reputation for linking prospective entrepreneurs to private- and public-sector funding sources. Over an eight-year period 280 businesses were supported, leading to the creation of 530 jobs.[28] The Provincial Communities Enterprise Project in Victoria is another example of a successful focus on the facilitation of private and co-operative enterprises through financial-planning advice, brokering loan arrangements and establishing partnerships with local government.[29]

In addition to advocacy, regulation and network facilitation there are numerous examples of local government and non-government organisations attempting to reduce dependence on external sources of investment by becoming directly involved in the establishment and maintenance of employment generating enterprises or through regional development and venture capital funds.

Such initiatives can take a variety of forms, including direct public ownership and control, community enterprises and cooperatives, hybrid forms of public and private ownership, or the establishment of private corporations in which shareholding is restricted to residents of particular groups or communities. An important common feature of such alternative forms of local enterprise is their capacity to be based on objectives other than the maximisation of short-term profitability. They can, for example, work towards broader social and environmental goals and establish longer time frames for returns on investment.

The recent history of attempts at direct local government economic intervention are not always reassuring. Over the last fifteen years reformist administrations such as the Labour-controlled Greater London Council in England, the New Democratic Party Government in Ontario, Canada, and a number of Australian Labor State governments have explored a range of approaches to supporting local economic development. The problems they encountered suggest that it is very difficult to overcome the economic and political dilemmas of generating democratic local employment programs while the regional economy and regional state finances are being over-whelmed by the pressures of international economic competitiveness and deregulated international financial markets.[30]

For some proponents of CED the promotion of local self reliance is the most important priority. Canadian community activist Maria Nozick, for example, argues that the goal of CED should be to create 'sustainable communities' with an emphasis on economic self reliance, ecological sustainability, community control, the meeting of individual needs (non material as well as material), and the fostering of a genuine sense of local community culture.[31]

She points to the First Nation community at Kingfisher Lake in Northern Ontario, Canada, which took over the local Hudson Bay Company trading store and channelled the profits into a series of local enterprises including laundromats, housing stock, fuel supply, electricity generation, a cooperative bank and a small airline. Nozick's central point is that

> Kingfisher Lake owes its success to a clear and focused strategy for community self reliance. One of the principles of self reliance evident in the Kingfisher Lake example is that community economic development starts by meeting people's basic needs – food, clothing travel – instead of pulling development ideas out of the air in the hope of developing an 'export' market.[32]

There is a strong ecological case for using local resources more effectively to maximise local community self reliance and it will continue to be an attractive option for many indigenous and remote communities. However, self-reliance strategies have become increasingly difficult in the context of globalised financial markets and the legal restrictions imposed by treaties such as NAFTA and GATT.[33] While CED projects must remain connected to their local context, they also need to build strong alliances and links with other CED projects and community organisations, both within and beyond their local area, if they are to survive and maintain their focus on broader objectives of social change.[34]

Some of the most interesting and creative local responses to globalised economic relations are in fact as much about making new connections as about preserving autonomy. A number of Community Shared Agriculture (CSA) projects in Canada have involved the establishment of urban locality or common-interest groups (for example, low-income groups or groups seeking affordable organic produce) that join together to purchase agricultural products directly from farmers.[35]

The group pays individual farmers or farming produce cooperatives on a yearly basis providing the benefit of a guaranteed income to the producers. In return, the farmers undertake to drop off an agreed share of their weekly production at several city collection points. Participation in the group involves a recognition that consumers will receive more in good seasons and less in bad seasons. Many CSA groups have the explicit aim of sensitising urban populations to the dilemmas and difficulties facing family farmers and farming communities.[36]

In Canada, Toronto health workers and consumers committed to alternative health procedures have been active in creating 'wellness networks' directly linking providers and service users. Education workers have been revisiting the 1970s traditions of learning exchanges and networks and have begun exploring the idea of alternative universities outside the mainstream education system. Housing workers, architects and urban planners have endeavoured to build on the strong Canadian tradition of housing co-operatives through a diverse range of CED and job-creation experiments in housing cooperatives, such as rooftop community gardens, energy and water conservation, child care, elder care and recreation work.

In 1984 a number of retrenched workers in the Kitchener Waterloo area of Ontario established 'The Working Centre' as a basis for organising responses to plant closures and increasing unemployment in the area.[37] The initial focus was on obtaining government funding for training and job-creation programs and raising venture capital for local employment projects, such as a recycling business and a community restaurant. The Centre has also become a focus for unemployed and employed workers wanting to raise broader questions about the future of work and alternative forms of production and distribution.

Much of this questioning has arisen from the Christian (largely Mennonite) culture of the local Ontario communities, and there are frequent references to the influence of Ghandian and Tolstoyan principles of 'living with less' and the idea of 'work as a gift' to be shared rather than bought and sold. This has led to the establishment of a network of community gardens, systems for linking agricultural and craft producers more directly to consumers, and a range of Local Exchange Trading Systems type schemes for moving out of the mainstream market economy.

While Australia has a limited tradition of community and union investment cooperatives, there is a long tradition of producer cooperatives in the dairy and wheat industries. In the Hunter Valley of New South Wales, the Metal Workers Union established the Hunter Valley Labour Cooperative in 1986. The Cooperative acts as a labour-placement broker, linking unemployed workers to employers requiring short-term work. There is a particularly strong emphasis on improving working conditions and environmental standards in local industries. By 1995 the Cooperative had a full-time staff of twenty and supported employment for over 600 workers at any one time.[38]

The most difficult dilemma for proponents of alternative local enterprises is the question of finance. Again and again the key question in considering the feasibility of local or community economic development proposals is 'How can this be financed?'. Where will the capital come from and what conditions will be attached? Are there workable alternatives to reliance on the mainstream banking and financial institutions?[39] The answer provided by Jack Quarter, author of a detailed study of alternative financial institutions in Canada, is that 'ultimately, the "bottom line" for [alternative finance] proposals is whether people, either in organisations or as individuals, want to direct their savings into investment vehicles utilising social criteria, or whether their only concern is the rate of return, regardless of the investment policies that generate it'.[40]

The wide variety of alternative-financing models explored in different settings include credit unions and cooperatives, ethical investment funds, community investment funds, community loan guarantee programs, community development bonds (in which shares are sold to finance investment in particular areas), and the strategic use of union pension funds.[41] The following examples suggest some possible starting points.

In Bangladesh the Grameen banking network was established in 1976 to provide an alternative banking system for poor villagers.[42] The objective was to improve access to loans for community enterprises and community development at low rates of repayment, with loan programs linked to extensive training and based on strict financial discipline. The bank is 25 per cent government owned and 75 per cent owned by its borrowers. Only borrowers may own shares in the bank and no one may own more than one share.

Borrowers operate in small groups where continued access to loans by group members is dependent upon all group members maintaining their repayments. By 1990 there were over 750 branches of the Grameen bank providing low-cost loans to almost 1 million borrowers for purposes ranging from small cooperative businesses to housing, health and legal services. Similar programs designed to provide loans funds for small-scale community enterprises have also begun to be explored in Australia.

VanCity, the largest credit union in Canada and one of the top twenty Canadian financial institutions, has drawn on the experience of the Grameen banking experiment to establish a system of Peer Loan Funds (or Loan Circles) in which groups of at least four borrowers agree to vouch for each other in order to obtain loans from the fund. These have been particularly successful as the basis for supporting women and members of First Nation and ethnic communities moving out of exploitative black-economy and sweated-labour arrangements into cooperative CED settings.[43]

In a number of Canadian provinces funds invested in government-guaranteed Community Loan Funds by local community members and organisations, such as trade unions, churches, schools and First Nation communities, can be used as security to borrow larger amounts of capital from banks that would otherwise not be prepared to lend without collateral.[44] Under the Ontario New Democratic Party Government's Community Investment Share Corporation Scheme, community organisations could buy shares in government-guaranteed investments targeted at CED projects that pay at least 75 per cent of total wages to employees working in Ontario.[45]

Some of the most significant experiments aimed at broadening the use of pension funds for community investment have been in Quebec, Canada, where the government centralised control of all public pension funds in 1966. By 1990 this fund had holdings of over $36 billion and annual investments of $2 billion, with an explicit commitment to balancing financial return with the promotion of Quebec's economic development.[46] The Confederation des Syndicats Nationaux (CSN), representing over 250 000 workers, has established several financial cooperatives with the aim of creating 'socialised entrepeneurship and finance'. The focus has been on both new worker cooperative enterprises and worker buy outs, such as the financing of a rubber-recycling plant drawing on the skills of retrenched Uniroyal workers in Montreal.

The Fonds de Solidarite des Travailleurs du Quebec (FTQ), started in 1984 by the Quebecois union movement, now describes itself as the 'largest development capital corporation in Quebec'.[47] The FTQ is a union-based ethical investment fund with a commitment to long-term employment and environmental objectives. Investors are drawn primarily from Quebec union members and shares cannot normally be resold until retirement or death.

The Crocus Investment Fund set up by the Manitoba union movement in 1991 represents an even more ambitious strategy for 'social entrepeneurship'.[48] The Fund encourages investment by union members with the explicit goal of supporting the gradual takeover of companies by their workers. It therefore actively intervenes in the corporate structure of businesses in which it has a substantial interest with the aim of transferring voting rights to the workers of the company. Its role then becomes that of a supportive banker and financial adviser. The famous Mondragon cooperatives of Spain utilise a similar system of encouraging members to save with the cooperative bank, which can then provide funds for investment by cooperative members.

In Australia, debates about broadening the objectives of superannuation funds and changes in the regulation of Australian financial institutions provide important opportunities for a new agenda of research and project development aimed at exploring the question: Are there workable local alternatives to reliance on the mainstream banking and financial institutions?[49]

In Coffs Harbour, New South Wales, the SuperVisioN Superannuation Fund was established in 1994 as a not-for-profit company with the mission of attracting local savings by guaranteeing that 25 per cent of savings would be reinvested in the local region. In late 1994 the Australian Council of Trade Unions (ACTU) convened a major conference exploring the broader potential of superannuation funds to create local employment and infrastructure through 'economically targeted investments'. The ACTU noted that 'the compulsory nature of superannuation suggests members should have a real say in choosing investment options. Member investment choice provides scope for greater direct participation of individual members in the management of their superannuation investments . . . This should be encouraged.'[50]

The democratisation of local economic relationships requires new forms of local governance.

Many of the attempts to create fairer and more accountable local economic and financial relationships reflect and illustrate the challenges involved in re-creating all the spheres and institutions of local governance. The increasing dominance of globalised corporate power over local and national state institutions calls for a spirited defence of the institutions of local democracy and local government.[51] In the Australian context, the reinvention of local governance depends upon a sober assessment of the limited scope of local decision making.

However, support for the democratic renewal of local governance needs to be based on a recognition of the limits of purely localised action. Part of the answer lies in the development of national and international alliances between government and non-government organisations at local, provincial, national and regional levels. And in a world of globalised power there will also need to be a renewal and democratisation of the institutions of governance at the global level.

Without being naive about romanticised visions of a modern Athenian polis, effective political responses to globalisation depend on a spirited defence and reinvention of democratic local political and economic institutions. The attacks on local government and local democracy in Australia should therefore be of major concern.[52]

Democratically accountable local governments must be defended as spaces for monitoring, regulating and challenging the local impact of decisions made by more distant and less accountable corporations and nation states. An enhanced regulatory role for local government is likely to be most effective if alliances and charters are developed between like-minded local governments in Australia and other countries. Such alliances can begin to share information and use their combined moral leverage and consumer power to have increased influence on public opinion and investment decisions.

Traditional local spaces such as the apartment block, the street, the playgroup, the neighbourhood house, the primary school, the sporting club, the community health centre and the library can all be valuable sites for defending and re-creating the importance of face-to-face relationships. But we also need to think far more creatively about newer forms of local space (such as the shopping mall), as well as the ambiguous potential for information technology to create and destroy local connections (including cyber localities).[53]

The most important role for local government will be to help provide the space and the resources for the exploration of new relationships of governance based on emerging forms of cooperation between local states, markets and non-government, 'civil society' organisations.

This needs to be based on a recognition of the changing forms of local governance with the development of many new hybrid relationships between the local state, the market and non-government, 'civil society' or 'third sector' organisations including locality based community organisations, interest based community organisations, community service providers, religious organisations, trade unions and social movements.[54] It would be interesting in this regard to re-examine the desirability of some form of the Whitlam Government's Australian Assistance Plan for encouraging a diversity of local community initiatives and alternative forms of local governance.

Some of these forms may arise from and be focussed on the 'very local'. At the level of the household, changing family and generational responsibilities might see a reworking of the ways in which housing costs and the responsibilities for paid and unpaid work are shared between different family members, creating new kinds of extended families and friendship networks.

Local community campaigns, local economic development projects, localised financial arrangements and local consumer cooperatives all merit support and experimentation. Some of these projects may be driven primarily by the goal of increased self-reliance – of preserving some realm of non-globalised relationships. Others may be concerned with the fostering of connections between producers and consumers at a variety of geographical levels.

Many of these initiatives can be built on the work of third-sector organisations and social movements. Many will be most successful if they are linked to similar projects and initiatives in other localities within and beyond Australia. And many will finally be reliant on supportive resourcing arrangements and regulatory environments at global, regional and national levels. It is vital that the emerging institutions of local civil society are nurtured, resourced and connected as a counterweight to the power of the globalised firm and as locations within which new relations of production and distribution can be explored. The critical point is that strong local communities need the backing of strong, democratic and effective forms of local government.

The democratisation of local governance requires new forms of political resistance at all levels.

In the context of mounting media hysteria about the collapse of global society into tribal barbarism and ethnic cleansing, it is vital to keep telling the stories of local solidarities, trust and resistance.

We can begin by remembering the acts of courageous individuals and small groups who have refused to accept that power resides only with the militarised state and the globalised corporation. Globalisation critic Paul Ekins provides a useful collection of such examples by drawing on the outcomes of the 'Right Livelihood Awards' for 'practical and exemplary solutions' to global and local problems.[55] He suggests that we should more often be telling the stories of the winners of these awards, of people such as Mike Cooley (for developing the possibilities of socially useful technology with the workers at Lucas Aerospace); Petra Kelly (co-founder of the German Greens); Bill Mollison (developer of the theory and practice of permaculture); Mordechai Vanunu (for revealing the extent of Israel's nuclear weapon's program) or Rigoberta Menchu (for challenging assaults on human rights in Guatemala). The point is not to create new cults of the heroic individual or romanticise the 'power of one', but to recognise that the actions of individuals still matter in both practical and symbolic ways.

Sandi Brockway learned her politics in the anti-Vietnam war protests of the 1960s and the anti-poverty campaigns of the 1970s.[56] Since then she has committed civil disobedience at Diablo nuclear power plant, Livermore nuclear weapons research laboratories, Concord Naval Weapons Station (protesting against arms shipments to Central America), and Vandenberg airforce base (protesting against the testing of MX missiles targeted at Kwajelein atoll in the Pacific Ocean). More recently, she has been the driving force behind the creation of 'Macrocosm USA Inc.', a non-profit clearing house that 'strives to present solutions and holistic approaches to urgent social and environmental problems'.

As well as producing traditional hard-copy information about the possibilities of local alternatives to local and global exploitation, Macrocosm USA has created an 'electronic hub' on the Internet designed to act as an accessible database, network and source of examples of 'world best practice' on local and global resistance, campaigns and alternative institutions.

In 1995 four English women – Joanna Wilson, Andrea Needham, Lotta Kronlid and Anie Zelter – cut through the security fence at British Aerospace's plant at Warton and attacked a Hawk fighter plane with hammers, causing $1.5 million worth of damage.[57] They left a twenty-minute video in the cockpit explaining that their reason for attacking the plane was that it was due to be exported to Indonesia and that this was a moral and practical protest against the repression of human rights and self-determination by the Indonesian Government in East Timor. In their defence they cited the Nuremberg principles of responsibility for action to prevent genocide over-riding national property laws. They were charged with trespass and damage to property. The jury found them not guilty.

In the Australian context, this book was begun at the time of the death of the inspirational Murri Island activist, Eddie Mabo, whose dogged legal campaign for land rights finally broke open the colonial legal fraud of *terra nullius* and laid the basis for a sweeping reconsideration of colonialism and reconciliation in Australia. The final drafts of this book were completed in 1998 at the time of the death of H.C. 'Nugget' Coombs, who was honoured by both indigenous and non-indigenous Australians as an individual who had demonstrated great courage and determination in pursuing principles of justice and democracy in a wide range of settings.

The recognition of new spheres of exploitation is given voice and presence through the emergence of locally grounded social movements and new alliances are being created between social movements and unionists, leading to the exploration of 'social movement unionism'.[58] Across the world women in households and villages and communities keep coming together to challenge sexual violence and the unequal sexual division of labour.[59] Local campaigns against environmental destruction extend from Tasmania's Franklin River to the Amazon basin, from Bhopal to Union Carbide, and from breastfeeding women in African villages to the front door of the Nestlé corporation.[60]

There is much that is inspiring in such stories of local resistance, but difficult questions remain about the effectiveness of local resistance in an age of global power. Thirty years ago the pioneering work of Frances Fox Piven and Richard Cloward began to document the factors associated with the success and failure of American social movements struggling for social change.[61] Their key conclusion was that the 'success of a movement depends not on its organisational prowess but on its ability to disrupt'.[62]

One implication of this finding is the concern that many social movements are readily co-opted and bought off by the actions of state and market institutions. The deeper problem is that *people cannot defy institutions to which they have no access and to which they make no contribution*.[63] As English social-theorist Leslie Sklair argues,

> the dilemma is that the only chance that people in social move-
> ments have to succeed is by disrupting the local agencies with
> which they come into direct contact in their daily lives, rather

than the more global institutions whose interests these agencies are serving directly, or, more often indirectly, while workers are often confused about whom (which representation of capital) to oppose when their interests (conditions of labour, livelihoods) are threatened. Increasingly as capitalism globalises, subordinate groups find difficulty in identifying their adversaries.[64]

Local action alone is not enough because too many local outcomes have distant causes. This means that structures and connections designed to bring local forms of resistance together and create alliances of local networks are a high priority. This is what author and activist Jeremy Brecher has in mind when he talks about the 'Lilliputian tactic' of tying down the corporate 'giants' of global corporate power with thousands of interconnected local grassroots movements and struggles. The aim is to counter the divide-and-rule, 'beggar thy neighbour' tactics of the race-to-the-bottom agenda by creating the conditions in which workers and citizens with lower wages and working conditions are lifted upwards rather than driving down the living standards of workers in more prosperous economies.

> The Lilliput Strategy requires grass-roots rebellions against downward levelling; coalition building; transnational networking; and the creation or reformation of international institutions. Only by combining their efforts can those resisting the effects of globalization in Chicago and Warsaw, Chiapas and Bangalore begin to bring the New World Economy under control.[65]

The dilemmas facing international social movements open up the broader question of political agency. Who are going to be the principal actors in the struggles to resist corporate globalisation? Political parties of the organised Left are going through a period of considerable ambivalence about policy and strategy. Most social democratic parties have embraced 'globalisation with a human face', in which communitarian values sit oddly with ongoing reductions in the role, resources and services of the public sector. The international trade union movement retains considerable power, but is often caught between meeting the immediate needs of its embattled and dwindling membership and supporting broader political and social objectives. Consumer groups too have demonstrated considerable influence when they are able to act effectively on an international scale, but there will always be too many differences of class, gender, race and geography to make consumerism alone a basis for a new kind of democratic international politics.

The question of political agency remains complex and will no doubt only be worked out in the context of particular struggles and campaigns. In this regard, some of the most interesting possibilities for forging new connections are to be found in the campaigns against the alleged employment and environmental practices of transnational corporations such as Nestlé, Nike and McDonald's. Such campaigns, which bring together workers, consumers and social movements in a range of national contexts and across national boundaries, provide one significant forum for exploring new kinds of political internationalism.

The nation state still matters.

As the rhetoric of 'think global: act local' becomes pervasive, it is tempting to accept that the opportunity for autonomous political action at the level of the nation state has effectively disappeared. As noted in chapter 2, many critics of corporate globalisation are deeply pessimistic about the capacity of nation states to operate as more than 'transmission belts' for global capital.

The prospect of building socialism – or social democracy – or Keynesian liberalism – in any one country is indeed more remote than ever. But the nation state has not disappeared or become irrelevant. While the nation state is only one of many levels at which economic, political and social relationships are formed and contested, political scientist M.J. Peterson argues that the struggle over state resources and policies will continue to be a crucial factor affecting the outcome of struggles at other geographical and political levels.

> While civil society operates outside the institutional apparatus of the state, it relies on the state for provision of security, a range of public services and various goods. It also depends on the state fostering, or at least not obstructing, the conditions under which it can flourish. These conditions include secure rights to participation and non interference with autonomous arranging of group enterprises and activities.[66]

One of the most important lessons from the last fifteen years in Australia is that if the people lose democratic control over key decision-making forums and processes of the national and regional state, they lose a great deal, for the most significant decisions in relation to capital formation, production and distribution will effectively have been corporatised.

The policy options and strategic choices at the level of the nation state are, in essence, similar to those discussed earlier in relation to the local-level state. National governments can and should support research that identifies the social and environmental impacts of restructuring and globalisation in different localities and regions. Such research will be strengthened by the establishment of national and international indicators that make visible the full extent of costs and benefits; winners and losers. International benchmarking based on creative social and environmental auditing can, in turn, facilitate a broader understanding of citizenship rights at national and international levels.

The objectives of national social policy need to include programs aimed at redistributing the social costs of restructuring. In Australia, as in many industrialised countries, there is also an urgent need for the articulation of new policy frameworks and institutions to fill the void left by the collapse of faith in traditional Keynesian welfare-state arrangements. The social-policy choices facing Australia are increasingly being framed in terms of United States and European labour-market models. It is therefore commonly argued that the maintenance of strong income-security programs and a legally regulated industrial relations system limit export competitiveness and prevent a significant reduction in unemployment levels. The preferred option is to pursue a fully deregulated labour market and accept a widening gap in wages and conditions as the price for strong employment growth.

An effective challenge to this unsatisfactory pair of choices will need to be based on the establishment of new cultural assumptions and industrial agreements that can support a broader sharing out of both paid and unpaid work, as well as forms of labour-market flexibility that operate *for* rather than *against* the interests of workers.[67] It will also need to be based on a determined defence of progressive taxation as a desirable and effective means of sharing the costs and burdens of citizenship. The key problem with debates about taxation remains that 'rather than being the dues we pay for the privileges of living in an organised society, taxes have been characterised as an unjustified imposition to be avoided if possible'.[68]

National economic policy needs to be based on a concerted effort to win international support for appropriate and effective regulation of financial markets and foreign-investment flows. Prudent financial regulation is an essential starting point for the introduction of strategies designed to encourage a higher proportion of Australian savings into long-term investment programs. Support for not-for-profit superannuation schemes that explicitly combine national and regional economic and environmental priorities with the objective of maximising individual rates of return can make an important contribution to this objective.[69] An interventionist range of industry policies will also be required so as to help balance investment priorities between export growth, employment generation and environmental sustainability.[70] Considerable attention will need to be paid to the development of new forms of public and private partnerships at local, national and international levels given that 'in this new era, the most successful states will be those which can augment their conventional power resources with collaborative power: engaging others – states, corporations and business associations – to form cooperative agreements and "consortia" for action'.[71]

As the communication and control of information comes to play an increasingly important economic and cultural role, it is particularly important that telecommunications remains accessible and that the diversity of the media is strengthened rather than further concentrated. This makes the future of Australian national institutions, such as Telstra and the Australian Broadcasting Corporation, as well as the emerging question of Internet access and control, particularly vital.

The outcomes of the Kyoto Climate Change Summit raised a series of intriguing questions about the ways in which the possibility and desirability of national government intervention in major investment decisions can vary depending upon the interests of the players involved. The *Age* newspaper's economic commentator, Kenneth Davidson, has noted that corporate executives and their political supporters consistently use the inevitability of globalisation to argue against the capacity of national governments to intervene to prevent the tide of global corporate power sweeping across borders.

> When it comes to ordinary Australians, the global juggernaut is apparently unstoppable, but when it comes to the mining industry, the global juggernaut is apparently capable of deflection.[72]

The Australian Government's Kyoto 'triumph' also signalled a questionable long-term reliance on mining and timber industries as the basis for Australian export growth at precisely the time when both economic and environmental factors are likely to see reduced demand for commodities and an increasing emphasis on information and service industries.

Many apologists for corporate globalisation will no doubt continue to attack any proposals for national state intervention. They will argue that all forms of globalisation are inevitable and irreversible although, interestingly, the editorial writers of the conservative economic journal, the *Economist*, have recognised that 'those who demand that the trend of global integration be halted and reversed are frightening precisely because, given the will, governments could do it'.[73] Supporters of more democratic and emancipatory responses to globalisation might also note the comments of Commandante Marcos, who has led the peasant communities of Chiapas in southern Mexico in the Zapatista resistance movement against what he has described as the first of many wars between the winners and losers of corporate globalisation. The Zapatistas have been particularly effective at using Internet technologies to build alliances with groups around the world. At the top of the Zapatista home page Commandante Marcos notes:

> the crash of these two winds will be born, its time has arrived, it has stoked the fire of history. Now the wind from above rules, but here comes the wind from below, here comes the storm . . . that is how it will be.

Chapter 11

Conclusion:
The Struggle Continues

In our stories of creativity, survival, and day to day heroism, alongside stories of invasion, migration, colonisation and conflict, we may find that it is what we share with other societies, in Europe, in Asia, in America and Africa, that matters to us most.
Ann Curthoys[1]

In the last fifteen years the deregulation and restructuring of the Australian economy has led to a dramatic shift in Australian political, social and cultural assumptions. The 1980s and 1990s have seen the old 'certainties' of protectionism, arbitration and the belief in a significant role for the public sector swept away in a wave of enthusiasm for the brave new world of global competitiveness. For some the acceptance of 'the power of markets and the internationalisation of Australia' is a transformation to be celebrated.[2] For many others the experience has been one of deepening inequality, insecurity and trauma as jobs, services and communities have disappeared.

Global Nation? has sought to question the view that there is only one way to approach the dilemmas of globalisation. In applying this argument to Australia, the starting point is to begin with a grounded critique of the real costs and dangers of taken-for-granted forms of the unregulated free-market globalisation of the Australian economy. A sustained critique of the dominance of neo-liberal, economic rationalist economics needs to be linked to the articulation of a language that can successfully convey the imagination of more desirable relationships between individuality and mutuality; solidarity and difference; ecology and economy.

Such challenges will only be effective if they are connected to the development of institutional forms that involve an appropriate reworking of the relationship between state, market and civil society. And such challenges will only avoid the irrelevance of utopianism if they are grounded in the lived experience and aspirations of the constituencies that have most to lose from the assumption that the expansion of free-market individualism and consumerism into every facet of human life in every corner of the globe is both inevitable and desirable.

In 1998 the prospects for the indigenous peoples of Australia seem bleaker than they have for many years. Australian Aborigines and Torres Strait Islanders know much about the devastating economic and cultural effects of two hundred years of globalisation. A colonial legacy of invasion, dispossession, disease and the theft of land and children has developed into a more modern, but no less poisonous, mix of widespread racism, funding cuts and ongoing attempts by Australian and transnational mining companies to maximise access to resources on Aboriginal lands.

But it is also instructive and inspiring to consider the ways in which indigenous resistance has been organised and has drawn on possibilities and institutions at a wide range of levels.

In the early 1990s Aboriginal parents and students in the northern suburbs of Melbourne successfully combined a determined local community campaign with State-level legal action based on anti-discrimination legislation to stop the closure of their local Northland Secondary College and the discontinuation of its special programs for Aboriginal students.

The Aboriginal and Torres Strait Islander Commission (ATSIC) process, for all its difficulties, has provided a means of exploring new forms of decision making and service delivery at regional levels, which may reflect Aboriginal and Torres Strait Islander communal boundaries more appropriately than any of the existing tiers of government.

A long campaign by the people of a small Torres Strait island led finally to the High Court of Australia and the Federal Parliament, where the Mabo judgement and the *Native Title Act* laid the foundations for challenging *terra nullius* and re-opening some sense of hope for many local communities.

As the attacks on Aboriginal and Torres Strait Islander peoples grow more savage, the pressure for international protest and sanctions become more intense. The United Nations Working Group on Indigenous Populations has become an important forum for sharing information and developing cooperative strategies. The largest festival of international competitiveness, the Sydney Olympic Games, has the potential to become a global stage on which local and national struggles for self-determination are pursued.

The future of justice for indigenous Australians will be deeply influenced by the transformed relationships of globalisation. But that future will also depend upon how individuals, groups and communities build cooperative connections, create democratic institutions, and develop effective political strategies at local, national, regional and global levels. It is therefore appropriate to conclude this book by quoting former Aboriginal and Torres Strait Islander Social Justice Commissioner, Mick Dodson.

> The struggle will continue in Geneva, just as it does now in Burketown and Bairnsdale. But as I have often said, and will continue to say, as long as there is injustice, people will fight against that injustice. It may be popular now to promote superficial notions of 'one nation' by marginalizing and excluding those Australians who do not fit the image. But we have a long experience of such things. And we will continue to foster and work towards a vision of Australia where vilifying indigenous Australians is not an acceptable way to create a national identity to be proud of, and where sacrificing our human rights is not seen as an acceptable price for reducing the budget deficit.[3]

Notes

1 Introduction

1 See Giddens, A. *Consequences of Modernity*, Polity Press, Cambridge, 1990.
2 Appadurai, A. *Modernity at Large: Cultural Dimensions of Globalization*, University of Minnesota Press, Minneapolis, 1997, p. 18.

2 Breaking the Spell?

1 Hirst, P. and Thompson, G. *Globalisation in Question*, Polity Press, Cambridge, 1996, p. 6.
2 EPAC, *Shaping Our Future*, Conference Proceedings of the Commonwealth Government National Strategies Conference, AGPS, Canberra, 1995, p. 5.
3 Downer, A. 'Globalisation or Globaphobia: Does Australia Have a Choice?', Speech to the National Press Club, 1 December 1997.
4 Bellchamber, G. 'Globalisation Issues: A Union Perspective', in *Globalisation: Issues for Australia*, AGPS, Canberra, 1995, p. 203.
5 Giddens, A. *Beyond Left and Right: The Future of Radical Politics*, Polity Press, Cambridge, 1994; McGrew, T. 'A Global Society', in Hall, S., Held, D. and McGrew, T. (eds), *Modernity and its Functions*, Polity Press, Cambridge, 1994; Harvey, D., *The Condition of Post Modernity*, Basil Blackwell, Oxford, 1989. See also Drache, D. and Gertler, M. (eds), *The New Era of Global Competition: State Policy and Market Power*, McGill–Queens University Press, Montreal, 1991; Featherstone, M. (ed.), *Global Culture: Nationalism, Globalization and Modernity* (A Theory, Culture and Society Special Issue), Sage, London, 1990; Camilleri, J. and Falk, J. *The End of Sovereignty? The Politics of a Shrinking and Fragmented World*, Edward Elgar, Aldershot, 1992.
6 See Soja, E. *Post Modern Geography*, Verso, London, 1989.
7 Robertson, R. *Globalisation: Social Theory's Global Culture*, Sage, London, 1992; Appadurai, A. *Modernity at Large: Cultural Dimensions of Globalization*, University of Minnesota Press, Minneapolis, 1997.

8 See Hirst and Thompson, *Globalisation in Question*; Glynn, A. and Sutcliffe, B., 'Global But Leaderless? The New Capitalist Order', in Miliband, R. and Panitch, L., *Socialist Register 1992*, Merlin Press, London, 1992, pp. 76–95; Held, D. *Democracy and the Global Order*, Polity Press, Cambridge, 1995.

9 See Robertson, *Globalisation*; Harvey, *Condition of Post Modernity*; Poster, M. *The Mode of Information*, Polity Press, Cambridge, 1990.

10 Held, D. 'Democracy: From City States to a Cosmopolitan Order?', in *Political Studies*, XL, Special Issue, 1992, p. 32.

11 Both cited in Bienefeld, M. 'Capitalism and the Nation State in the Dog Days of the Twentieth Century', in Miliband, R. and Panitch, L. (eds), *Between Globalism and Nationalism*, Merlin Press, London, 1994, p. 109.

12 Sheridan, G. 'Background Tips to Reading Global Situation', *Weekend Australian*, 3 January 1995, p. 9.

13 Sweeney, S. 'What is the "New Labor Internationalism"? Comments on Upward Harmonization, Social Charters and Globalization from Below', Paper presented to the Sixteenth Annual North American Labor History Conference on International and Comparative Labor History, Wayne State University, Detroit, 27–29 October 1994; Brecher, J., Childs, J. and Cutler, J. (eds), *Global Visions: Beyond the New World Order*, Black Rose Books, Montreal, 1993; Sengenberger, W. 'The Role of Labour Market Regulation in Industrial Restructuring', in Standing, G. and Tokman, V. (eds), *Towards Social Adjustment: Labour Market Issues in Structural Adjustment*, International Labour Organisation, Geneva, 1991, pp. 235–50.

14 United Nations Research Institute for Social Development (UNRISD), *States of Disarray: The Social Effects of Globalization*, UNRISD, London, 1995.

15 Standing, G. and Tokman, V. (eds), *Towards Social Adjustment: Labour Market Issues in Structural Adjustment*, ILO, Geneva, 1991, pp. 235–50; Yeatman, A., 'Women's Citizenship Claims, Labour Market Policy and Globalisation', *Australian Journal of Political Science*, 27, 1992, pp. 449–61.

16 Sassen, S. *The Mobility of Labor and Capital: A Study in International Investment and Labor Flow*, Cambridge University Press, Cambridge, 1990.

17 Featherstone, *Global Culture*; Robertson, *Globalisation*; Yeatman, A. 'Multi-culturalism, Globalisation and Rethinking the Social', *Australian and New Zealand Journal of Sociology*, 30, 3, 1994, pp. 247–53.

18 Pieterse, J. 'Globalisation as Hybridisation', *International Sociology*, 9, 2, June 1994, pp. 161–84.

19 See Deleuze, G. and Guattari, F., *A Thousand Plateaus: Capitalism and Schizo-phrenia*, University of Minneapolis Press, Minneapolis, 1987.

20 See Appadurai, *Modernity at Large*.

21 Beck, U. *Risk Society*, Sage, London, 1993.

22 Kenichi Ohmae, *The End of the Nation State*, Free Press, New York, 1995.

23 Ibid. p. 39.

24 Ibid. p. 16.

25 See, for example, Dale, R. 'Global Agenda', *Time*, 13 March 1995, pp. 56–60; Drucker, P. *Global Shift: The Internationalization of Economic Activity*, Guilford Press, New York, 1992; O'Hara-Deveraux, M. and Johansen, R. *Global Work: Bridging Distance, Culture and Time*, Jossey Bass Publications, San Francisco,

1994; EPAC, *Globalisation: Issues for Australia*, AGPS, Canberra, 1995; Rhinesmith, S. *A Manager's Guide to Globalization: Six Keys to Success in a Changing World*, Business One Irwin, Homewood, Ill., 1993.

26 Bora, B. 'The Implications of Globalisation for Australian Foreign Investment Policy', in EPAC, *Globalisation*, p. 97.

27 O'Hara-Deveraux and Johansen, *Global Work*, p. 1.

28 Davis, B. 'Globalisation: Who's At It?', in EPAC, *Globalisation*, p. 195.

29 Gibson, B. 'What Distinguishes Australia in the International Marketplace', in *Business Council Bulletin*, 120, June 1995, pp. 68–71.

30 Cited in Brecher, J. 'After NAFTA: Global Village or Global Pillage?', *The Nation*, December 1993, p. 686.

31 Cited in Parry, G. 'The Interweaving of Foreign and Domestic Policy-Making', *Government and Opposition*, 28, 2, 1993, p. 143.

32 Reich, R. *The Work of Nations*, Vintage Books, New York. p. 1.

33 Dahrendorf, R. 'Economy, Opportunity, Civil Society and Political Liberty', in C. Hewitt de Alcantara (ed.), *Social Futures, Global Visions*, Basil Blackwell/ UNRISD, Oxford, 1996, p. 24.

34 Thurow, L. *The Future of Capitalism*, Allen & Unwin, St Leonards, NSW, 1996, p. 216.

35 Van Liemt, G. 'Economic Globalisation: Labour Options and Business Strategies in High Labour Cost Countries', *International Labour Review*, 131, 4–5, 1992, pp. 453–70.

36 See Panitch, L. 'Globalisation and the State' in Miliband, R. and Panitch, L. (eds), *Between Globalism and Nationalism: Socialist Register 1994*, Merlin Press, London, 1994.

37 Lind, M. *The Next American Nation*, Free Press, New York, 1995.

38 Fukuyama, F. *Trust: The Social Virtues and the Culture of Prosperity*, Free Press, New York, 1995.

39 Cited in Ryan, C. 'It Seemed Like a Good Idea', *Australian Financial Review*, 17–18 January 1998, p. 25.

40 Carroll, J. and Manne, R. *Shutdown: The Future of Economic Rationalism and How To Save Australia*, Text Publishing, Melbourne, 1992 and Santamaria, B. 'Capitalism's Oligarchy', *Weekend Australian*, 2–3 March 1996, p. 26.

41 Hewitt, J. 'The IMF Pill May Be More Curse Than Cure', *Age*, 14 January 1998, p. A11 and Hewitt, J. 'Facing Crisis in Asia the US Goes MIA', *Age*, 26 December 1997, p. A17.

42 Cox, R. 'Multilateralism and World Order', *Review of International Studies*, 18, 1992, pp. 161–80.

43 Castells, M. *The Informational City*, Basil Blackwell, Oxford, 1990, p. 348.

44 Brecher, J. 'After NAFTA: Global Village or Global Pillage?', *The Nation*, December 1993, p. 686.

45 See, for example, Dangschat, J. and Fasenfest, D. '(Re)structuring Urban Poverty: The Impact of Globalization on its Extent and Spatial Concentration', *Research in Community Sociology*, 5, 1995, pp. 35–61.

46 See, for example, Martin H. and Schuman, H. *The Global Trap*, Zed Books, London, 1977; Marcuse, P. 'Globalisation's Forgotten Dimension', *Polis*, 3, July 1995, pp. 42–50; Seabrook, J. *Pioneers of Change: Experiments in Creating a Humane Society*, New World Publishers, Philadelphia, 1993.

47 See Thrift, N. 'A Hyperactive World', in Johnson, R., Taylor, P. and Watts, M. (eds), *Geographies of Global Change*, Basil Blackwell, Oxford, 1995.

48 Giddens, A. *The Consequences of Modernity*, Polity Press, Cambridge, 1991.

49 See UNRISD, *States of Disarray*.

50 Walker, M. 'Global Taxation Paying for Peace', *World Policy Journal*, X, 2, Summer 1993, pp. 7–12.

51 See, for example, Ekins, P. *A New World Order: Grassroots Movements for Social Change*, Routledge, London, 1992.

3 Transforming the Global Economy?

1 O'Hara-Deveraux, M. and Johansen, R. *Global Work: Bridging Distance, Culture and Time*, Jossey Bass Publications, San Francisco, 1994, p. xi.

2 United Nations Research Institute for Social Development (UNRISD), *States of Disarray: The Social Effects of Globalization*, UNRISD Report for the World Summit for Social Development, Banson, London, 1995, p. 24.

3 Hirst, P. and Thompson, G. *Globalization in Question*, Polity Press, Cambridge, 1996; Glynn, A. and Sutcliffe, B. 'Global but Leaderless? The New Capitalist Order', in Miliband, R. and Panitch, L. *Socialist Register 1992*, Merlin Press, London, 1992.

4 This discussion draws on the following sources: Hirst and Thompson, *Globalization in Question*; Hoogvelt, A. *Globalisation and the Post Colonial World: The New Political Economy of Development*, Macmillan, London, 1997; Mitchell, J. 'The Nature and Government of the Global Economy', in McGrew, A., Lewis, P. et al. (eds), *Global Politics: Globalization and the Nation State*, Polity Press, Cambridge, 1992; Cavanagh, J., Wysham, D and Arruda, M. (eds), *Beyond Bretton Woods: Alternatives to the Global Economic Order*, Pluto Press, London, 1994; Waters, M. *Globalization*, Routledge, London, 1995.

5 Marx, K. and Engels, F. *The Communist Manifesto*, trans. Samuel Moore, Penguin, London, 1968, p. 83.

6 See Hirst and Thompson, *Globalization in Question*.

7 An excellent and more detailed critical overview of the major debates about the development of the postwar global economy and its relationship to Australia is included in Bell, S. *Ungoverning the Economy*, Oxford University Press, Melbourne, 1997.

8 See Hirst and Thompson, *Globalization in Question*; Fagan, R. and Webber, M. *Global Restructuring: The Australian Experience*, Oxford University Press, Melbourne, 1994.

9 Cited in Cid, C. *Something's Wrong Somewhere: Globalisation, Community and the Moral Economy of the Farm Crisis*, Fernwood, Halifax, 1995.

10 See Amin, A. (ed.), *Post-Fordism: A Reader*, Basil Blackwell, Oxford, 1995; Lash, S. and Urry, J. *Economies of Signs and Space*, Sage, London, 1994.

11 See Fagan and Webber, *Global Restructuring*.

12 Hirst and Thompson, *Globalization in Question*.

13 See Dunkley, G. *The Free Trade Adventure: The Uruguay Round and Globalism – A Critique*, Melbourne University Press, Melbourne, 1997.

14 See Grinspun, R. and Cameron, M. (eds), *The Political Economy of North American Free Trade*, McGill-Queens University Press, Montreal, 1993.

15 See Dunkley, *The Free Trade Adventure*; Jackson, J. 'The World Trade Organisation: Watershed Innovation or Cautious Small Step Forward?', in Arndt, S. and Milner, C. *The World Economy: Global Trade Policy 1995*, Basil Blackwell, Oxford, 1995.

16 Koechlin, T. 'The Globalization of Investment', *Contemporary Economic Policy*, XIII, January 1995, pp. 92–9.

17 Chuppe, T., Haworth, H. and Watkins, M. 'Global Finance: Causes, Consequences and Prospects for the Future', *Global Finance Journal*, 1, pp. 1–20.

18 See Bell, *Ungoverning the Economy*, p. 101–3.

19 Korten, D. *When Corporations Rule the World*, Kumarian Press, Connecticut and Berrett Koehler Publications, San Francisco, 1996, p. 189.

20 Cited in da Silva, W. 'Money's Making the World Go Round', *Sunday Age*, 26 March 1996, p. 7.

21 Sinclair, T. 'Passing Judgement: Credit Rating Processes as Regulatory Mechanisms of Governance in the Emerging World Order', *Review of International Political Economy*, 1, 1, Spring 1994, pp. 133–60.

22 Watts, R. 'Dancing to Whose Tune? The Future of Work: Employment and Australian Government Policy, 1983–1997', Paper delivered to South West Sydney Community Sector Conference, Bankstown, 26–27 November 1997, p. 46.

23 Hutton, W. 'Mexico Plight Should Dent Tory Complacency', *Guardian Weekly*, 5 February 1996, p. 4.

24 See, for example, Hiscock, G. 'Paper Tigers Burnout', *Weekend Australian*, 1–2 November 1997, p. 21.

25 See Toohey, B. 'Banks Uneasy Over IMF Asia Campaign', *Australian Financial Review*, 9 December 1997, p. 19.

26 Ranald, P. *Disciplining Governments: What the MAI Would Mean for Australia*, Public Sector Resource Research Centre, University of NSW and Evatt Foundation, Sydney, 1998.

27 Krugman, P. and Venables, A. 'Globalization and the Inequality of Nations', *Quarterly Journal of Economics*, CX, No. 4, November 1995, pp. 857–80.

28 Fagan and Webber, *Global Restructuring*.

29 Williamson cited in Reich, R. *The Work of Nations*, Vintage Books, New York, 1992, p. 19.

30 See Elix, D. 'Operating in a Global Environment', *Business Council Bulletin*, 120, June 1995, pp. 36–9.

31 Zimmerman, L. 'Globalisation: Can Australia Compete?, *Practising Manager*, 11, 3, October 1991, p. 23.

32 Korten, D. *When Corporations Rule the World*, Kumarian Press, Connecticut and Berrett-Koehler, San Francisco, 1995.

33 Hirst and Thompson, *Globalization in Question*.

34 Elix, 'Operating in a Global Environment'.

35 Gibson, B. 'What Distinguishes Australia in the International Marketplace?', *Business Council Bulletin*, 120, June 1995, pp. 68–71.

36 Kanter, R. *When Giants Learn to Dance: Mastering the Challenges of Strategy: Management and Careers in the 1990s*, Simon & Schuster, New York, 1989, p. 19.

37 Cited in Rhinesmith, S. *A Manager's Guide to Globalization: Six Keys to Success in a Changing World*, Business One Irwin, Homewood, Ill., 1993, p. 8.

38 See O'Hara-Deveraux and Johansen, *Global Work: Bridging Distance, Culture and Time*.

39 Elix, 'Operating in a Global Environment', p. 39.
40 Ibid. p. 39.
41 See Panitch, L. 'Globalisation and the State' and Albo, G. 'Competitive Austerity and the Impasse of Capitalist Employment Policy', in Miliband, R. and Panitch, L. (eds), *Between Globalism and Nationalism: Socialist Register 1994*, Merlin Press, London, 1994.
42 Korten, *When Corporations Rule the World*.
43 See Lloyd, P. 'Global Integration', *Australian Economic Review*, 1st Quarter 1993, pp. 35–48.
44 Houghton, J. 'Globalization: Unleashing the Power of People', *Executive Speeches*, 6, 1995, p. 3.
45 Cited in Watson, B. *Commentary*, No. 10, 1995, p. 12.
46 Cited in Rhinesmith, *A Manager's Guide to Globalization*, p. 8.
47 See Porter, M. *Competitive Advantage of Nations*, Macmillan, London, 1990; Best, M. *The New Competition: Institutions of Industrial Restructuring*, Polity Press, Cambridge, 1990.
48 Dunning, J. (ed.), *Governments, Globalization and International Business*, Oxford University Press, New York, 1997.
49 Ibid.
50 See Ormerod, P. 'National Competitiveness and State Intervention', *New Political Economy*, 1, 1, 1966; van Liemt, G. 'Economic Globalisation: Labour Options and Business Strategies in High Labour Cost Countries', *International Labour Review*, 131, 4–5, 1992, 453–70.
51 'Goodman, J. and Pauly, L. 'The Obsolescence of Capital Controls?', *World Politics*, October 1993, pp. 50–82; Pryke, M. and Lee, R. 'Place Your Bets: Towards an Understanding of Globalisation, Socio-financial Engineering and Competition within a Financial Centre', *Urban Studies*, 32, 2, 1995, pp. 329–44.

4 Onto the Global Racetrack?

1 Commonwealth of Australia, *Working Nation: Policies and Programs*, AGPS, Canberra, 1994, p. 52.
2 Costello, P. The Menzies Lecture, Monash University, 12 November 1997.
3 Cited in *Australian Financial Review*, 11 October 1993, p. 22.
4 See Castles, F. *Australian Public Policy and Economic Vulnerability*, Allen & Unwin, Sydney, 1988; Ravenhill, J. 'Australia and the Global Economy', in Bell, S. and Head, B (eds), *State, Economy and Public Policy in Australia*, Oxford University Press, Melbourne, 1994.
5 The following discussion draws on a range of sources including Castles, *Australian Public Policy and Economic Vulnerability* and Catley, B. *Globalising Australian Capitalism*, Cambridge University Press, Cambridge, 1996.
6 Bell, S. *Ungoverning the Economy*, Oxford University Press, Melbourne, 1997.
7 Whitlam, E.G. 'A Tribute to the Modest Member', Address to the Centre for Independent Studies, Bert Kelly Lecture Series, 1997.
8 For general overviews of the economic developments and policies of the period 1983 to 1996 see Bell and Head, *State, Economy and Public Policy in Australia;* Bell, S. 'The Politics of Economic Adjustment: Explaining the Transformation of Industry State Relationships in Australia', *Political Studies XLIII*, 1995,

pp. 22–47; Ewer, P., Hampson, I., Lloyd, C. Rainford, J., Rix, S. and Smith, M. *Politics and the Accord*, Pluto Press, Sydney, 1991.

9 Kasper, W. 'Advancing into the 21st Century: Visions and Challenges Facing the Downunder Economy', *Australian Economic Review*, 4th quarter, 1992, pp. 51–64.

10 Kelly, P. *The End of Certainty*, Allen & Unwin, Sydney, 1992, p. 76.

11 See Pitchford, J. 'A Sceptical View of Australia's Current Account and Debt Problem', *Australian Economic Review*, 2nd Quarter, 1989, pp. 5–13.

12 Cited in Kelly, *The End of Certainty*, p. 222.

13 Cited in Ewer et al. *Politics and the Accord*, p. 63.

14 See Vines, D. 'Unfinished Business: Australian Protectionism, Australian Trade Liberalisation and APEC', *Australian Economic Review*, 1st Quarter, 1995, pp. 35–52; Devos, S. 'Regional Integration', *OECD Observer*, 192, February/March 1995, pp. 4–7; Anderson, K. 'The GATT's Review of Australian Trade Policy', in Arndt, S. and Milner, C. *The World Economy: Global Trade Policy 1995*, Basil Blackwell, Oxford, 1995.

15 *Hilmer Report*, National Competition Policy, AGPS, Canberra, 1993.

16 See Stilwell, F. 'Wages Policy and the Accord', in Mahony, G. (ed.), *The Australian Economy Under Labor*, Allen & Unwin, Sydney, 1993.

17 Bell, *Ungoverning the Economy*, p. 148.

18 See INDECS, *State of Play 8*, Allen & Unwin, Sydney, 1995, p. 104.

19 Commonwealth of Australia, *One Nation*, AGPS, Canberra, 1992.

20 Commonwealth of Australia, *Working Nation: Policies and Programs*, AGPS, Canberra, 1994.

21 Ibid. p. 57.

22 See, for example, Costa, M. and Duffy, M. *Labor Prospects and the Nineties*, Federation Press, Sydney, 1991.

23 See ACTU and Trade Development Council, *Australia Reconstructed: A Report by the Mission Members to the ACTU and the TDC*, AGPS, Canberra, 1987.

24 See Frankel, B. *From Prophets the Deserts Come*, Arena Press, Melbourne, 1992.

25 Bell, *Ungoverning the Economy*, p. 88. See also Phipps, A. and Sheen, J. 'Macro-economic Policy and Employment Growth in Australia', *Australian Economic Review*, 1, January/March 1995, pp. 86–104; Gupta, D. 'The Global Macro Economic Environment in the 1990s Facing Australian Corporations: An Explanation', *Australian Journal of Corporate Law*, 3, 1, 1993, pp. 89–100; Fraser, M. 'Australia is Failing the Economic Test', *Australian*, 13 September 1995.

26 See INDECS, *State of Play 8*.

27 Colebatch, T. 'How Did the Economy Get Into This Much Trouble?', *Age*, 2 February 1995.

28 See Colebatch, T. 'The Banana Republic Threat Stays With Us', *Age*, 15 May 1996. See also Clark, G. 'Time to Challenge the Fantasy of Free Trade' *Age*, 13 July 1996.

29 Cited in Steketee, M. 'Great Deregulator Loses Faith in Markets', *Weekend Australian*, 29–30 April 1995, p. 10.

30 Probert, B. 'Restructuring and Globalisation: What Do They Mean?', *Arena*, April–May 1992, p. 21.

31 See, for example, Hill, H. and McKern, B. 'Australia', in Dunning, J. (ed.), *Governments, Globalization and International Business*, Oxford University Press, New York, 1997.

32 Liberal Party of Australia, *Meeting the Challenges. The New Global Economy: Liberal and National Party Trade Strategies for the Future*, Liberal Party of Australia, Melbourne, 1996, p. 1.

33 Ravenhill, J. 'Foreign Economic Policies', in Galligan, B., McAllister, I. and Ravenhill, J. (eds), *New Developments in Australian Politics*, Macmillan, Melbourne, 1997; Watts, R. 'Dancing to Whose Tune? The Future of Work: Employment and Australian Government Policy, 1983–1997', Paper delivered to South West Sydney Community Sector Conference, Bankstown, 26–27 November 1997.

34 Costello, P. The Menzies Lecture, Monash University, 12 November 1997.

35 Crooks, M. 'An August Budget Marriage: Australia's Conservative Parties Wed the New Right', *Just Policy*, 8, November 1996, pp. 43–6; De Carvalho, D. 'Budget 1996: The Re-appearing Middle', *Just Policy*, 8, November 1996, pp. 47–50.

36 Commonwealth of Australia, *Commission of Audit Report*, AGPS, Canberra, 1996.

37 Costello, P., Address to Metal Trades Industry Association (unpublished).

38 See Livingstone, C. 'The Workplace Relations Act', *Arena*, 24, August/September 1996, pp. 20–2.

39 Both quotes from Colebatch, T. 'Howard Signals Hard Line on Federal Support for Industry', *Age*, 4 December 1997, p. A9.

40 Mortimer Report, *Going for Growth: Business Programs for Investment, Innovation and Export*, Department of Industry, Science and Technology, Canberra, 1997; Goldsworthy Report, *The Global Information Economy: The Way Ahead*, Information Industries Task Force, AGPS, Canberra, 1997; Metal Trades Industry Association (MTIA) and Economic Intelligence Unit, *Make or Break: A Report for the MTIA*, Economic Intelligence Unit, Sydney, 1997.

41 Department of Industry, Science and Tourism, *Investing for Growth*, AGPS, Canberra, 1997.

42 See Dwyer, M. 'Imports Trigger Shock Deficit', *Australian Financial Review*, 3 February 1997, p. 1.

43 Zimmerman, L. 'Globalisation: Can Australia Compete?, *Practising Manager*, 11, 3, October 1991, pp. 21–8; Whiteman, J. 'Globalisation and Strategic Trade Policy', *Prometheus*, 8, June 1990, pp. 35–49.

44 Salmon, I. A Business Perspective, Address to Making it Work (National Summit on the Future of Work in Australia), Sydney, 24 May 1996.

45 Watson, B. *Commentary*, No. 10, 1995, p. 13.

46 Yetton, P., Davis, J. and Swan, P. *Going International: Export Myths and Strategic Realities*, Report to the Australian Manufacturing Council, AGSM, Sydney, 1992, p. 72.

47 Zimmerman, 'Globalisation: Can Australia Compete?', p. 23.

48 See Brett, J. 'Politics and Business Parted', *Age*, 17 July 1997, p. A15.

49 Stewardson, B. 'The Globalisation of BHP' in Economic Planning Advisory Commission, *Globalisation: Issues for Australia*, AGPS, Canberra, 1995.

50 Ibid. p. 25.

51 Stewardson, 'The Globalisation of BHP', p. 59

52 Maiden, M., 'Shock as BHP Boss Quits', *Age*, 5 March 1998, p. 1.

53 Brett, 'Politics and Business Parted'.

54 Zimmerman, 'Globalisation: Can Australia Compete?'.

55 Cited in Summons, M. 'The Competitive Edge: How We Can Compete', *Australian Business*, 27 February 1991, p. 44.

56 Cited in Carvana, L. 'ICI Blasts Rivals with Global Deal', *Australian*, 24 December 1997, p. 19.
57 Courvisanos, J. 'Transnational Corporate Planning and National Industrial Planning: The Case of the Ford Motor Company in Australia', *Journal of Australian Political Economy*, 34, December 1994, pp. 53–76.
58 Clark, G. 'Global Interdependence and Regional Development: Business Linkages and Corporate Governance in a World of Financial Risk', *Transnational Institute of British Geography*, 18, 1993, pp. 309–25.
59 Ibid. p. 312.
60 Marceau, J. 'Will the Souffle Rise? Australian Business Recipes in the New World Economic Order', *Prometheus*, 10, 2, December 1992, p. 189.

5 The Price of Competitiveness?

1 United Nations Research Institute for Social Development (UNRISD)/United Nations Development Project (UNDP), 'Adjustment, Globalisation and Social Development', Report of the UNRISD/UNDP International Seminar on Economic Restructuring and Social Policy, UNRISD, New York, 1995, p. 8.
2 Cited in Steketee, M. 'Great Deregulator Loses Faith in Markets', *Weekend Australian*, 29–30 April 1995, p. 10.
3 Cover story, *Economist*, 18–24 January 1997.
4 *Economist*, 18–24 January 1997, p. 13. For a similar argument from a senior World Bank economist see Zia Qureshi, 'Globalisation: New Opportunities, Tough Challenges', *Finance and Development*, 33, March 1996, pp. 30–3.
5 See UNRISD, *States of Disarray: The Social Effects of Globalization*, Report for the World Summit for Social Development, Banson, London, 1995.
6 Robinson, W. 'Globalisation: Nine Theses on Our Epoch', *Race and Class*, 38, 2, 1996, pp. 13–31.
7 Brah, A. 'Questions of Difference and International Feminism', in Aaron, J. and Walby, S. (eds), *Out of the Margins*, Falmer Press, London, 1991, p. 168.
8 See Martin Jones, D. *Political Development in Pacific Asia*, Polity Press, Cambridge, 1997.
9 I would like to thank Joe Camilleri for a number of thoughtful comments on these issues.
10 See UNRISD, *States of Disarray*.
11 See Khor, M. 'Experts Attack Shift in Global Health Strategy', *Third World Network Features*, Third World Network, Penang, 1995.
12 Robinson, 'Globalisation'.
13 Ibid.
14 See 'Is This Man Worth $200m?', *Financial Review, Weekend Review*, 29 April 1994.
15 See Kearney, M. 'The Local and the Global: The Anthropology of Globalization and Transnationalism', *Annual Review of Anthropology*, 24, 1995, pp. 547–65.
16 UNRISD/UNDP, 'Adjustment, Globalisation and Social Development', p. 8.
17 Lind, M. *The Next American Nation*, Free Press, New York, 1995, p. 14.
18 See Rifkin, J. *The End of Work*, Tarcher/Putnam, New York, 1995.
19 UNRISD/UNDP, 'Adjustment, Globalisation and Social Development'.
20 Ellingsen, P. 'The Holy Grail of Higher Growth Brings Polarisation', *Age*, 4 March 1995, p. 21.

21 See Hamilton, C. 'Workers in the Globalised World: The End of the Post War Consensus', Australian Council of Social Service *(ACOSS) Impact Supplement*, December 1996.

22 Cited in Runyan, A. 'The Places of Women in Trading Places: Gendered Global/ Regional Regimes and Internationalised Feminist Resistance', in Kofman, E. and Youngs, G. (eds), *Globalization Theory and Practice*, Pinter, London, 1996, p. 239.

23 The quote is from Jenson, J. 'Some Consequences of Economic and Political Restructuring and Readjustment', *Social Politics*, 3, 1, Spring 1996, p. 3. See also Connelly, M. 'Gender Matters: Global Restructuring and Adjustment', *Social Politics*, 3, 1, Spring 1996, pp. 12–31; Cohen, M. 'The Return of the Robber Barons: The Dangers for Women in the New World Economy', *Refractory Girl*, 49, Spring 1995, pp. 40–6; Peterson, V. 'The Politics of Identification in the Context of Globalisation, *Women's Studies International Forum*, 19, 1/2, pp. 5–15; Standing, G. 'Global Feminization Through Flexible Labour', *World Development*, 17, 7, 1989, pp. 1077–95; Riley, M. and Mejia, R. 'Gender in the Global Trading System', *Development*, 40, 3, 1997, pp. 30–6.

24 See Pettman, J. 'An International Political Economy of Sex', in Kofman and Youngs (eds), *Globalization Theory and Practice*.

25 Pellerin, H. 'Global Restructuring in the World Economy and Migration: The Globalization Migration Dynamics', *International Journal*, XLVIII, Spring 1993, pp. 241–55.

26 See Bryson, L. *Welfare and the State: Who Benefits?*, Macmillan, London, 1992.

27 See Cerny, P. *The Changing Architecture of Politics: Structure, Agency and the Future of the State*, Sage, London, 1990.

28 Cass, B. *Income Support for the Unemployed in Australia: Towards A More Active Society*, Social Security Review Issues Paper No. 4, AGPS, Canberra, 1988; Commonwealth of Australia, *Working Nation: Policies and Programs*, AGPS, Canberra, 1994.

29 Langmore, J. and Quiggan, J. *Work for All: Full Employment in the Nineties*, Melbourne University Press, Melbourne, 1994.

30 See Bell, S. *Ungoverning the Economy*, Oxford University Press, Melbourne, 1997, p. 115.

31 See Delaney, A. 'Working at Home on the Global Assembly Line', in Wiseman, J. (ed.), *Alternatives to Globalisation: An Asia-Pacific Perspective*, Community Aid Abroad, Melbourne, 1997.

32 Mitchell, D. 'Family Policy', in Galligan, B., McAllister, I. and Ravenhill, J. (eds), *New Developments in Australian Politics*, Macmillan, Melbourne, 1997; Cass, B. 'A Family Policy Audit', *Just Policy*, 6, May 1996, pp. 26–35.

33 See Steketee, M. 'Decline of the Welfare State', *Weekend Australian*, 4 January 1997, p. 17.

34 Cited in Steketee, M. 'Decline of the Welfare State'.

35 Costello, P. The Menzies Lecture, Monash University, 12 November 1997.

37 For the positive interpretation see, for example, Travers, P. and Richardson, S. *Living Decently: Material Well-being in Australia*, Oxford University Press, Melbourne, 1993; Hope, D. 'Poverty Doesn't Spell Underclass', *Weekend Australian Magazine*, 3–4 June 1995; Harding, A. 'Equity, Redistribution and the Tax Transfer System Since the Early 1980s', in Hogan, M. and Dempsey, K. (eds), *Equity and Citizenship Under Keating*, Sydney University Press, Sydney, 1995. More critical

perspectives can be found in Saunders, P. *Welfare and Inequality: National and International Perspectives on the Australian Welfare State*, Cambridge University Press, Cambridge, 1994; Bryson, L. 'The Welfare State and Economic Adjustment', in Bell, S. and Head, B. (eds), *State, Economy and Public Policy in Australia*, Oxford University Press, Melbourne, 1994.

38 Bell, *Ungoverning the Economy*, p. 93.

39 Harding, A. *The Suffering Middle: Trends in Income Inequality in Australia 1982 to 1993–94*, National Centre for Social and Economic Modelling (NATSEM) Discussion Paper No. 21, NATSEM, University of Canberra, 1997, p. 19. See also Economic Planning Advisory Commission (EPAC), *Income Distribution in Australia: Recent Trends and Research*, EPAC Paper No. 7, AGPS, Canberra, 1995; Stilwell, F. *Economic Inequality*, Pluto Press, Leichhardt, NSW, 1993; Evatt Foundation, *The State of Australia*, Evatt Foundation, Sydney, 1996; Marcuse, P. *Is Australia Different? Globalization and the New Urban Poverty*, Australian Housing and Urban Research Institute (AHURI) Occasional Paper No. 3, AHURI, Melbourne 1996.

40 See, for example, *Business Review Weekly* (special issue on The Rich 200) 20 May 1996; Eccleston, R. 'The Wages of Inequality', *Weekend Australian*, 16–17 September 1995, p. 24.

41 See Bread for the World Institute, *Hunger 1995*, Seventh Annual Report on the State of World Hunger, Bread for the World Institute, Washington DC, October, 1996.

42 Figures based on Harding, *The Suffering Middle*.

43 Gregory, R. and Hunter, B. *The Macro Economy and the Growth of Ghettos and Urban Poverty in Australia*, Discussion Paper No. 25, Australian National University Centre for Economic Policy Research, Canberra, 1995. See also Troy, P. *The Perils of Urban Consolidation*, Federation Press, Annandale, NSW, 1996; Peel, M. 'Governing the Urban Future', *Australian Rationalist*, No. 40, Autumn/Winter 1996, pp. 15–23.

44 Gregory and Hunter, *The Macro Economy and the Growth of Ghettos and Urban Poverty in Australia*, p. 4.

45 EPAC, *Income Distribution in Australia*, pp. 80 and 69.

46 See Edwards, A. and Magarey, S. (eds), *Women in a Restructuring Australia*, Allen & Unwin, Sydney, 1995.

47 See McKenzie, D. 'Managers Win Wage Rise Race'; *Weekend Australian*, 17–18 January 1998, p. 1.

48 Cited in McKenzie, 'Managers Win Wage Rise Race'.

49 See Fincher, R. and Niewenhuysen, N. (eds), *Australian Poverty: Then and Now*, Melbourne University Press, Melbourne, 1998. The quote is from Walker, M. 'Poor Jump to 30% of Population', *Age*, 14 March 1998, p. 30.

50 Cited in Gun, M. 'Downward Envy: Why Middle Australia Hates the Poor', *Weekend Australian*, Weekend Review, 2–3 November 1996, p. 2.

51 Ibid.

52 Hamilton, 'Workers in the Globalised World', p. 6.

53 Deveson, I., 'The Challenge of Change for Australians', *Business Council Bulletin*, May 1993, p. 29.

54 Cited in *Sunday Age* (Property section), 26 March 1995, p. 1.

55 Cited in Smith, R. 'Caught in the Current', *Time Australia*, 15 May 1995, p. 22.
56 Cain, J., *Age*, 11 April 1993, p. 8.
57 After widespread public outrage Kennett finally agreed to allow the elections to proceed but still argued that he could see no threat to democracy from the proposal to cancel elections!

6 Wired to the World?

1 Cited in the *Age*, 6 March 1996, p. 10.
2 Castells, M. *The Power of Identity*, Basil Blackwell, Oxford, 1997, p. 317.
3 Cited in Robins, K. 'The New Spaces of Global Media', in Johnson, R., Taylor, P. and Watts, M. (eds), *Geographies of Global Change*, Basil Blackwell, Oxford, 1996, p. 250.
4 Saatchi and Saatchi, *Annual Report 1986*, cited in Barker, C. *Global Television*, Basil Blackwell, Oxford, 1997, p. 157.
5 See, for example, Castells, *The Power of Identity*.
6 McLuhan, M. and Powers, B. *The Global Village: Transformations in World Life and Media in the 21st Century*, Oxford University Press, New York, 1989.
7 See Anderson, B. *Imagined Communities*, Verso, London, 1991.
8 See Harvey, D. *The Condition of Post Modernity*, Basil Blackwell, Oxford, 1989.
9 See McLuhan and Powers, *The Global Village*.
10 Adorno, T. and Horkheimer, M. *Dialectic of Enlightenment*, trans. J. Cumming, Continuum, New York, 1972, p. 159.
11 Althusser, L. *Lenin and Philosophy and Other Essays*, New Left Books, London, 1971, p. 146.
12 See, for example, Benjamin, W. *Illuminations*, Fontana, London, 1973.
13 Poster, M. 'A Second Media Age', *Arena Journal*, New Series, 3, 1994, pp. 49–91.
14 House of Representatives Standing Commitee on Long Term Strategies, *Australia as an Information Society: Grasping New Paradigms*, AGPS, Canberra, 1991, p. vii.
15 Castells, M. *The Informational City*, Basil Blackwell, Oxford, 1991, p. 17. See also Castells, M. 'The Net and the Self: Working Notes for a Critical Theory of the Informational Society', *Critique of Anthropology*, 16, 1, March 1996, pp. 9–38.
16 Thompson, J. *The Media and Modernity*, Stanford University Press Stanford, CA, 1995.
17 Fist, S. *Future Telecommunications: The Price of Driving on the Information Superhighway*, Summit Paper for the Australian Consumer Council (ACC), Sydney, 1996, p. 3.
18 Petrie, D. Director of Advanced Technology for Microsoft, The Media Report, ABC Television, 1 May 1997.
19 Cited in Brand, S. *The Media Lab: Inventing the Future at MIT*, Penguin, New York, 1988, p. 206.
20 See Arnst, C. and Edmonson, G. 'The Global Free For All', *Business Week*, 26 September 1995, p. 16.
21 Trebing, H. and Estabrooks, M. 'The Globalisation of Telecommunications: A Study in the Struggle to Control Markets and Technology', *Journal of Economic Issues*, xxix, 2, June 1995.

22 Robins, K. 'The New Spaces of Global Media', Johnson, R., Taylor, P. and Watts, M. (eds), *Geographies of Global Change*, Basil Blackwell, Oxford, 1996; Nordenstreng, K. and Schiller, H. (eds), *Beyond National Sovereignty: International Communication in the 1990s*, Ablex, Norwood, NJ, 1993; Schiller, H. 'Not Yet the Post Imperialist Era', *Critical Studies in Mass Communication*, 8, 1, March 1991, pp. 13–28.

23 See 'The US Global Information Infrastructure: Agenda for Cooperation, *Presidents and Prime Ministers*, 4, May–June 1995, pp. 37–9.

24 Yoshiko Kurisaki, 'Globalization or Regionalization? An Observation of Current PTO Activities', *Telecommunications Policy*, December 1993, pp. 699–706.

25 Cited in Barker, *Global Television*, p. 59.

26 Levitt, T. *The Marketing Imagination*, Free Press, New York, 1983, p. 28.

27 Cited in Papathanassopolous, S. 'The Fast Growing Internationalisation of Television', *Media Information Australia*, No. 71, February 1994, p. 44.

28 Gerbner, S. *The Media Report*, ABC Radio National, 29 August 1997.

29 Ibid.

30 Neil, A. 'How King Rupert Tarnished His Crown', *Age*, 4 March 1998, p. A15.

31 See Shaw, M. *Civil Society and Media in Global Crises: Representing Distant Violence*, Pinter, London, 1996.

32 Gerbner, *The Media Report*.

33 Maguire, J. 'Sport, Identity Politics and Globalization: Diminishing Contrasts and Increasing Varieties', *Sociology of Sport Journal*, 11, 4 December 1994, pp. 398–427; Rowe, D., Lawrence, G., Miller, T. and McKay, J. 'Global Sport?: Core Concern and Peripheral Vision', *Media Culture and Society*, 16, 44, October 1994, pp. 661–75.

34 'NBA Out to Conquer the World', *Sunday Age Sportsweek*, 16 November 1997, p. 16. See also Wagner, E. 'Sport in Asia and Africa: Americanisation or Mundialisation?', *Sociology of Sport Journal*, 7, 4 December 1990, pp. 399–402.

35 See Kearney, M. 'The Local and the Global: The Anthropology of Globalization and Transnationalism', *Annual Review of Anthropology*, 24, 1995, pp. 547–65; Seabrook, J. 'The Cultural Pollution of the South', *Third World Network Features*, Third World Network, Penang, 1996.

36 Hoskins, C., McFayden, S., Finn, P. and Jackel, A. 'Film and Television Co-productions: Evidence from Canadian–European experience', *European Journal of Communication*, 10, 2, pp. 221–43.

37 Papathanassopoulous, S. 'The Fast Growing Internationalisation of Television', *Media Information Australia*, 7, 1, February 1994, pp. 39–45.

38 Pieterse, J. 'Globalisation as Hybridisation', *International Sociology*, 9, 2, June 1994, p. 169.

39. Gillespie, M. *Television, Ethnicity and Cultural Change*, Routledge, London, 1995.

40 Barker, *Global Television*, p. 191.

41 Cited in Mangan, P. 'World At Their Feet', *Sunday Age Sportsweek*, 16 November 1997, p. 19.

42 See Cunningham, S. and Turner, G. (eds), *The Media in Australia*, 2nd edn, Allen & Unwin, Sydney, 1997; Langdale, J. 'Social and Economic Perspectives on Australia's Communications Future', *Prometheus*, 14, 1, June 1996, pp. 39–50; Fist, *Future Telecommunications*.

43 See Chadwick, P. *Media Mates: Carving up Australia's Media*, Macmillan, Melbourne, 1989.

44 See Murphy, D. 'Lord of the Rings', *Bulletin*, 23 December 1997, pp. 23–5.

45 Carlyon, L. 'Ink Inc.', *Sunday Age*, 11 May 1997, p. 17.

46 Given, J. *The Media Report*, ABC Radio National, 11 September 1997.

47 Mansfield Review, *The Challenge of a Better Australian Broadcasting Commission*, AGPS, Canberra, 1997.

48 Kostanzo, P. *The Media Report*, ABC Radio National, 24 April 1997.

49 Cutler, T. *The Media Report*, ABC Radio National, 24 April 1997. Walker, D. 'Why Selling Telstra Doesn't Matter', *Age*, 8 June 1996, p. A23.

50 See Crofts, S. 'Global Neighbours', in Allan, R. (ed.), *To be Continued . . . Soap Opera Around the World*, Routledge, London and New York, 1995.

51 Fist, *Future Telecommunications*.

52 Commonwealth of Australia, *Creative Nation*, AGPS, Canberra, 1995.

53 See, for example, Broadcast Services Expert Group, *Networking Australia's Future*, AGPS, Canberra, 1993.

54 McChesney, R. 'The Internet and US Communication Policy Making in Historical and Critical Perspective', *Journal of Communications*, 46, 1, Winter 1996, pp. 98–124.

55 Brants, K., Huizenga, M. and Van Meerten, R. 'The New Canals of Amsterdam: An Excercise in Local Electronic Democracy', *Media Culture and Society*, 18, 2, April 1996, pp. 233–47; Sassi, S. 'Self Willed and Odd Thing Called the Net: Remarks on the Quality of the Networked World', *Nordicom Review*, 1, 1995 pp. 49–58; Morley, D. and Robins, K. *Spaces of Identity: Global Media, Electronic Landscapes and Cultural Boundaries*, Routledge, New York, 1995.

56 See, for example, the *Media Report* programs on the use of information technology by remote indigenous communities, ABC Radio National, 20 and 27 June 1996.

57 Shields, P. 'State, National Identity and Media', *Peace Review*, 8, 1, March 1996, pp. 89–96; Hedges, I. ' Transnational Corporate Culture and Cultural Resistance', *Socialism and Democracy*, 9, 1, 18, Spring 1995, pp. 151–64; Donner, W. and Hedges, I. 'Media Wars', *Socialism and Democracy*, 9, 1, 18, Spring 1995, pp. 139–50.

58 Keane, J. Structural Transformation of the Public Sphere', *Communications Review*, 11, 1, 1995, pp. 1–22; Poster, M. 'Post Modern Virtualities', *Body and Society* 1, 3–4, November 1994, pp. 79–95.

59 Ernie, J. 'On the Limits of Wired Identity in the Age of Global Media', *Identities*, 2, 4, April 1996, pp. 419–28; Aronowitz, S. *Technoscience and Cyberculture*, Routledge, New York, 1996; Sardar, Z. 'Cyberspace as the Darker Side of the West', *Futures*, 27, 7, September 1995, pp. 777–94.

7 Nowhere to Hide?

1   Cited in an interview with Noronha, F. 'Globalisation Killing Environment Says Prominent Indian Green', fred@bom2.vsnl.net.in

2   Cited in Dayton, L. 'Ecologist Condemns Australia's "Moronic" Greenhouse Stance', *Age*, 2 December 1997, p. A11.

3   Cited in Savva, N. 'Solar Protest Sparks Fears on Security', *Age*, 21 October 1997, p. A1.

4   Howard, J. 'Climate Change and a Forecast of Economic Winter', *Age*, 7 October 1997, p. A10.

5 Gore, A. *Earth in the Balance: Ecology and the Human Spirit*, Plume, New York, 1995, p. 269.

6 See Porter, G. and Brown, J. *Global Environmental Politics*, Westview Press, Boulder, Co, 1996.

7 See, for example, Erhlich P. *The Population Bomb*, Pan, London, 1968.

8 Carson, R. *Silent Spring*, Houghton Mifflin, Boston, 1987.

9 See Matas, R. 'How the Arctic's Being Poisoned', *Globe and Mail*, 27 June 1995, p. A10.

10 Yearley, S. *Sociology, Environmentalism, Globalisation*, Sage, London, 1996.

11 See Mahlman, J., Albritton, D. and Watson, R. *State of Scientific Understanding of Climate Change*, Office of Science and Technology Policy, Washington, DC, 1993.

12 Williamson, R. and Ceretig, M. 'Salmon Free For All Left Stocks in Peril', *Globe and Mail*, 8 October 1994, p. 3.

13 See Porter and Brown, *Global Environmental Politics*.

14 Cited in Noronha, 'Globalisation Killing Environment Says Prominent Indian Green'.

15 Cited in Taylor, A. *Choosing Our Future: A Practical Politics of the Environment*, Routledge, London, 1994, p. 59.

16 See Flavin, C. 'The Legacy of Rio', in World Watch Institute, *State of the World 1997*, Earthscan, London, 1997; Redclift, M. *Wasted: Counting the Costs of Global Consumption*, Earthscan, London, 1996.

17 See *Time*, Special Issue on 'Our Precious Planet', November 1997.

18 See World Wildlife Fund (WWF), *State of the Climate*, WWF, London, 1997.

19 Eckersley, R. 'Greening the Modern State' in James, P. (ed.), *The State in Question: Transformations of the Australian States*, Allen & Unwin, Sydney, 1996, pp. 84 and 106.

20 Vogler, J. 'Regimes and the Global Commons: Space, Atmosphere and Oceans', in McGrew, A. and Lewis, P. et al., *Global Politics*, Polity Press, Cambridge, 1992; Hempel, L. *Environmental Governance: The Global Challenge*, Island Press, Washington, 1995; Lipshutz, R. (with Judith Mayer), *Global Civil Society and Global Environmental Governance*, State University of New York Press, Albany, NY, 1996.

21 Kennedy, D. 'GATTastrophe', *Habitat Australia*, April 1995, pp. 42–3.

22 See Zarsky, L. APEC and the Environment, Presentation to Conference on Taking Australia into Asia: Trade, Investment and Human Rights, Community Aid Abroad 23 February 1996.

23 Wapner, P. 'International Activism and Global Civil Society', *Dissent*, Summer 1994, pp. 389–93; Esteva, G. and Prakash, M. 'From Global to Local Thinking', *Ecologist*, 24, 5, 1994, pp. 162–3.

24 Schoon, N. 'How Greenpeace Toppled Goliath', *Vancouver Sun*, 24 June 1995, p. 10.

25 Chatterjee, P. and Finger, M. *The Earth Brokers*, Routledge, New York, 1994, p. 7.

27 See Norberg-Hodge, H. 'Globalisation versus Community', in Goldsmith, E., Khor, M., Norberg-Hodge, H. and Vandana Shiva, et al., *The Future of Progress: Reflections on Environment and Development*, Resurgence, Devon, 1995.

28 See Flannery, T. *The Future Eaters*, Reed Books, Melbourne, 1994.

28 State of the Environment Advisory Council, *State of the Environment 1996*, CSIRO Publishing, Melbourne, 1996, p. 10.

29 See Rolls, E. *They All Ran Wild*, Angus & Robertson, Sydney, 1969.
30 See Walker, K. *The Political Economy of Environmental Policy: An Australian Introduction*, University of NSW Press, Sydney, 1994; Papadakis, E. *Politics and the Environment: The Australian Experience*, Allen & Unwin, Sydney, 1993; Holland, I. 'The New Ethic', in Smith, J. (ed.), *The Unique Continent*, University of Queensland Press, Brisbane, 1992.
31 Commonwealth Government, *Building a Competitive Australia*, AGPS, Canberra, 1991.
32 See Eckersley, 'Greening the Modern State' for a helpful discussion of this period.
33 State of the Environment Advisory Council, *State of the Environment 1996*.
34 Gawenda, M. 'Old Fears Shape New Era', *Age*, 26 May 1997, p. A15; Bone, P. 'Room For More in Big Empty Land, But How Many?', *Age*, 27 February 1995, p. A12.
35 Davidson, K. 'No Leg to Stand on Over Greenhouse Gas', *Age*, 28 June 1997, p. B3.
36 See Kinrade, P. 'Head in the Clouds Over Greenhouse', *Age*, 20 June 1997; Colebatch, T. 'Hot Air Clouding the Global Warming Debate', *Age*, 28 June 1997, p. A35.
37 Howard, J. 'Climate Change and a Forecast of Economic Winter', *Age*, 7 October 1997, pp. 39–45.
38 Kelly, P. 'Greenhouse: Why Flat Targets Won't Work', *Australian*, 4 June 1997, p. 13.
39 Skelton, R. 'Mining Chief's Warming Challenge', *Age*, 16 October 1997, p. A12.
40 Davidson, K. 'No Leg to Stand on Over Greenhouse Gas', *Age*, 28 June 1997, p. B3.
41 Harris, S. *Environment and Sustainable Development: An Australian Social Science Perspective*, Occasional Paper, Academy of the Social Sciences, Canberra, 1993.
42 Dyer, H. 'Eco Cultures: Global Culture in the Age of Ecology', *Millennium*, 22, 3, 1993, pp. 484–504.

8 Where in the World?

1 Cited in Gordon, M. 'APEC The Next Challenge', *Weekend Australian*, 19–20 November 1994, p. 26.
2 Howard, J. 'Politics and Patriotism: A Reflection on the National Identity Debate, Address delivered at the Grand Hyatt Hotel, Melbourne, 13 December 1995.
3 See Held, D. *Democracy and the Global Order*, Polity Press, Cambridge, 1995; Hobsbawn, E. *Nations and Nationalism Since 1780*, Cambridge University Press, Cambridge, 1990.
4 Anderson, B. *Imagined Communities*, Verso, London, 1991.
5 See Cerny, P. *The Changing Architecture of Politics: Structure, Agency and the Future of the State*, Sage, London and Newbury Park, CA, 1990.
6 Hoogvelt, A. *Globalisation and the Post Colonial World: The New Political Economy of Development*, Macmillan, London, 1997.
7 Camilleri, J. and Falk, J. *The End of Sovereignty? The Politics of a Shrinking and Fragmenting World*, Edward Elgar, Aldershot, 1992; Macmillan, J. and Linklater, A. *Boundaries in Question: New Directions in International Relations*, Cassell, London, 1995.
8 Ohmae, K. *The End of the Nation State*, Free Press, New York, 1995.
9 See Dunkley, G. *The Free Trade Adventure: The Uruguay Round and Globalism – A Critique*, Melbourne University Press, Melbourne, 1997.

10 Asher, A. *Background Briefing*, ABC Radio National, 30 November 1997.

11 Panitch, L. 'Globalisation and the State', in Miliband, R. and Panitch, L. (eds), *Between Globalism and Nationalism: Socialist Register 1994*, Merlin Press, London, 1994, p. 74. (Italics in original.)

12 Dunkley, *The Free Trade Adventure*.

13 See Cable, V. 'The Diminished Nation-State: A Study in the Loss of Economic Power', *Daedalus*, 124, 2, Spring 1995, pp. 23–53; Strange, S. 'The Defective State', *Daedalus*, 124, 2, Spring 1995, pp. 55–74.

14 See, for example, James, P., Crook, S., Pakulski, J. and Waters, M. *Postmodernization: Change in Advanced Society*, Sage, London, 1992; Hinkson, J. 'The State of Postmodernity', in James, P. (ed.), *The State in Question: Transformations of the Australian State*, Allen & Unwin, Sydney, 1996.

15 See Huntington, S. *The Clash of Civilisations: The Remaking of World Order*, Simon & Schuster, New York, 1996.

16 Ibid.

17 Pieterse, J. 'Globalisation as Hybridisation', *International Sociology*, 9, 2, June 1994, p. 179.

18 Held, *Democracy and the Global Order*, p. 137.

19 Coombs, H.C. *The Return of Scarcity*, Cambridge University Press, Cambridge, 1990, p. 113–14.

20 James, P. 'As Nation and State: A Post Modern Republic Takes Shape', in James, *The State in Question*, p. 225.

21 McQueen, H. *A New Britannia*, Penguin Books, Melbourne, 1986, p. 3.

22 Catley, B. *Globalising Australian Capitalism*, Cambridge University Press, Cambridge, 1996.

23 Kelly, P. *The End of Certainty*, Allen & Unwin, Sydney, 1992.

24 Cited in Kelly, P. 'A Nation Reborn', *Weekend Australian*, 25–26 January 1997, p. 10.

25 Woolcott, R. 'Advance Australia Where?' *Weekend Australian*, 25–26 January 1997, p. 28.

26 Cited in Middleton, K., 'Keating's Good Citizen', *Age*, 27 April 1995.

27 See Kelly, *The End of Certainty*.

28 Evans, G. 'International Treaties: Their Impact on Australia', Keynote Address, International Treaties Conference, Canberra, 4 September 1995.

29 Evans, G. and Grant, B. *Australia's Foreign Relations in the World of the 1990s*, Melbourne University Press, Melbourne, 1991.

30 See Frankel, B. *From Prophets the Deserts Come*, Arena Press, Melbourne, 1992.

31 Commonwealth of Australia, *The National Interest: White Paper on Foreign Affairs and Trade*, AGPS, Canberra, 1997.

32 Cited in Sheridan, G. 'Howard's New Horizons', *Weekend Australian*, 14–15 December 1996, p. 21.

33 Cited in Gordon, M. 'John Howard's Defensive Diplomacy', *Weekend Australian*, 21–22 September 1996, p. 19.

34 Simons Report, *One Clear Objective: Poverty Reduction Through Sustainable Development*, AGPS, Canberra, 1997.

35 'A National Identity Crisis', *Economist*, 14 December 1996, p. 35.

36 See Yeatman, A. 'Multiculturalism, Globalisation and Rethinking the Social', *Australian and New Zealand Journal of Sociology*, 30, 3, 1994, pp. 247–53;

Yeatman, A. 'Women's Citizenship Claims, Labour Market Policy and Global-isation', *Australian Journal of Political Science*, 27, 1992, pp. 449–61.

37 See, for example, Hudson, W. and Bolton, G. (eds), *Creating Australia: Changing Australian History*, Allen & Unwin, Sydney, 1997; Stokes, G. (ed.), *The Politics of Identity in Australia*, Cambridge University Press, Cambridge, 1997.

38 See Jupp, J. 'Immigration and National Identity: Multiculturalism', in Stokes, G. *The Politics of Identity in Australia*, Burgman, V. and Willis, M. *Illusions of Identity: The Art of Nation*, Hale & Iremonger, Sydney, 1993; White, R. *Inventing Australia*, Allen & Unwin, Sydney, 1981.

39 Lake, M. 'Feminists Creating Citizens', Hudson and Bolton, *Creating Australia*; Grimshaw, P., Lake, M., McGrath, A. and Quartlly, M. *Creating a Nation: 1788–1900*, McPhee Gribble, Melbourne, 1994.

40 See Coombs, *The Return of Scarcity*.

41 See Sharp, N. *No Ordinary Judgement: Mabo the Murray Islander's Land Case*, Arena, Melbourne, 1994; Rowse, T. *After Mabo: Interpreting Indigenous Traditions*, Melbourne University Press, Melbourne, 1993.

42 Flanagan, R. 'Everyone Suffers in the Politics of Hate', *Age*, 3 December 1997, p. A15.

9 Alternative Strategies?

1 Peniche, S. 'From Civil Society to Continental Solidarity', *Crossroads*, November 1994, p. 16.

2 Gerbner, S. *Media Report*, ABC Radio National, 29 August 1996.

3 See, for example, Marcuse, P. 'Globalisation's Forgotten Dimension', *Polis*, 3, July 1995, pp. 42–50.

4 Held, D. 'Democracy: From City States to a Cosmopolitan Order?', *Political Studies*, XL, Special Issue, 1992, pp. 10–39.

5 See, for example, Marcuse, 'Globalisation's Forgotten Dimension'.

6 Reich, R. *The Work of Nations*, Vintage Books, New York, 1992; Sassen, S. *The Mobility of Labor and Capital: A Study in International Investment and Labor Flow*, Cambridge University Press, Cambridge, 1990.

7 Palmé Commission, *Common Security: A Programme for Disarmament*, Inde-pendent Commission on Disarmament and Security Issues, Simon & Schuster, New York, 1982; Brandt Commission, *North South, A Programme for Survival, Common Crisis*, Independent Commission on International Development Issues, 1980; Brundtland Commission, *Our Common Future*, World Commission on Environment and Development, Oxford University Press, Oxford, 1987.

8 Falk, R. 'The Making of Global Citizenship', Brecher, J., Childs, J. and Cutler, J. (eds), *Global Visions: Beyond the New World Order*, Black Rose Books, Montreal, 1993, p. 50. See also Stern Pettersson, M. 'Reading the Project, "Global Civilization: Challenges for Sovereignty, Democracy, and Security" ', *Futures*, 25, 2, 1993, pp. 123–38.

9 See Yeatman, A. *Bureaucrats, Technocrats, Femocrats*, Allen & Unwin, Sydney, 1990.

10 Falk, 'The Making of Global Citizenship', p. 50.

11 Ibid. p. 48.

12 See McKay, H. *Reinventing Australia*, Angus & Robertson, Pymble, NSW, 1993.

13 See, for example, Harvey, D. *The Condition of Post Modernity*, Polity Press, Basil Blackwell, Oxford, 1989; Beck, U. *Risk Society: Towards a New Modernity*, Sage, London, 1992.

14 See Beilharz, P. *Transforming Labor: Labour Tradition and the Labor Decade in Australia*, Cambridge University Press, Cambridge, 1994.

15 Cited in Whitlam, E. G. *The Road to Reform: Labor in Government*, 1975 Chifley Memorial Lecture, Melbourne University ALP Club, 1975, p. 6.

16 See Wiseman, J. 'The Development and Outcomes of the Victorian Social Justice Strategy', in Costar, B. and Considine, M. *Trials in Power: Cain, Kirner and Victoria 1982–1992*, Melbourne University Press, Melbourne, 1992.

17 See Beilharz, P. 'Social Justice and Social Democracy', *Australian and New Zealand Journal of Sociology*, 25, 1, May 1989, pp. 85–99.

18 Cited in Gun, M. 'Downward Envy: Why Middle Australia Hates the Poor', *Weekend Australian, Weekend Review*, 2–3 November 1996, p. 2.

19 Pusey, M. *Economic Rationalism in Canberra*, Cambridge University Press, Cambridge, 1991.

20 Cited in Hirst, M. 'No More "Po Mo" Propaganda', *Australian Higher Education Supplement*, 26 July 1995.

21 Bauman, Z. *Modernity and Ambivalence*, Polity Press, Cambridge, 1991, p. 256.

22 See, for example, Fraser, N. *Unruly Practices: Power, Discourse and Gender in Contemporary Social Theory*, Polity Press, Cambridge, 1989; Edgar, D. 'Restoring the Common Good', *Age*, 28 December 1996, p. A11.

23 Rustin, M. 'Life Beyond Liberalism', in Osborne, P. (ed.), *Socialism and the Limits of Liberalism*, Verso, London, 1991, pp. 171 and 176.

24 Korten, D. *When Corporations Rule the World*, Kumarian Press, Connecticut and Berrett Koehler, San Francisco, 1996.

25 Ekins, P. *A New World Order: Grassroots Movements for Social Change*, Routledge, London, 1992, p. 36.

26 See LeQuesne, C. *Reforming World Trade*, Oxfam, Oxford, 1996; Goncalves, R. and Goncalves, L. 'Alternatives to the World Trading System', in Cavanagh, J. Wysham, D. and Arruda, M. (eds), *Beyond Bretton Woods: Alternatives to the Global Economic Order*, Pluto Press, London, 1994; Atkinson, J. *GATT: What do the Poor Get?*, Community Aid Abroad (CAA) Background Report No. 5, CAA, Melbourne, 1994.

27 The following discussion in relation to global financial relations draws primarily on the following sources: Crotty, J. and Epstein, G. 'In Defence of Capital Controls', in Panitch, L. (ed.), *Are There Alternatives: The Socialist Register 1996*, Merlin, London, 1996; Wachtel, H. 'Taming Global Money', in Cavanagh, J., Wysham, D. and Arruda, M. *Beyond Bretton Woods*; Miller, M. 'Where is Globalization Taking Us? Why We Need a New "Bretton Woods" ', *Futures*, 27, 2, 1995, pp. 125–44; Brecher, J. 'Global Capital Mobility', *Z Papers*, 1, 2, 1992, pp. 17–21; Mendez, R. *International Public Finance: A New Perspective on Global Relations*, Oxford University Press, New York, 1992.

28 Fraser, M. 'Why Our Future is Uncertain', *Australian*, 7 January 1998, p. 10.

29 Goodman, J. and Pauly, L. 'The Obsolescence of Capital Controls? Economic Management in an Age of Global Markets', *World Politics*, 46, October 1993,

pp. 50–82; Chuppe, T., Haworth, H. and Watkins, M. 'Global Finance: Causes, Consequences and Prospects for the Future', *Global Finance Journal*, 1, 1, 1989, pp. 1–20.

30 Bienefeld, M. 'Capitalism and the Nation State in the Dog Days of the Twentieth Century', in Miliband, R. and Panitch, L. (eds), *Between Globalism and Nationalism*, Merlin Press, London, 1994, p. 102.

31 See Tobin, J. 'A Tax on International Currency Transactions', in United Nations, *Human Development Report*, 1994; Tobin, J. 'A Proposal for International Monetary Reform', *Eastern Economic Journal*, 4, 1978, pp. 153–9; Walker, M. 'Global Taxation Paying for Peace', *World Policy Journal*, X, 2, Summer 1993, pp. 7–12.

32 Chenoweth, N. and Burke, F., 'News Corp Tax Inquiry Goes Global', *Australian Financial Review*, 5 February 1998, p. 1.

33 Robertson, I. 'Globalization and Democracy: Free Trade Gives Freedom Only to Capital', *Canadian Centre for Policy Alternatives Monitor*, November 1995, p. 2.

34 Cassani, R. 'Financing Civil Society for a Global Responsibility', *Futures*, 27, 2, March 1995, pp. 215–21.

35 Crotty and Epstein, 'In Defence of Capital Controls'.

36 Roberts, S. 'Global Regulation and Trans State Organization', in Johnson, R., Taylor, P. and Watts, M. (eds), *Geographies of Global Change*, Basil Blackwell, Oxford, 1995; Peterson, M. 'Transnational Activity, International Society and World Politics', *Millennium: Journal of International Studies*, 21, 3, pp. 371–88.

37 Crotty and Epstein, 'In Defence of Capital Controls', p. 135.

38 See Sally, R. 'Multinational Enterprises, Political Economy and Institutional Theory: Domestic Embeddedness in the Context of Internationalization', *Review of International Political Economy*, 1, 1, Spring 1994, pp. 161–92.

39 Cited in Rae, H. and Reus-Smit, C. (eds), *The United Nations: Between Sovereignty and Global Governance*, Summary of the Proceedings of a Landmark International Conference, Latrobe University, July 1995, School of Politics, Latrobe University, Melbourne, 1996, p. 1.

40 Ofuatey-Kodjoe, W. 'The United Nations and the Protection of Individual and Group Rights', *International Social Science Journal*, 47, 2, June 1995, pp. 315–31.

41 See, for example, Ferris, P. (ed), *The Challenge to Intervene: A New Role for the United Nations?*, Life and Peace Institute, Upsala, Sweden, 1993; Cleveland, H. and Bloomfield, L. *Rethinking International Cooperation*, University of Minnesota Press, Minneapolis, 1988; Lillich, B. *International Human Rights: Problems of Law, Policy and Practice*, 2nd edn, Little, Brown and Company, Boston, 1991.

42 Lambert, R. and Casperz, D. 'International Labour Standards: Challenging Globalization Ideology', *Pacific Review*, 8, 4, 1995, pp. 569–88.

43 See, for example, Cavanagh, Wysham and Arruda, *Beyond Bretton Woods*.

44 Korten, D. *When Corporations Rule the World*, Kumarian Press and Berrett Koehler, Connecticut and San Francisco, 1996, p. 181.

45 Montanari, I. 'Harmonization of Social Policies and Social Regulation in the European Community', *European Journal of Political Research*, 27, 1, 1995, pp. 21–45.

46 Cited in Benchley, F. 'Dock War Could Go Global', *Australian Financial Review*, 7–8 February 1998, p. 3.

47 AFP, 'Hawke Leads Global Crusade Against Rio', *Australian Financial Review*, 9 February 1998, p. 8.

48 Sklair, L. 'Social Movements and Global Capitalism', *Sociology*, 29, 3, August 1995, pp. 495–512.

49 Cox, R. 'The Global Political Economy and Social Choice', Drache, D. and Gertler, M. (eds), *The New Era of Global Competition: State Policy and Market Power*, McGill-Queens University Press, Montreal, 1991, p. 349.

50 Pollert, A. 'The Challenge for Trade Unionism: Sectoral Change, "Poor Work" and Organising the Unorganised', in Panitch, L. (ed.), *Are There Alternatives*.

51 See, for example, Thompson, E.P. *Double Exposure*, Merlin Press, London, 1985; Barish, J. 'Co-alition Building, Post NAFTA', *Crossroads*, November 1994, pp. 23–4.

52 Lambert and Casperz, 'International Labour Standards'.

53 Atkinson, J. *APEC: Winners and Losers*, Australian Council for Overseas Aid, (ACFOA) Development Dossier 34, Community Aid Abroad (CAA) Background Report No. 7, ACFOA/CAA, Canberra and Melbourne, 1995.

54 See Evatt Foundation, *Unions 2000: A Blueprint for Trade Union Activism*, Evatt Foundation, Sydney, 1995.

10 Alternative Directions?

1 Mahon, R. 'The "New" Canadian Political Economy Revisited: Production, Space, Identity', in Jenson, J., Mahon, R. and Beinefeld, M. *Production, Space, Identity: Political Economy Faces the 21st Century*, Canadian Scholars' Press, Toronto, 1993, pp. 13–14.

2 Mlinar, Z. (ed.), *Global and Territorial Identities*, Aldershot, Avebury, 1992, p. 2.

3 Little, S. 'Back to the Future: The Networked Household in the Global Economy', Urban Research Program Working Paper No. 52, Australian National University, Canberra, March 1996.

4 Collier, R. 'Review of Seabrook's, J. *Pioneers of Change: Experiments in Creating a Humane Society*, in *International Journal of Group Tensions*, 25, 1, 1995, p. 109.

5 See, for example, Brecher, J., Childs, J. and Cutler, J. (eds), *Global Visions: Beyond the New World Order*, Black Rose Books, Montreal, 1993; Ekins, P. *A New World Order: Grassroots Movements for Social Change*, Routledge, London, 1992; Nozick, M. *No Place Like Home: Building Sustainable Communities*, Canadian Council on Social Development, Ottowa, 1992; Lipietz, A. *Towards a New Economic Order: Postfordism, Ecology and Democracy*, Polity Press, Cambridge, 1989; Costello, N., Michie, J. and Milne, S. *Beyond the Casino Economy*, Verso, London, 1989; Burns, D., Hambleton, R. and Hoggett, P. *The Politics of Decentralization*, Macmillan, New York, 1994; Dag Hammasrkjold Foundation (DHF), *Another Development: Approaches and Strategies*, DHF, Uppsala, 1977.

6 See Ife, J. *Community Development: Creating Community Alternatives*, Longman, Melbourne, 1995; Schumacher, E. *Small is Beautiful: A Study of Economics as if People Mattered*, Abacus, London, 1974; Gyford, J. *The Politics of Local Socialism*, Allen & Unwin, London, 1985; Bookchin, M. *From Urbanization to Cities: Towards a New Politics of Citizenship*, Cassell, London, 1995.

7 See, for example, Repo, M. 'The Fallacy of Community Control' in Cowley, J., Kaye, A., Mayo, M. and Thompson, M. (eds), *Community or Class Struggle*, State 1,

London, 1977; Bryson, L. and Mowbray, M. ' "Community": The Spray on Solution', *Australian Journal of Social Issues*, 16, 4, 1981 pp. 255–67; Mowbray, 'The Medicinal Properties of Localism: A Historical Perspective', Thorpe, R. and Petruchenia, J. (eds), *Community Work and Social Change*, Routledge & Kegan Paul, London, 1985.

8 Sklair, L. 'Social Movements and Global Capitalism', *Sociology*, 29, 3, August 1995, pp. 495–512.

9 Hay, C. 'Re-stating the Problem of Regulation and Re-regulating the Local State', *Economy and Society*, 24, 3, 1995, pp. 387–407.

10 Mlinar, Z. 'Local Responses to Global Change', *Annals of the American Academy*, 540, July 1995, pp. 145–57.

11 Sassoon, A. (ed.), *Women and the State: The Shifting Boundaries of Public and Private*, Hutchinson, London, 1987.

12 Mlinar, 'Local Responses to Global Change'. See also Hay, 'Re-stating the Problem of Regulation and Re-regulating the Local State'.

13 Wellman, B. and Berkowitz, S. (eds), *Social Structures: A Network Approach*, Cambridge University Press, New York, 1988.

14 See, for example, Seabrook, J. *Pioneers of Change: Experiments in Creating a Humane Society*, New World Publishers, Philadelphia, 1993.

15 Shragge, E. *Community Economic Development*, Black Rose Books, Montreal, 1993; Boothroyd, P. and Davis, C. 'Community Economic Development: Three Approaches', *Journal of Planning Education and Research*, 12, 3, 1993, pp. 230–40.

16 Pickvance, C. and Pretecaille, E. (eds), *State Restructuring and Local Power*, Pinter, London, 1991; Robertson, J. 'The Fallacy of Single Level Control: Local Economies in a Changing Global Environment', *Futures*, 25, 2, 1995, pp. 169–77; McKinsey & Co. *Lead Local, Compete Global*, McKinsey, Sydney, 1994.

17 Cooke, P. and Morgan, K. 'The Network Paradigm: New Departures in Corporate and Regional Development', *Environment and Planning D Society and Space*, 11, 1993, pp. 543–64; Trigilia, C. 'The Paradox of the Region: Economic Regulation and the Representation of Interests', *Economy and Society*, 20, 3, August 1991, pp. 306–27; McKinsey & Co. *Lead Local, Compete Global*.

18 Shuman, M. 'Lilliputian Power: A World Economy as if Communities Mattered', in Cavanagh, J., Wysham, D. and Arruda, M. (eds), *Beyond Bretton Woods: Alternatives to the Global Economic Order*, Pluto Press, London, 1994, p. 188.

19 Ibid.

20 Ibid.

21 Petrella, R. 'Europe Between Competitive Innovation and a New Social Contract', *International Social Science Journal*, 47, 1, March 1995, pp. 11–23; Barnett, R. and Cavanagh, J. 'A Global New Deal', in Cavanagh, Wysham and Arruda, *Beyond Bretton Woods*.

22 See Craig Smith, N. *Morality and the Market: Consumer Pressure for Corporate Accountability*, Routledge, London, 1990.

23 For further discussion of the Seikatsu Club, see Ekins, P. *A New World Order: Grassroots Movements for Social Change*, Routledge, London, 1992; Sklair, 'Social Movements and Global Capitalism', *Sociology*, 29, 3, August 1995, pp. 495–512; 'Seikatsu Consumers Co-operative, Co-operative Action based on "Han" ' Seikatsu Club, Tokyo, 1992.

24 Cited in Ekins, *A New World Order*, p. 132.
25 See Petrella, 'Europe Between Competitive Innovation and a New Social Contract'.
26 Eisenschitz, A. and Gough, J. *The Politics of Local Economic Policy: The Problems and Possibilities of Local Initiative*, Macmillan, London, 1993; Boothroyd, P. and Davis, C. 'Community Economic Development: Three Approaches', *Journal of Planning Education and Research*, 12, 3, 1993, pp. 230–40; Government of Canada, National Welfare Grants Program, *Community Economic Development in Canada*, Government of Canada (Human Resources Development), Ottawa, 1993; Hudson, J. and Galaway, B. (eds), *Community Economic Development*, Thompson Educational Publishing, Toronto, 1994.
27 Vaneveld, E. *Communities at Work: Lessons from Australian and OECD Experience of Employment Development Initiatives*, Brotherhood of St Laurence, Melbourne, 1998.
28 Ibid.
29 See O'Neil, K. *Signposts for Future Employment*, Brotherhood of St. Laurence, Melbourne, 1998.
30 Campbell, B. and Jaques, M. 'Goodbye to the GLC', *Marxism Today*, April 1986, pp. 6–9; Murray, R. 'Public Sector Possibilities', *Marxism Today*, July 1986, pp. 28–32.
31 Nozick, M. *No Place Like Home: Building Sustainable Communities*, Canadian Council on Social Development, Ottawa, 1992.
32 Ibid, p. 62.
33 Drache, D. and Gertler, M. (eds), *The New Era of Global Competition: State Policy and Market Power*, McGill-Queens University Press, Montreal, 1991.
34 Shragge, E. *Community Economic Development*, Black Rose Books, Montreal, 1993, p. 3.
35 See Our Local Economy (OLE), *How Can We Grow Our Local Economy With Real Meaning*, Town Hall Week 1994 Report, OLE, Toronto, 1994.
36 Nozick, *No Place Like Home*, p. 62. Note also Roberts, W., Bacher, J. and Nelson, B. *Get a Life: A Green Cure for Canada's Economic Blues*, Get a Life Publishing, Toronto, Ontario, 1994.
37 See *Good Work News*, 'The Working Centre', Kitchener, Ontario, 1994.
38 See O'Neil, *Signposts for Future Employment*.
39 Newman, L., Lyon, D. and Philp, W. *Community Economic Development: An Approach for Urban Based Economies*, Report No. 16, Institute of Urban Studies, University of Winnipeg, Canada, 1986, provides a useful overview of a wide range of CED financing mechanisms including worker investments, targeted pension funds investments, ethical investment schemes, community investment programs, community bonds, tax subsidies for non-profit and CED investments, direct public subsidies and government purchasing.
40 Quarter, J. *Canada's Social Economy*, Lorimer, Toronto, 1992, p. 163.
41 See Dahn, S. The Missing Link: A Directory of Financing Initiatives for Small Business Generated Community Economic Development (unpublished), Churchill Fellowship Report, Melbourne, 1992.
42 See Shuman, M. 'Lilliputian Power: A World Economy as if Communities Mattered', in Cavanagh, J. Wysham, D. and Arruda, M. (eds), *Beyond Bretton Woods: Alternatives to the Global Economic Order*, Pluto Press, London, 1994.

43 VanCity Community Brochure, cited in Quarter, *Canada's Social Economy*, p. 156.
44 Government of Ontario, Ministry of Municipal Affairs, *Community Loan Fund Program Handbook*, Government of Ontario, 1994.
45 Government of Ontario, Ministry of Municipal Affairs, *Community Investment Shares Program Handbook*, Government of Ontario, 1994. See also, Parsons, G. *Community Bonds: A New Approach to Community Economic Development*, Community Bonds Office, Saskatchewan Government, Regina, 1993.
46 See Mendell, M. and Evoy, L. 'Democratizing Capital: Alternative Investment Strategies', in Shragge, *Community Economic Development*.
47 Fonds de Solidarite des Travailleurs du Quebec, *Class A Shares: Seventh Edition*, FTQ, Montreal, 1990, p. 3.
48 Shragge, *Community Economic Development*.
49 Australian Council of Trade Unions (ACTU), *Superannuation: Investing in a Nation's Savings*, Paper presented to Super 2000: Investing in the Community conference, Evatt Foundation, Sydney, 1994; Toohey, B. 'Driving a Hard Bargain', *Financial Review*, 22 August 1995, p. 13; Toohey, B. 'The Politics of the Industry Super Funds', *Financial Review*, 23 August 1995, p. 13.
50 ACTU, *Superannuation: Investing in a Nation's Savings*, p. 5.
51 See Mlinar, Z. 'Local Responses to Global Change', *Annals of the American Academy*, 540, July 1995, pp. 145–57; Jacob, B., Ostroski, K. and Teune, H. (eds), *Democracy and Local Governance: Ten Empirical Studies*, Matsunaga Institute for Peace, University of Hawaii, Honolulu, 1993; Burns, D., Hambleton, R. and Hoggett, P. *The Politics of Decentralization*, Macmillan, New York, 1994.
52 See Mowbray, M. 'The Medicinal Properties of Localism'.
53 Goss, J. 'The Magic of the Mall: An Analysis of Form, Function and Meaning in the Contemporary Retail Built Environment', *Annals of the Association of American Geographers*, 83, 1993, pp. 18–47.
54 Anheier, H. and Seibel, W. (eds), *The Third Sector: Comparative Studies of Non-profit Organisations*, Walter de Gruyter, Berlin and New York, 1990; Lipietz-Pestoff, V. 'Third Sector and Co-operative Services: An Alternative to Privatization', *Journal of Consumer Policy*, 15, 1992, pp. 21–45; Salamon, L. 'On Market Failure, Voluntary Failure, and Third Party Government: Towards a Theory of Government Non-profit Relations in the Modern Welfare State', *Journal of Voluntary Action Research*, 16, 1987, pp. 20–49; Streeck, W. and Schmitter, P. *Private Interest Government: Beyond Market and State*, Sage, London, 1985; Walzer, M. *The Civil Society*, The Gunnar Myrdal Lecture, Stockholm, 1990.
55 Ekins, *A New World Order*.
56 See Brockway, S. (ed.), *Macrocosm USA: An Environmental, Political and Social Handbook with Directories*, Macrocosm USA, Cambria, California, 1995.
57 See Wainwright, M., Fairhall, D. and Vidal, J. 'Peace Women Cleared Over Jet Attack', *Guardian*, 31 July 1996, p. 1.
58 See Mittelman, J. 'The Globalisation Challenge: Surviving at the Margins', *Third World Quarterly*, 15, 3, 1994, pp. 427–43; Burgman, V. *Power and Protest: Movements for Change in Australian Society*, Allen & Unwin, St Leonards, NSW, 1993; Eder, K. *The New Politics of Class: Social Movements and Cultural Dynamics in Advanced Societies*, Sage, London, 1993; Castells, M. *The City and the Grassroots: A Cross Cultural Theory of Urban Social Movements*, Westview Press, Boulder, Co,

1983; Omvedt, G. *Reinventing Revolution: New Social Movements and the Socialist Tradition in India*, M.E. Sharpe, Armonk, 1993; Pakulski, J. *Social Movements: The Politics of Moral Protest*, Longman Cheshire, Melbourne, 1991.

59 Alpert, A. and Elliott, J. 'Maquila Menace', *Dollars and Sense*, November/December 1995, pp. 28–33.

60 See Brecher, J., Childs, J. and Cutler, J. (eds.), *Global Visions: Beyond the New World Order*, Black Rose Books, Montreal 1993; Kelly, P. *Fighting for Hope*, Chatto & Windus, London, 1984.

61 Piven, F. and Cloward, R. *Poor People's Movements: Why They Succeed, How They Fail*, Vintage, New York, 1979.

62 Sklair, L. 'Social Movements and Global Capitalism', *Sociology*, 29, 3, August 1995, p. 498.

63 Piven and Cloward, *Poor People's Movements*, p. 23 (italics in original).

64 Sklair, 'Social Movements and Global Capitalism'. See also, Gould, K., Weinberg, A. and Schnaiberg, A. 'Natural Resource Use in a Transnational Treadmill: International Agreements, National Citizenship Practices and Sustainable Development', *Humboldt Journal of Social Relations*, 21, 1, 1995, pp. 61–93.

65 Brecher, J. and Costello, T. 'Taking on the Multinationals', *Nation*, 19 December 1994, p. 760.

66 Peterson, M. 'Transnational Activity, International Society and World Politics', *Millenium: Journal of International Studies*, 21, 3, p. 376.

67 Langmore, J. and Quiggan, J. *Work for All: Full Employment in the Nineties*, Melbourne University Press, Melbourne, 1994.

68 Hamilton, C. 'Workers in the Globalised World: The End of the Post War Consensus', in ACOSS IMPACT supplement, December 1996, p. 6.

69 See Coombs, H.C. *The Return of Scarcity*, Cambridge University Press, Cambridge, 1990.

70 See Bell, S. *Ungoverning the Economy*, Oxford University Press, Melbourne, 1997.

71 Weiss, L. 'Globalization and the Myth of the Powerless State', *New Left Review*, 225, September/October 1997, p. 26.

72 Davidson, K. 'Kyoto "Triumph" is a Long Term Defeat', *Age*, 15 December 1997, p. A11.

73 *Economist*, 17 October, 1995, p. 16.

11 Conclusion

1 Curthoys, A. 'History and Identity', in Hudson, W. and Bolton, G. (eds), *Creating Australia: Changing Australian History*, Allen & Unwin, Sydney, 1997, p. 36.

2 Kelly, P. *The End of Certainty*, Allen & Unwin, Sydney, 1992, p. 2.

3 Dodson, M. 'It's Time for Justice', *Frontline*, No. 37–38, August–September 1996, p. 6.

Bibliography

Adorno, T. and Horkheimer, M. *Dialectic of Enlightenment*, trans. J. Cumming, Continuum, New York, 1972.

AFP 'Hawke Leads Global Crusade Against Rio', *Australian Financial Review*, 7–8 February 1998, p. 8.

Albo, G. 'Competitive Austerity and the Impasse of Capitalist Employment Policy', in R. Miliband and L. Panitch (eds), *Between Globalism and Nationalism: Socialist Register 1994*, Merlin Press, London, 1994.

Alpert, A. and Elliott, J. 'Maquila Menace', *Dollars and Sense*, November/December 1995, pp. 28–33.

Althusser, L. *Lenin and Philosophy and Other Essays*, New Left Books, London, 1971.

Amin, A. (ed.) *Post-Fordism: A Reader*, Basil Blackwell, Oxford, 1995.

Anderson, B. *Imagined Communities*, Verso, London, 1991.

Anderson, K. 'The GATT's Review of Australian Trade Policy', in Arndt, S. and Milner, C., *The World Economy: Global Trade Policy 1995*, Basil Blackwell, Oxford, 1995.

Anheier, H. and Seibel, W. (eds) *The Third Sector: Comparative Studies of Non-profit Organisations*, Walter de Gruyter, Berlin and New York, 1990.

Appardurai, A. *Modernity at Large: Cultural Dimensions of Globalization*, University of Minnesota Press, Minneapolis, 1997.

Arnst, C. and Edmonson, G. 'The Global Free For All', *Business Week*, 26 September 1995, p. 16.

Aronowitz, S. *Technoscience and Cyberculture*, Routledge, New York, 1996.

Atkinson, J. *APEC: Winners and Losers*, Australian Council for Overseas Aid (ACFOA) Development Dossier 34/Community Aid Abroad (CAA) Background Report No. 7, ACFOA/CAA, Canberra and Melbourne, 1995.

Atkinson, J. *GATT: What Do the Poor Get?*, Community Aid Abroad (CAA) Background Report No. 5, CAA, Melbourne, 1994.

Australian Council of Trade Unions and Trade Development Council *Australia Reconstructed: A Report by the Mission Members to the ACTU and the TDC*, AGPS, Canberra, 1987.

Australian Council of Trade Unions *Superannuation: Investing in a Nation's Savings*, Presented to Super 2000: Investing in the Community conference, Evatt Foundation, Sydney, 1994.

Australian Episcopal Conference of the Roman Catholic Church *Common Wealth for Common Good*, Collins Dove, North Blackburn, Victoria, 1992.

Australian Science and Technology Council *The Networked Nation*, AGPS, Canberra, 1994.

Barish, J. 'Co-alition Building, Post NAFTA', *Crossroads*, November 1994, pp. 23–4.

Barker, C. *Global Television: An Introduction*, Basil Blackwell, Oxford, 1997.

Barnett, R. and Cavanagh, J. 'A Global New Deal', in Cavanagh, J., Wysham, D. and Arruda, M. (eds), *Beyond Bretton Woods: Alternatives to the Global Economic Order*, Pluto Press, London, 1994.

Bauman, Z. *Modernity and Ambivalence*, Polity Press, Cambridge, 1991.

Beck, U. *The Risk Society*, Sage, London, 1989.

Beilharz, P. 'Social Democracy and Social Justice', *Australian and New Zealand Journal of Sociology*, 25, 1, May 1989, pp. 85–99.

Beilharz, P. *Transforming Labor*, Cambridge University Press, Cambridge, 1994.

Bell, S. 'The Politics of Economic Adjustment: Explaining the Transformation of Industry State Relationships in Australia', *Political Studies XLIII*, 1995, pp. 22–47.

Bell, S. and Head, B. (eds) *State, Economy and Public Policy in Australia*, Oxford University Press, Melbourne, 1994.

Bell, S. *Ungoverning the Economy*, Oxford University Press, Melbourne, 1997.

Bellchamber, G. 'Globalisation Issues: A Union Perspective', in Economic Planning Advisory Commission, *Globalisation: Issues for Australia*, AGPS, Canberra, 1995.

Benchley, F. 'Dock War Could Go Global', *Australian Financial Review*, 7–8 February 1998, p. 3.

Benjamin, W. *Illuminations*, Fontana, London, 1973.

Best, M. *The New Competition: Institutions of Industrial Restructuring*, Polity Press, Cambridge, 1990.

Bone, P. 'Room for More in Big Empty Land, But How Many?', *Age*, 27 February 1995, p. 11.

Bookchin, M. *From Urbanization to Cities: Towards a New Politics of Citizenship*, Cassell, London, 1995.

Boothroyd, P. and Davis, C. 'Community Economic Development: Three Approaches', *Journal of Planning Education and Research*, 12, 3, 1993, pp. 230–40.

Bora, B. 'The Implications of Globalisation for Australian Foreign Investment Policy', in EPAC, *Globalisation: Issues for Australia*, AGPS, Canberra, 1995.

Brah, A. 'Questions of Difference and International Feminism', in Aaron, J. and Walby, S. (eds), *Out of the Margins*, Falmer Press, London, 1991.

Brand, S. *The Media Lab: Inventing the Future at MIT*, Penguin, New York, 1988.

Brandt Commission *North South: A Programme for Survival, Common Crisis*, Independent Commission on International Development Issues, 1980.

Brants, K., Huizenga, M. and Van Meerten, R. 'The New Canals of Amsterdam: An Exercise in Local Electronic Democracy', *Media Culture and Society*, 18, 2, April 1996, pp. 233–47.

Bread for the World Institute *Hunger 1995, Seventh Annual Report on the State of World Hunger*, Bread for the World Institute, Washington, DC, October, 1996.

Brecher, J. 'Global Capital Mobility', *Z papers*, 1, 2, 1992, pp. 17–21.

Brecher, J., Childs, J. and Cutler, J. (eds) *Global Visions: Beyond the New World Order*, Black Rose Books, Montreal, 1993.

Brecher, J. 'After NAFTA: Global Village or Global Pillage?', *Nation*, December 1993, pp. 685–9.

Brecher, J. and Costello, T. 'Taking on the Multinationals', *Nation*, 19 December 1994, p. 760.

Brett, J. 'Politics and Business Parted', *Age*, 17 July 1997, p. A15.

Brett, J., Gillespie, J. and Goot, M. (eds) *Developments in Australian Politics*, Macmillan, Melbourne, 1994.

Brockway, S. (ed.) *Macrocosm USA: An Environmental, Political and Social Handbook with Directories*, Macrocosm USA Inc., Cambria, CA, 1995.

Brundtland Commission *Our Common Future*, World Commission on Environment and Development, Oxford University Press, Oxford, 1987.

Bryson, L. 'The Welfare State and Economic Adjustment', in Bell S. and Head B. (eds), *State, Economy and Public Policy in Australia*, Oxford University Press, Melbourne, 1994.

Bryson, L. and Mowbray, M. ' "Community": The Spray on Solution', *Australian Journal of Social Issues*, 16, 4, 1981, pp. 225–67.

Bryson, L. *Welfare and the State: Who Benefits?*, Macmillan, London, 1992.

Burgman, V. *Power and Protest: Movements for Change in Australian Society*, Allen & Unwin, Sydney, 1993.

Burns, D., Hambleton, R. and Hoggett, P. *The Politics of Decentralization*, Macmillan, New York, 1994.

Cable, V. 'The Diminished Nation-State: A Study in the Loss of Economic Power', *Daedalus*, 124, 2, Spring 1995, pp. 23–53.

Cain, J. *Age*, 11 April 1993, p. 8.

Camilleri, J. and Falk, J. *The End of Sovereignty? The Politics of a Shrinking and Fragmenting World*, Edward, Elgar, Aldershot, 1992.

Campbell, B. and Jaques, M. 'Goodbye to the GLC', *Marxism Today*, April 1986, pp. 6–9.

Carlyon, L. 'Ink Inc.', *Sunday Age*, 11 May 1997, p. 17.

Carroll, J. and Manne, R. *Shutdown: The Future of Economic Rationalism and How To Save Australia*, Text Publishing, Melbourne, 1992.

Carson, R. *Silent Spring*, Houghton Mifflin, Boston, 1987.

Cass, B. 'A Family Policy Audit', *Just Policy*, 6, May 1996, pp. 26–35.

Cass, B. *Income Support for the Unemployed in Australia: Towards A More Active Society*, Social Security Review Issues Paper No. 4, AGPS, Canberra, 1988

Cassani, R. 'Financing Civil Society for Global Responsibility', *Futures*, 27, 2, March 1995, pp. 215–21.

Castells, M. 'The Net and the Self: Working Notes for a Critical Theory of the Informational Society', *Critique of Anthropology*, 16, 1 March 1996, pp. 9–38.

Castells, M. *The City and the Grassroots: A Cross Cultural Theory of Urban Social Movements*, Westview Press, Boulder, Co, 1983.

Castells, M. *The Informational City*, Basil Blackwell, Oxford, 1991.

Castells, M. *The Power of Identity*, Basil Blackwell, Oxford, 1997.

Castles, F. *Australian Public Policy and Economic Vulnerability*, Allen & Unwin, Sydney, 1988.

Catley, B. *Globalising Australian Capitalism*, Cambridge University Press, Cambridge, 1996.

Cavanagh, J., Wysham, D. and Arruda, M. (eds) *Beyond Bretton Woods: Alternatives to the Global Economic Order*, Pluto Press, London, 1994.

Cerny, P. *The Changing Architecture of Politics: Structure, Agency and the Future of the State*, Sage, London, 1990.

Chadwick, P. *Media Mates: Carving Up Australia's Media*, Macmillan, Melbourne, 1989.

Chatterjee, P. and Finger, M. *The Earth Brokers*, Routledge, New York, 1994.

Chenoweth, N. and Burke, F. 'News Corp Tax Inquiry Goes Global', *Australian Financial Review*, 5 February 1998, p. 1.

Chuppe, T., Haworth, H. and Watkins, M. 'Global Finance: Causes, Consequences and Prospects for the Future, *Global Finance Journal*, 1, 1, 1989, pp. 1–20.

Cid, C. *Something's Wrong Somewhere: Globalisation, Community and the Moral Economy of the Farm Crisis*, Fernwood, Halifax, 1995.

Clark, G. 'Global Interdependence and Regional Development: Business Linkages and Corporate Governance in a World of Financial Risk', *Transnational Institute of British Geography*, 18, 1993, pp. 309–25.

Clark, G. 'Time to Challenge the Fantasy of Free Trade', *Age*, 13 July 1996, p. 29.

Cleveland, H. and Bloomfield, L. *Rethinking International Cooperation*, University of Minnesota Press, Minneapolis, 1988.

Cohen, M. 'The Return of the Robber Barons: The Dangers for Women in the New World Economy, *Refractory Girl*, 49, Spring 1995, pp. 40–6.

Colebatch, T. 'How Did the Economy Get Into This Much Trouble?', *Age*, 2 February 1995, p.15.

Colebatch, T. 'Hot Air Clouding the Global Warming Debate', *Age*, 28 June 1997, p. A35.

Colebatch, T. 'Howard Signals Hard Line on Federal Support for Industry', *Age*, 4 December 1997, p. A9.

Colebatch, T. 'The Banana Republic Threat Stays With Us', *Age*, 15 May 1996, p. 1.

Collier, R. 'Review of Seabrook, J. *Pioneers of Change: Experiments in Creating a Humane Society*', *International Journal of Group Tensions*, 25, 1, Spring 1995, pp. 103–13.

Committee on Employment Opportunities *Restoring Full Employment: A Discussion Paper*, Canberra, AGPS, 1993.

Commonwealth of Australia *Building a Competitive Australia*, AGPS, Canberra, 1991.

Commonwealth of Australia *Commission of Audit Reports*, AGPS, Canberra, 1996.

Commonwealth of Australia *Creative Nation*, AGPS, Canberra, 1995.

Commonwealth of Australia *One Nation*, AGPS, Canberra, 1992.

Commonwealth of Australia *The National Interest: White Paper on Foreign Affairs and Trade*, AGPS, Canberra, 1997.

Commonwealth of Australia *Working Nation: Policies and Programs*, AGPS, Canberra, 1994.

Connelly, M. 'Gender Matters: Global Restructuring and Adjustment', *Social Politics*, 3, 1, Spring 1996, pp. 12–31.

Cooke, P. and Morgan, K. 'The Network Paradigm: New Departures in Corporate and Regional Development', *Environment and Planning D Society and Space*, 11, 1993, pp. 543–64.

Coombs, H.C. *The Return of Scarcity*, Cambridge University Press, Cambridge, 1990.

Costa, M. and Duffy, M. *Labor Prospects and the Nineties*, Federation Press, Sydney, 1991.

Costello, N., Michie, J. and Milne, S. *Beyond the Casino Economy*, Verso, London, 1989.

Costello, P. The Menzies Lecture, Monash University, 12 November 1997.

Courvisanos, J. 'Transnational Corporate Planning and National Industrial Planning: The Case of the Ford Motor Company in Australia', *Journal of Australian Political Economy*, 34, December 1994, pp. 53–76.

Cox, R. 'Multilateralism and World Order', *Review of International Studies*, 18, 1992, pp. 161–80.

Cox, R. 'The Global Political Economy and Social Choice', in Drache, D. and Gertler, M. (eds), *The New Era of Global Competition: State Policy and Market Power*, McGill–Queens University Press, Montreal, 1991.

Craig Smith, N. *Morality and the Market: Consumer Pressure for Corporate Accountability*, Routledge, London, 1990.

Crofts, S. 'Global neighbours', in R. Allan (ed.), *To Be Continued . . . Soap Opera Around the World*, Routledge, London and New York, 1995.

Crooks. M. 'An August Budget Marriage: Australia's Conservative Parties Wed the New Right', *Just Policy*, 8, November 1996, pp. 43–6.

Crotty, J. and Epstein, G. 'In Defence of Capital Controls', in Panitch, L. (ed.), *Are There Alternatives: The Socialist Register 1996*, Merlin, London, 1996.

Cunningham, S. and Turner, G. (eds) *The Media in Australia*, 2nd edn, Allen & Unwin, Sydney, 1997.

Curthoys, A. 'History and Identity', in Hudson W. and Bolton G. (eds), *Creating Australia: Changing Australian History*, Allen & Unwin, Sydney, 1997.

da Silva, W. 'Money's Making the World Go Round', *Sunday Age*, 26 March 1996, p. 7.

Dag Hammasrkjold Foundation (DHF) *Another Development: Approaches and Strategies*, DHF, Uppsala, 1977.

Dahn, S. *The Missing Link: A Directory of Financing Initiatives for Small Business Generated Community Economic Development*, Churchill Fellowship Report, unpublished, Melbourne, 1992.

Dahrendorf, R. *Economy, Opportunity, Civil Society and Political Liberty*, in C. Hewitt de Alcantara (ed.), *Social Futures Global Visions*, Basil Blackwell/United Nations Research Institute for Social Development, Oxford, 1996, p. 24.

Dale, R. 'Global Agenda', *Time*, 13 March 1995, pp. 56–60.

Dangschat, J. and Fasenfest, D. '(Re)structuring Urban Poverty: The Impact of Globalization on its Extent and Spatial Concentration', *Research in Community Sociology*, 5, 1995, pp. 35–61.

Davidson, K. 'Kyoto "Triumph" is a Long Term Defeat', *Age*, 15 December 1997, p. 11.

Davidson, K. 'No Leg to Stand on Over Greenhouse Gas', *Age*, 28 June 1997, p. B3.

Davis, B. 'Globalisation: Who's At It?', in EPAC, *Globalisation: Issues for Australia*, AGPS, Canberra, 1995.

Dayton, L. 'Ecologist Condemns Australia's "Moronic" Greenhouse Stance', *Age*, 2 December 1997, p. A11.

De Carvalho, D. 'Budget 1996: The Re-appearing Middle', *Just Policy*, 8, November 1996, pp. 47–50.

Delaney, A. 'Working at Home on the Global Assembly Line', in Wiseman, J. (ed.), *Alternatives to Globalisation: An Asia-Pacific Perspective*, Community Aid Abroad, Melbourne, 1997.

Deleuze, G. and Guattari, F. *A Thousand Plateaus: Capitalism and Schizophrenia*, University of Minneapolis Press, Minneapolis, 1987.

Department of Industry, Science and Tourism *Investing for Growth*, AGPS, Canberra, 1997.

Deveson, I. 'The Challenge of Change for Australians, *Business Council Bulletin*, May, 1993, pp. 26–9.

Devos, S. 'Regional Integration', *OECD Observer*, 192, February/March 1995, pp. 4–7.

Dodson, M. 'It's Time For Justice', *Frontline*, 37–38, August/September 1996, p. 6.

Donner, W. and Hedges, I. 'Media Wars', *Socialism and Democracy*, 9, 1, 18, Spring 1995, pp. 139–50.

Downer, A. 'Globalisation or Globaphobia: Does Australia Have a Choice?', Speech to the National Press Club, 1 December 1997.

Drache, D. and Gertler, M. (eds) *The New Era of Global Competition: State Policy and Market Power*, McGill–Queens University Press, Montreal, 1991.

Drucker, P. *Global Shift: The Internationalization of Economic Activity*, Guilford Press, New York, 1992.

Dunkley, G. *The Free Trade Adventure: The Uruguay Round and Globalism – A Critique*, Melbourne University Press, Melbourne, 1997.

Dunning, J. (ed.) *Governments, Globalization and International Business*, Oxford University Press, New York, 1997.

Dyer, H. Eco Cultures: Global Culture in the Age of Ecology, *Millenium*, 22, 3, 1993, pp. 484–504.

Eccleston, R. 'The Wages of Inequality', *Weekend Australian*, 16–17 September 1995, p. 24.

Eckersley, R. 'Greening the Modern State', in James, P. (ed.), *The State in Question: Transformations of the Australian State*, Allen & Unwin, Sydney, 1996.

Economic Planning Advisory Commission (EPAC) *Income Distribution in Australia: Recent Trends and Research*, EPAC Paper No. 7, AGPS, Canberra, 1995.

Economic Planning Advisory Commission *Regional Trading Agreements*, Background Paper No. 40, AGPS, Canberra, 1994.

Economic Planning Advisory Commission *Shaping Our Future*, Conference Proceedings of the Commonwealth Government National Strategies Conference, AGPS, Canberra, 1995.

Economic Planning and Advisory Committee *Globalisation: Issues for Australia*, AGPS, Canberra, 1995.

Economist, 'A National Identity Crisis', *Economist*, 14 December 1996, p. 35.

Eder, K. *The New Politics of Class: Social Movements and Cultural Dynamics in Advanced Societies*, Sage, London, 1993.

Edgar, D. 'Restoring the Common Good', *Age*, 28 December 1996, p. A11.

Edwards, A. and Magarey, S. (eds) *Women in a Restructuring Australia*, Allen & Unwin, Sydney, 1995.

Eisenschitz, A. and Gough, J. *The Politics of Local Economic Policy: The Problems and Possibilities of Local Initiative*, Macmillan, London, 1993.

Ekins, P. *A New World Order: Grassroots Movements for Social Change*, Routledge, London, 1992.

Elix, D. 'Operating in a Global Environment', *Business Council Bulletin*, 120, June 1995, pp. 36–9.

Ellingsen, P. 'The Holy Grail of Higher Growth Brings Polarisation', *Age*, 4 March 1995, p. 21.

Erhlich, P. *The Population Bomb*, Pan, London, 1968.

Ernie, J. 'On the Limits of Wired Identity in the Age of Global Media', *Identities 1996*, 2, 4 April 1996, pp. 419–28.

Esping-Anderson, G. *The Three Worlds of Welfare Capitalism*, Polity Press, Cambridge, 1989.

Esteva, G. and Prakash, M. 'From Global to Local Thinking', *Ecologist*, 24, 5, 1994, pp. 162–3.

Evans, G. 'International Treaties: Their Impact on Australia', Keynote Address, International Treaties Conference, Canberra, 4 September 1995.

Evans, G. and Grant, B. *Australia's Foreign Relations in the World of the 1990s*, Melbourne University Press, Melbourne, 1991.

Evatt Foundation *The State of Australia*, Evatt Foundation, Sydney, 1996.

Evatt Foundation *Unions 2000: A Blueprint for Trade Union Activism*, Evatt Foundation, Sydney, 1995.

Ewer, P., Hampson, I., Lloyd, C., Rainford, J., Rix, S. and Smith, M. *Politics and the Accord*, Pluto Press, Sydney, 1991.

Fagan, R. and Webber, M. *Global Restructuring: The Australian Experience*, Oxford University Press, Melbourne, 1994.

Falk, R. 'The Making of Global Citizenship', in Brecher, J., Childs, J. and Cutler, J. (eds), *Global Visions: Beyond the New World Order*, Black Rose Books, Montreal, 1993.

Featherstone, M. (ed.) *Global Culture: Nationalism, Globalization and Modernity* (A Theory, Culture and Society Special Issue), Sage, London, 1990.

Ferris, P. (ed.) *The Challenge to Intervene: A New Role for the United Nations?*, Life and Peace Institute, Upsala, Sweden, 1993.

Fincher, R. and Nieuwenhuysen, N. (eds) *Australian Poverty: Then and Now*, Melbourne University Press, Melbourne, 1998.

Fist, S. *Future Telecommunications: The Price of Driving on the Information Superhighway*, Summit Paper for the Australian Consumer Council (ACC), ACC, Sydney, 1996.

Flanagan, R. 'Everyone Suffers in the Politics of Hate', *Age*, 3 December 1997, p. A15.

Flannery, T. *The Future Eaters*, Reed Books, Melbourne, 1994.

Flavin, C. 'The Legacy of Rio', in World Watch Institute, *State of the World 1997*, Earthscan, London, 1997.

Fonds de Solidarite des Travailleurs du Quebec (FTQ) *Class A Shares: Seventh Edition*, FTQ, Montreal, 1990.

Frankel, B. *From Prophets the Deserts Come*, Arena, Melbourne, 1992.

Fraser, M. 'Australia is Failing the Economic Test', *Australian*, 13 September 1995.

Fraser, M. 'Why Our Future is Uncertain', *Australian*, 7 January 1998, p. 10.

Fraser, N. *Unruly Practices: Power, Discourse and Gender in Contemporary Social Theory*, Polity Press, Cambridge, 1989.

Fukuyama, F. *Trust: The Social Virtues and the Culture of Prosperity*, Free Press, New York, 1995.

Fukuyama, F. *The End of History and the Last Man*, Penguin, London, 1992.

Garnaut, R. *Australia and the Northeast Asian Ascendancy*, AGPS, Canberra, 1989.

Gawenda, M. 'Old Fears Shape New Era', *Age*, 26 May 1997, p. A15.

Gibson, B. 'What Distinguishes Australia in the International Marketplace', *Business Council Bulletin*, 120, June 1995, pp. 68–71.

Giddens, A. *Beyond Left and Right: The Future of Radical Politics*, Polity Press, Cambridge, 1994.

Giddens, A. *The Consequences of Modernity*, Polity Press, Cambridge, 1992.

Gillespie, M. *Television, Ethnicity and Cultural Change*, Routledge, London, 1995.

Glynn, A. and Sutcliffe, B. 'Global But Leaderless? The New Capitalist Order', in Miliband, R. and Panitch, L., *Socialist Register 1992*, Merlin Press, London 1992, pp. 76–95.

Goldsworthy Report *The Global Information Economy: The Way Ahead*, Information Industries Task Force, AGPS, Canberra, 1997.

Goncalves, R. and Goncalves, L. 'Alternatives to the World Trading System', in Cavanagh, J., Wysham, D. and Arruda, M. (eds), *Beyond Bretton Woods: Alternatives to the Global Economic Order*, Pluto Press, London, 1994.

Good Work News, The Working Centre, Kitchener, Ontario, 1994.

Goodman, J. and Pauly, L. 'The Obsolescence of Capital Controls?', *World Politics*, October 1993, 50–82.

Gordon, M. 'APEC: The Next Challenge', *Weekend Australian*, 19–20 November 1994, p. 26.

Gordon, M. 'John Howard's Defensive Diplomacy', *Weekend Australian*, 21–22 September 1996, p. 19.

Gore, A. *Earth in the Balance: Ecology and the Human Spirit*, Plume, New York, 1993.

Goss, J. 'The Magic of the Mall: An Analysis of Form, Function and Meaning in the Contemporary Retail Built Environment', *Annals of the Association of American Geographers*, 83, 1993, pp. 18–47.

Gould, K., Weinberg, A. and Schnaiberg, A. 'Natural Resource Use in a Transnational Treadmill: International Agreements, National Citizenship Practices and Sustainable Development', *Humboldt Journal of Social Relations*, 21, 1, 1995, pp. 61–93.

Government of Canada, National Welfare Grants Program *Community Economic Development in Canada*, Government of Canada (Human Resources Development), Ottawa, 1993.

Gregory, R. and Hunter, B. 'The Macro Economy and the Growth of Ghettos and Urban Poverty in Australia', Discussion paper No. 25, ANU Centre for Economic Policy Research, Canberra, 1995.

Grimshaw, P., Lake, M., McGrath, A. and Quartly, M. *Creating a Nation: 1788–1900*, McPhee Gribble, Melbourne, 1994.

Grinspun, R and Cameron, M. (eds) *The Political Economy of North American Free Trade*, McGill–Queens University Press, Montreal, 1993.

Gun, M. 'Downward Envy: Why Middle Australia Hates the Poor', *Weekend Australian*, *Weekend Review*, 2–3 November 1996, p. 2.

Gupta, D. 'The Global Macro Economic Environment in the 1990s Facing Australian Corporations: An Explanation', *Australian Journal of Corporate Law*, 3, 1, 1993, pp. 89–100.

Gyford, J. *The Politics of Local Socialism*, Allen & Unwin, London, 1985.

Hamilton, C. 'Workers in the Globalised World: The End of the Post War Consensus', Australian Council of Social Services (ACOSS) Impact supplement, December 1996, p. 6.

Harding, A. 'Equity, Redistribution and the Tax Transfer System Since the Early 1980s', in Hogan, M. and Dempsey, K. (eds), *Equity and Citizenship Under Keating*, Sydney University Press, Sydney, 1995.

Harding, A. *The Suffering Middle: Trends in Income Inequality in Australia 1982 to 1993–94*, Discussion Paper No. 21, National Centre for Social and Economic Modelling, University of Canberra, Canberra, 1997.

Harris, R. 'Globalisation, Trade and Income', *Canadian Journal of Economics*, 26, 1993, p. 773.

Harris, S. 'Environment and Sustainable Development: An Australian Social Science Perspective', Occasional Paper, Academy of the Social Sciences, Canberra, 1993.

Harvey, D. *The Condition of Post Modernity*, Basil Blackwell, Oxford, 1989.

Hay, C. 'Re-stating the Problem of Regulation and Re-regulating the Local State', *Economy and Society*, 24, 3, 1995, pp. 387–407.

Hedges, I. ' Transnational Corporate Culture and Cultural Resistance', *Socialism and Democracy*, 9, 1, 18, Spring 1995, pp. 151–64.

Held, D. 'Democracy: From City States to a Cosmopolitan Order?', *Political Studies*, XL, Special Issue, 1992, pp. 10–39.

Held, D. (ed.) *States and Societies*, Martin Robertson, London, 1983.

Held, D. *Democracy and the Global Order*, Polity Press, Cambridge, 1995.

Hempel, L. *Environmental Governance: The Global Challenge*, Island Press, Washington, DC, 1995.

Hewitt, J. 'The IMF Pill May be More Curse than Cure', *Age*, 14 January 1998, p. A11.

Hill, H. and McKern, B. 'Australia', in Dunning, J. (ed.), *Governments, Globalization and International Business*, Oxford University Press, New York, 1997.

Hilmer Report *National Competition Policy*, AGPS, Canberra, 1993.

Hinkson, J. 'The State of Postmodernity', in James, P. (ed.), *The State in Question: Transformations of the Australian State*, Allen & Unwin, Sydney, 1996.

Hirst, P. and Thompson, G. 'The Problem of "Globalization": International Economic Relations, National Economic Management and the Formation of Trading Blocs', *Economy and Society*, 21, 4, November 1992, pp. 357–96.

Hirst, P. and Thompson, G. *Globalization in Question*, Polity Press, Cambridge, 1996.

Hobsbawn, E. *Nations and Nationalism Since 1780*, Cambridge University Press, Cambridge, 1990.

Hoogvelt, A. *Globalisation and the Post Colonial World: The New Political Economy of Development*, Macmillan, London, 1997.

Hope, D. 'Poverty Doesn't Spell Underclass', *Australian Magazine*, 3–4 June 1995, pp. 6–10.

Hoskins, C., McFayden, S., Finn. P. and Jackel, A. 'Film and Television Co-productions: Evidence from Canadian–European Experience', *European Journal of Communication*, 10, 2, 1995, pp. 221–43.

Houghton, J. 'Globalization: Unleashing the Power of People', *Executive Speeches*, 6, 1995, p. 3.

House of Representatives Standing Commitee on Long Term Strategies *Australia as an Information Society: Grasping New Paradigms*, AGPS, Canberra, 1991.

Howard, J. 'Climate Change and a Forecast of Economic Winter', *Age*, 7 October 1997, p. A10.

Howard, J. 'Politics and Patriotism: A Reflection on the National Identity Debate (unpublished), Address Delivered at the Grand Hyatt Hotel, Melbourne, 13 December 1995.

Hudson, J. and Galaway, B. (eds) *Community Economic Development*, Thompson Educational Publishing, Toronto, 1994.

Hudson, W. and Bolton, G. (eds) *Creating Australia: Changing Australian History*, Allen & Unwin, Sydney, 1997.

Huntington, S. *The Clash of Civilisations: The Remaking of World Order*, Simon & Schuster, New York, 1996.

Hutton, W. 'Mexico Plight Should Dent Tory Complacency', *Guardian Weekly*, 5 February 1996, p. 4.

Ife, J. *Community Development: Creating Community Alternatives*, Longman, Melbourne, 1995.

INDECS *State of Play* 8, Allen & Unwin, Sydney, 1995.

International Labor Organisation (ILO) *World Labour Report*, ILO, Geneva, 1995.

Jackson, J. 'The World Trade Organisation: Watershed Innovation or Cautious Small Step Forward?', in Arndt, S. and Milner, C., *The World Economy: Global Trade Policy 1995*, Basil Blackwell, Oxford, 1995.

Jacob, B., Ostroski, K. and Teune, H. (eds) *Democracy and Local Governance: Ten Empirical Studies*, Matsunaga Institute for Peace, University of Hawaii, Honolulu, 1993.

James, P. 'As Nation and State: A Post Modern Republic Takes Shape', in James, P. (ed.), *The State in Question: Transformations of the Australian State*, Allen & Unwin, Sydney, 1996.

James, P., Crook, S., Pakulski, J. and Waters, M. *Postmodernization: Change in Advanced Society*, Sage, London, 1992.

Jenson, J. 'Some Consequences of Economic and Political Restructuring and Readjustment', *Social Politics*, 3, 1, Spring 1996.

Johnson, H. *Dispelling the Myth of Globalization: The Case for Regionalization*, Prager, New York, 1991.

Johnston, R., Taylor, P. and Watts, M. (eds) *Geographies of Global Change*, Basil Blackwell, Oxford, 1996.

Jupp, J. 'Immigration and National Identity: Multiculturalism', in Stokes, G. (ed.), *The Politics of Identity in Australia*, Cambridge University Press, Cambridge, 1997.

Kanter, R. *When Giants Learn to Dance: Mastering the Challenges of Strategy: Management and Careers in the 1990s*, Simon & Schuster, New York, 1989.

Kasper, W. 'Advancing into the 21st Century: Visions and Challenges Facing the Downunder Economy', *Australian Economic Review*, 4th Quarter, 1992, pp. 51–64.

Keane, J. 'Structural Transformation of the Public Sphere', *Communications Review*, 11, 1, 1995. pp. 1–22.

Kearney, M. 'The Local and the Global: The Anthropology of Globalization and Transnationalism', *Annual Review of Anthropology*, 24, 1995, pp. 547–65.

Kelly, P. 'A Nation Reborn', *Weekend Australian*, 25–26 January 1997, p. 1.

Kelly, P. 'Greenhouse: Why Flat Targets Won't Work', *Australian*, 4 June 1997, p. 13.

Kelly, P. *Fighting for Hope*, Chatto & Windus, London, 1984.

Kelly, P. *The End of Certainty*, Allen & Unwin, Sydney, 1992.

Kenichi Ohmae *The End of the Nation State*, Free Press, New York, 1995.

Kennedy, D. 'GATT-astrophe', *Habitat Australia*, April 1995, pp. 42–43.

Khor, M. 'Experts Attack Shift in Global Health Strategy', *Third World Network Features*, Third World Network, Penang, 1995.

King, D. (ed.) *Culture, Globalization and the World System: Contemporary Conditions for the Representation of Identity*, Macmillan and State University of New York, Basingstoke and Binghampton, 1991.

Kinrade, P. 'Head in the Clouds Over Greenhouse', *Age*, 20 June 1997, p. 17.

Koechlin, T. 'The Globalization of Investment', *Contemporary Economic Policy*, XIII, January 1995, pp. 92–9.

Korten, D. *When Corporations Rule the World*, Kumarian Press and Berrett Koehler, Connecticut and San Francisco, 1996.

Krugman, P. and Venables, A. 'Globalization and the Inequality of Nations', *Quarterly Journal of Economics*, CX, 4, November 1995, pp. 857–80.

Lake, M. 'Feminists Creating Citizens', in Hudson, W. and Bolton, G. (eds), *Creating Australia: Changing Australian History*, Allen & Unwin, Sydney, 1997.

Lambert, R. and Casperz, D. 'International Labour Standards: Challenging Globalization Ideology', *Pacific Review*, 8, 4, 1995, pp. 569–88.

Langdale, J. 'Social and Economic Perspectives on Australia's Communications Future', *Prometheus*, 14, 1, June 1996, pp. 39–50.

Langmore, J. and Quiggan, J. *Work for All: Full Employment in the Nineties*, Melbourne University Press, Melbourne, 1994.

Lash, S. and Urry, J. *Economies of Signs and Space*, Sage, London, 1994.

Lepani, B., Freed, G., Murphy, P. and McGillivray, A. *Australia in the Global Economy*, AGPS, Canberra, 1995.

LeQuesne, C. *Reforming World Trade*, Oxfam, Oxford, 1996.

Liberal Party of Australia *Meeting the Challenges. The New Global Economy: Liberal and National Party Trade Strategies for the Future*, Liberal Party of Australia, Melbourne, 1996.

Liepitz, A. *Towards a New Economic Order: Postfordism, Ecology and Democracy*, Polity Press, Cambridge, 1989.

Lillich, B. *International Human Rights: Problems of Law, Policy and Practice*, 2nd edn, Little, Brown & Company, Boston, 1991.

Lind, M. *The Next American Nation*, Free Press, New York, 1995.

Lipshutz, R. (with Judith Mayer) *Global Civil Society and Global Environmental Governance*, State University of New York Press, Albany, NY, 1996.

Little, S. 'Back to the Future: The Networked Household in the Global Economy', Urban Research Program Working Paper No. 52, Australian National University, Canberra, March 1996.

Livingstone, C. 'The Workplace Relations Act', *Arena*, 24, August/September 1996, pp. 20–2.

Lloyd, P. 1993 'Global Integration', *Australian Economic Review*, 1st Quarter, pp. 35–48.

Lowe, P. and Dwyer, J. (eds) *International Integration of the Australian Economy*, Reserve Bank of Australia, Sydney, 1994.

Luard, E. *The Globalization of Politics: The Changed Focus of Political Action in the Modern World*, New York University Press, New York, 1990.

Lyotard, J. *The Post Modern Condition*, University of Minnesota Press, Minnesota, 1984.

MacKay, H. *Reinventing Australia*, Angus & Robertson, Sydney, 1993.

Macmillan, J. and Linklater, A. *Boundaries in Question: New Directions in International Relations*, Cassell, London, 1995.

Maguire, J. 'Sport, Identity, Politics and Globalization: Diminishing Contrasts and Increasing Varieties', *Sociology of Sport Journal*, 11, 4, December 1994, pp. 398–427.

Mahlman, J., Albritton, D. and Watson, R. *State of Scientific Understanding of Climate Change*, Office of Science and Technology Policy, Washington, DC, 1993.

Mahon, R. 'The "New" Canadian Political Economy Revisited: Production, Space, Identity', in Jenson, J., Mahon, R. and Beinefeld, M., *Production, Space, Identity: Political Economy Faces the 21st Century*, Canadian Scholars' Press, Toronto, 1993.

Mangan, P. 'World at their Feet', *Sunday Age, Sportsweek*, 16 November 1997, p. 19.

Mansfield Review *The Challenge of a Better Australian Broadcasting Corporation*, AGPS, Canberra, 1997.

Marceau, J. 'Will the Souffle Rise? Australian Business Recipes in the New World Economic Order', *Prometheus*, 10, 2, December 1992, pp. 183–203.

Marcuse, P. 'Globalisation's Forgotten Dimension', *Polis*, 3, July 1995, pp. 42-50.

Marcuse, P. 'Is Australia Different? Globalization and the New Urban Poverty', Australian Housing and Urban Research Institute, Occasional Paper No. 3, AHURI, Melbourne, 1996.

Martin, H. and Schuman, H. *The Global Trap*, Zed Books, London, 1997.

Martin Jones, D. *Political Development in Pacific Asia*, Polity Press, Cambridge, 1997.

Marx, K and Engels, F. *The Communist Manifesto*, English edn, trans. Samuel Moore, Penguin Books, Harmondsworth, 1968.

Marx, K. *The First International and After*, ed. Fernbach, D., Penguin Books, Harmondsworth, 1981.

Matas, R. 'How the Arctic's Being Poisoned', *Globe and Mail*, 27 June 1995, p. A10.

McChesney, R. 'The Internet and US Communication Policy Making in Historical and Critical Perspective, *Journal of Communications*, 46, 1, Winter 1996, pp. 98–124.

McCluhan, M. and Powers, B. *The Global Village: Transformations in World Life and Media in the 21st Century*, Oxford University Press, New York, 1989.

McKenzie, D. 'Managers Win Wage Rise Race', *Weekend Australian*, 17–18 January 1998, p. 1.

McKinsey and Co. *Lead Local Compete Global: Unlocking the Growth Potential of Australia's Regions*, Department of Housing and Regional Development, Canberra, 1994.

McQueen, H. *A New Britannia*, Penguin, Melbourne, 1986.

Meadows, D. 'Who Causes Environmental Pollution?' *International Society of Ecological Economics Newsletter*, 8 July 1995.

Mendez, R. *International Public Finance: A New Perspective on Global Relations*, Oxford University Press, New York, 1992.

Metal Trades Industry Association (MTIA) and Economic Intelligence Unit *Make or Break: A Report for the MTIA*, Economic Intelligence Unit, North Sydney, 1997.

Middleton, K. 'Keating's Good Citizen', *Age*, 27 April 1995.

Miller, M. 'Where is Globalization Taking Us? Why We Need a New "Bretton Woods" ', *Futures*, 27, 2, 1995, pp. 125–44.

Ministry of Municipal Affairs, *Community Investment Shares Program Handbook*, Government of Ontario, 1994.

Ministry of Municipal Affairs, *Community Loan Fund Program Handbook*, Government of Ontario, 1994.

Mitchell, D. 'Family Policy', in Galligan, B., McAllister, I. and Ravenhill, J. (eds), *New Developments in Australian Politics*, Macmillan, Melbourne, 1997.

Mitchell, J. 'The Nature and Government of the Global Economy', in McGrew, A., Lewis, P. et al., *Global Politics: Globalization and the Nation State*, Polity Press, Cambridge, 1992.

Mittelman 'The Globalisation Challenge: Surviving at the Margins', *Third World Quarterly*, 15, 3, 1994, pp. 427–43.

Mlinar, Z. 'Local Responses to Global Change', *Annals of the American Academy*, 540, July 1995, pp. 145–57.

Mlinar, Z. (ed.) *Global and Territorial Identities*, Aldershot, Avebury, 1992.

Morley, D. and Robins, K. *Spaces of Identity: Global Media, Electronic Landscapes and Cultural Boundaries*, Routledge, New York, 1995.

Mortimer Report *Going For Growth: Business Programs for Investment, Innovation and Export*, Department of Industry Science and Technology, Canberra, 1997.

Mowbray, M. 'The Medicinal Properties of Localism: A Historical Perspective', in Thorpe, R. and Petruchenia, J. (eds), *Community Work and Social Change*, Routledge & Kegan Paul, London, 1985.

Murphy, D. 'Lord of the Rings', *Bulletin*, 23 December 1997, pp. 23–5.

Murray, R. 'Public Sector Possibilities', *Marxism Today*, July 1986, pp. 28–32.

Neil, A. 'How King Rupert Tarnished His Crown', *Age*, 4 March 1998, p. A15.

Newman, L., Lyon, D. and Philp, W. *Community Economic Development: An Approach for Urban Based Economies*, Report No. 16, Institute of Urban Studies, University of Winnipeg, Canada, 1986.

Norberg-Hodge, H. 'Globalisation versus Community' in Goldsmith, E., Khor, M., Norberg Hodge, H. and Vandanna Shiva, et al. *The Future of Progress: Reflections on Environment and Development*, Resurgence, Devon, 1995.

Nordenstreng, K. and Schiller, H. (eds) *Beyond National Sovereignty: International Communication in the 1990s*, Ablex, Norwood, NJ, 1993.

Nozick, M. *No Place Like Home: Building Sustainable Communities*, Canadian Council on Social Development, Ottawa, 1992.

O'Hara-Deveraux, M. and Johansen, R. *Global Work: Bridging Distance, Culture and Time*, Jossey Bass Publications, San Francisco, 1994.

O'Neil, K. *Signposts for Future Employment*, Brotherhood of St. Laurence, Melbourne, 1998.

Ofuatey-Kodjoe, W. 'The United Nations and the Protection of Individual and Group Rights', *International Social Science Journal*, 47, 2, June 1995, pp. 315–31.

Okin, S. *Justice, Gender and the Family*, Basic Books, New York, 1989.

Omvedt, G. *Reinventing Revolution: New Social Movements and the Socialist Tradition in India*, M.E.Sharpe, Armonk, 1993.

Ormerod, P. 'National Competitiveness and State Intervention', *New Political Economy*, 1, 1, 1966.

Osborne, P. (ed.) *Socialism and the Limits of Liberalism*, Verso, London, 1991.

Our Local Economy (OLE), *How Can We Grow Our Local Economy With Real Meaning*, Town Hall Week 1994 Report, OLE, Toronto, 1994.

Pakulski, J. *Social Movements: The Politics of Moral Protest*, Longman Cheshire, Melbourne, 1991.

Palme Commission (Independent Commission on Disarmament and Security Issues) *Common Security: A Programme for Disarmament*, Simon & Schuster, New York, 1982.

Panitch, L. 'Globalisation and the State', in Miliband, R. and Panitch L. (eds), *Between Globalism and Nationalism: Socialist Register 1994*, Merlin Press, London, 1994.

Papadakis, E. *Politics and the Environment: the Australian Experience*, Allen & Unwin, Sydney, 1993.

Papathanassopoulous, S. 'The Fast Growing Internationalisation of Television', *Media Information Australia* 7, 1 February 1994, pp. 39–45.

Parry, G. 'The Interweaving of Foreign and Domestic Policy-Making', *Government and Opposition*, 28, 2, 1993, p. 143.

Parsons, G. *Community Bonds: A New Approach to Community Economic Development*, Community Bonds Office, Saskatchewan, 1993.

Peel, M. 'Governing the Urban Future', *Australian Rationalist*, 40, Autumn/Winter 1996, pp. 15–23.

Peet, R. *Global Capitalism: Theories of Societal Development*, London, Routledge, 1991.

Pellerin, H. 'Global Restructuring in the World Economy and Migration: The Globalization Migration Dynamics', *International Journal*, XLVIII, Spring, 1993, pp. 241–55.

Peniche, S. 'From Civil Society to Continental Solidarity', *Crossroads*, November 1994, p. 16.

Pestoff, V. 'Third Sector and Co-operative Services: An Alternative to Privatization', *Journal of Consumer Policy*, 15, 1992, pp. 21–45.

Peterson, M. 'Transnational Activity, International Society and World Politics', *Millennium: Journal of International Studies*, 21, 3, pp. 371–88.

Peterson, V. 'The Politics of Identification in the Context of Globalisation', *Women's Studies International Forum*, 19, 1/2, pp. 5–15.

Petrella, R. 'Europe Between Competitive Innovation and a New Social Contract', *International Social Science Journal*, 47, 1, March 1995, pp. 11–23.

Pettman, J. 'An International Political Economy of Sex', in Kofman, E. and Youngs, G. (eds), *Globalization Theory and Practice*, Pinter, London, 1996.

Phipps, A. and Sheen, J. 'Macroeconomic Policy and Employment Growth in Australia', *Australian Economic Review*, 1, January/March 1995, pp. 86–104.

Pickvance, C. and Pretecaille, E. (eds) *State Restructuring and Local Power*, Pinter, London, 1991.

Pieterse, J. 'Globalisation as Hybridisation', *International Sociology*, 9, 2, June 1994, pp. 161–84.

Pitchford 'A Sceptical View of Australia's Current Account and Debt Problem', *Australian Economic Review*, 2nd Quarter, 1989, pp. 5–13.

Piven, F. and Cloward, R. *Poor People's Movements: Why They Succeed, How They Fail*, Vintage, New York, 1979.

Pollert, A. 'The Challenge for Trade Unionism: Sectoral Change, "Poor Work" and Organising the Unorganised', in Panitch, L. (ed.), *Are There Alternatives: The Socialist Register 1996*, Merlin, London, 1996.

Porter, G. and Brown, J. *Global Environmental Politics*, Westview Press, Boulder, Co, 1996.

Porter, M. *Competitive Advantage of Nations*, Macmillan, London, 1990.

Poster, M. 'A Second Media Age', *Arena Journal*, New Series, 3, 1994, pp. 49–91.

Poster, M. 'Post Modern Virtualities', *Body and Society* 1, 3–4, November 1994, pp. 79–95.

Poster, M. *The Mode of Information*, Polity Press, Cambridge, 1990.

Prescott, J. 'The Challenge of the Task Ahead: Defining the Milestones, *Australian Business Council Bulletin*, May 1993, pp. 70–4.

Probert, B. 'Restructuring and Globalisation: What Do They Mean?', *Arena*, April/May 1992, p. 21.

Pryke, M. and Lee, R. 'Place Your Bets: Towards an Understanding of Globalisation, Socio-financial Engineering and Competition within a Financial Centre', *Urban Studies*, 32, 2, 1995, pp. 329–44.

Pusey, M. *Economic Rationalism in Canberra*, Cambridge University Press, Cambridge, 1991.

Quarter, J. *Canada's Social Economy*, Lorimer, Toronto, 1992.

Rae, H. and Reus-Smit, C. (eds) *The United Nations: Between Sovereignty and Global Governance*, Summary of Proceedings, July 1995, School of Politics, Latrobe University, Melbourne, 1996.

Ranald, P. *Disciplining Governments: What the MAI Would Mean for Australia*, Public Sector Research Centre (University of New South Wales and Evatt Foundation), Sydney, 1998.

Ravenhill, J. 'Australia and the Global Economy', in Bell, S. and Head, B. (eds), *State, Economy and Public Policy in Australia*, Oxford University Press, Melbourne, 1994.

Ravenhill, J. 'Foreign Economic Policies', in Galligan, B., McAllister, I. and Ravenhill, J. (eds), *New Developments in Australian Politics*, Macmillan, Melbourne, 1997.

Redclift, M. *Wasted: Counting the Costs of Global Consumption*, Earthscan, London, 1996.

Reich, R. *The Work of Nations*, Vintage Books, New York, 1992.

Repo, M. 'The Fallacy of Community Control', in Cowley, J., Kaye, A., Mayo, M. and Thompson, M. (eds), *Community or Class Struggle*, State 1, London, 1977.

Rhinesmith, S. *A Manager's Guide to Globalization*, Business One Irwin, Homewood, Ill., 1993.

Richardson, B. 'The Globalisation of BHP', in EPAC, *Globalisation: Issues for Australia*, AGPS, Canberra, 1995.

Rifkin, J. *The End of Work*, Tarcher/Putnam, New York, 1995.

Riley, M. and Mejia, R. 'Gender in the Global Trading System', *Development*, 40, 3, 1997, pp. 30–6.

Rimmer, S. *Australian Labour Market and Microeconomic Reform*, Latrobe University Press, Melbourne, 1994.

Roberts, W., Bacher, J. and Nelson, B. *Get a Life: A Green Cure for Canada's Economic Blues*, Get a Life Publishing, Toronto, 1994.

Robertson, I. 'Globalization and Democracy: Free Trade Gives Freedom Only to Capital', *Canadian Centre for Policy Alternatives Monitor*, November 1995.

Robertson, J. 'The Fallacy of Single Level Control: Local Economies in a Changing Global Environment', *Futures*, 25, 2, 1995, pp. 169–77.

Robertson, R. *Globalization: Social Theory and Culture*, Sage, London, 1992.

Robins, K. 'The New Spaces of Global Media', in Johnson, R., Taylor, P. and Watts, M. (eds), *Geographies of Global Change*, Basil Blackwell, Oxford, 1996.

Robinson, W. 'Globalisation: Nine Theses on Our Epoch', *Race and Class*, 38, 2, 1996, pp. 13–31.

Rolls, E. *They All Ran Wild*, Angus & Robertson, Sydney, 1969.

Roniger, L. 'Public Life and Globalization as Cultural Vision', *Canadian Review of Sociology and Anthropology*, 32, August 1995, pp. 259–85.

Rowe, D., Lawrence, G., Miller, T. and McKay J. 'Global Sport?: Core Concern and Peripheral Vision', *Media Culture and Society*, 16, 44, October 1994, pp. 661–75.

Rowe, W. and Schelling, V. *Memory and Modernity: Popular Culture in Latin America*, Verso, London, 1991.

Rowse, T. *After Mabo: Interpreting Indigenous Traditions*, Melbourne University Press, Melbourne, 1993.

Runyan, A. 'The Places of Women in Trading Places: Gendered Global/Regional Regimes and Internationalised Feminist Resistance', in Kofman, E. and Youngs, G. (eds), *Globalization Theory and Practice*, Pinter, London, 1996, p. 239.

Ryan, C. 'It Seemed Like a Good Idea', *Australian Financial Review*, 17–18 January 1998, p. 25.

Salamon, L. 'On Market Failure, Voluntary Failure, and Third Party Government: Towards a Theory of Government Non-profit Relations in the Modern Welfare State', *Journal of Voluntary Action Research*, 16, 1987, pp. 20–49.

Sally, R. 'Multinational Enterprises, Political Economy and Institutional Theory: Domestic Embeddedness in the Context of Internationalization', *Review of International Political Economy*, 1, 1, Spring 1994, pp. 161–92.

Salmon, I. A Business Perspective, Address to Making it Work: National Summit on the Future of Work in Australia (unpublished), Sydney, 24 May 1996.

Santamaria, B. 'Capitalism's Oligarchy', *Weekend Australian*, 2–3 March 1996, p. 26.

Sardar, Z. 'Cyberspace as the Darker Side of the West', *Futures*, 27, 7, September 1995, pp. 777–94.

Sassen, S. *The Mobility of Labor and Capital: A Study in International Investment and Labor Flow*, Cambridge University Press, Cambridge, 1990.

Sassi, S. 'Self Willed and Odd Thing Called the Net: Remarks on the Quality of the Networked World', *Nordicom Review*, 1, 1995, pp. 49–58.

Sassoon, A. (ed.) *Women and the State: The Shifting Boundaries of Public and Private*, Hutchinson, London, 1987.

Saunders, P. *Welfare and Inequality: National and International Perspectives on the Australian Welfare State*, Cambridge University Press, Cambridge, 1994.

Savva, N. 'Solar Protest Spark Fears on Security', *Age*, 21 October 1997, p. A1.

Schiller, H. 'Not Yet the Post Imperialist Era', *Critical Studies in Mass Communication*, 8, 1, March 1991, pp. 13–28.

Schiller, H. *Mass Communications and American Empire*, 2nd edn, Westview Press, Boulder, Co, 1992.

Schoon, N. 'How Greenpeace Toppled Goliath', *Vancouver Sun*, 24 June 1995.

Schumacher, E. *Small is Beautiful: A Study of Economics as if People Mattered*, Abacus, London, 1974.

Seabrook, J. 'The Cultural Pollution of the South', *Third World Network Features*, Third World Network, Penang, 1996.

Seabrook, J. *Pioneers of Change: Experiments in Creating a Humane Society*, New World Publishers, Philadelphia, 1993.

Seidman, S. (ed.) *Jurgen Habermas on Society and Politics: A Reader*, Beacon Press, Boston, 1989.

Seikatsu Consumers Co-operative, Co-operative Action based on 'Han' Seikatsu Club, Tokyo, 1992.

Sengenberger, W. 'The Role of Labour Market Regulation in Industrial Restructuring', in Standing, G. and Tokman, V. (eds), *Towards Social Adjustment: Labour Market Issues in Structural Adjustment*, International Labour Organisation, Geneva, 1991.

Sharp, N. *No Ordinary Judgement: Mabo the Murray Islander's Land Case*, Arena, Melbourne, 1994.

Shaw, M. *Civil Society and Media in Global Crises: Representing Distant Violence*, Pinter, London, 1996.

Sheridan, G. 'Howard's New Horizons', *Weekend Australian*, 14–15 December 1996, p. 21.

Sheridan, G. 'Background Tips to Reading Global Situation', *Weekend Australian*, 3 January 1995, p. 9.

Shields, P. 'State, National Identity and Media', *Peace Review*, 8, 1, March 1996, pp. 89–96.

Shragge, E. *Community Economic Development*, Black Rose Books, Montreal, 1993.

Simons Report *One Clear Objective: Poverty Reduction Through Sustainable Development*, AGPS, Canberra, 1997.

Sinclair. T. 'Passing Judgement: Credit Rating Processes as Regulatory Mechanisms of Governance in the Emerging World Order', *Review of International Political Economy*, 1, 1, Spring 1994, pp. 133–58.

Skelton, R. 'Mining Chief's Warming Challenge', *Age*, 16 October 1997, p. A12.

Sklair, L. 'Social Movements and Global Capitalism', *Sociology*, 29, 3, August 1995, pp. 495–512.

Smith, J. (ed.) *The Unique Continent*, University of Queensland Press, Brisbane, 1992.

Smith, R. 'Caught in the Current', *Time Australia*, 15 May 1995, pp. 20–4.

Soja, E. *Post Modern Geography*, Verso, London, 1989.

Spiegel, L. 'The Suburban Home Companion: Television and the Neighbourhood Ideal in Post War America', in Colimina, B. (ed.), *Sexuality and Space*, Princeton Architectural Press, Princeton, 1992.

Standing, G. 'Global Feminization through Flexible Labour', *World Development*, 17, 7, 1989, pp. 1077–95 .

Standing, G. and Tokman, V. (eds) *Towards Social Adjustment: Labour Market Issues in Structural Adjustment*, International Labour Organisation, Geneva, pp. 235–50.

State of the Environment Advisory Council, *State of the Environment 1996*, CSIRO Publishing, Melbourne, 1996.

Steketee, M. 'Decline of the Welfare State', *Weekend Australian*, 4–5 January 1997, p. 17.

Steketee, M. 'Great Deregulator Loses Faith in Markets', *Weekend Australian*, 29–30 April 1995, p. 10.

Stern Pettersson, M. 'Reading the Project, "Global Civilization: Challenges for Sovereignty, Democracy, and Security" ', *Futures*, 25, 2, 1993, pp. 123–38.

Stewardson, B. 'The Globalisation of BHP', in EPAC, Globalisation: Issues for Australia, AGPS, Canberra, 1995.

Stilwell, F. 'Wages Policy and the Accord', in Mahony, G. (ed.), *The Australian Economy Under Labor*, Allen & Unwin, Sydney, 1993.

Stilwell, F. *Economic Inequality*, Pluto, Leichhardt, NSW, 1993.

Stokes, G. (ed.) *The Politics of Identity in Australia*, Cambridge University Press, Cambridge, 1997.

Strange, S. 'The Defective State', *Daedalus*, 124, 2, Spring 1995, pp. 55–74.

Streeck, W. and Schmitter, P. *Private Interest Government: Beyond Market and State*, Sage, London, 1985.

Summons, M. 'The Competitive Edge: How We Can Compete', *Australian Business*, 27 February 1991, p. 44.

Sunday Age, Sportsweek, 'NBA Out to Conquer the World', 16 November 1997, p. 3.

Sweeney, S. 'What is the "New Labor Internationalism"? Comments on Upward Harmonization, Social Charters and Globalization from Below', Paper Presented to the Sixteenth Annual North American Labor History Conference on International and Comparative Labor History, Wayne State University Detroit, 27–29 October 1994.

Taylor, A. *Choosing Our Future: A Practical Politics of the Environment*, Routledge, London, 1994.

Taylor, P. *World Geography, World Economy, Nation State and Locality*, Longman, 1989.

Thompson, E.P. *Double Exposure*, Merlin Press, London, 1985.

Thompson, J. *The Media and Modernity*, Stanford University Press, Stanford, Ca, 1995.

Thrift, N. 'A Hyperactive World' in Johnson, R., Taylor, P. and Watts, M. (eds), *Geographies of Global Change*, Basil Blackwell, Oxford, 1995.

Thurow, L. *Head to Head: The Coming Economic Battle Among Japan, Europe and America*, Allen & Unwin, Sydney, 1992.

Thurow, L. *The Future of Capitalism*, Allen & Unwin, Sydney, 1996.

Time Magazine, Special Issue on 'Our Precious Planet', November 1997.

Tobin, J. 'A Proposal for International Monetary Reform', *Eastern Economic Journal*, 4, 1978, pp. 153–9.

Tobin, J. 'A Tax on International Currency Transactions', in United Nations, *Human Development Report*, 1994.

Toohey, B. 'Banks Uneasy over IMF Asia Campaign', *Financial Review*, 9 December 1997, p. 19.

Toohey, B. 'Driving a Hard Bargain', *Financial Review*, 22 August 1995, p. 13.

Toohey, B. 'The Politics of the Industry Super Funds', *Financial Review*, 23 August 1995, p. 13.

Travers, P. and Richardson, S. *Living Decently: Material Well-being in Australia*, Oxford University Press, Melbourne, 1993.

Trebing, H. and Estabrooks, M. 'The Globalisation of Telecommunications: A Study in the Struggle to Control Markets and Technology', *Journal of Economic Issues*, xxix, 2, June 1995.

Trigilia, C. 'The Paradox of the Region: Economic Regulation and the Representation of Interests', *Economy and Society*, 20, 3, August 1991, pp. 306–27.

Troy, P. *The Perils of Urban Consolidation*, Federation Press, Sydney, 1996.

United Nations Department for Policy Co-ordination and Sustainable Development *Women in a Changing Global Economy*, United Nations, New York, 1994.

United Nations Research Institute for Social Development and United Nations Development Program (UNRISD/UNDP) *Adjustment, Globalisation and Social Development*, UNRISD, New York, 1995.

United Nations Research Institute for Social Development *States of Disarray: The Social Effects of Globalization*, Banson, London, 1995.

Van Boven, T. The International Human Rights Agenda: A Challenge to the United Nations (mimeo), University of Limburgh, Maastricht, 1989.

Van Liemt, G. 'Economic Globalisation: Labour Options and Business Strategies in High Labour Cost Countries', *International Labour Review*, 131, 4–5, 1992, pp. 453–70.

Van Parijs, P. (ed.) *Arguing for A Basic Income*, London, Verso, 1992.

Vaneveld, E. *Communities at Work: Lessons from Australian and OECD Experience of Employment Development Initiatives*, Brotherhood of St Laurence, Melbourne, 1998.

Vines, D. 'Unfinished Business: Australian Protectionism, Australian Trade Liberalisation and APEC', *Australian Economic Review*, 1st Quarter, 1995, pp. 35–52.

Vogler, J. 'Regimes and the Global Commons: Space, Atmosphere and Oceans', in McGrew, A., Lewis, P. et al. *Global Politics*, Polity Press, Cambridge, 1992.

Wachtel, H. 'Taming Global Money', in Cavanagh, J., Wysham, D. and Arruda, M. (eds), *Beyond Bretton Woods: Alternatives to the Global Economic Order*, Pluto Press, London, 1994.

Wainwright, M., Fairhall, D. and Vidal, J. 'Peace Women Cleared Over Jet Attack', *Guardian*, 31 July 1996, p. 1.

Walker, D. 'Why Selling Telstra Doesn't Matter', *Age*, 8 June 1996 p. A23.

Walker, K. *The Political Economy of Environmental Policy: An Australian Introduction*, University of New South Wales Press, Sydney, 1994.

Walker, M. 'Global Taxation Paying for Peace', *World Policy Journal*, X, 2, Summer, 1993, pp. 7–12.

Walker, M. 'Poor Jump to 30% of Population', *Age*, 14 March 1998, p. 30.

Wallace, I. *The Global Economic System*, Unwin Hyman, London and Boston, 1990.

Wallerstein, I. *The Modern World System II*, Academic, New York, 1980.

Walzer, M. *The Civil Society*, The Gunnar Myrdal Lecture, Stockholm, 1990.

Waters, M. *Globalization*, Routledge, London, 1995.

Watson, B. *Commentary*, No. 10, 1995, p. 13.

Watts, R. 'Dancing to Whose Tune? The Future of Work: Employment and Australian Government Policy, 1983–1997', Paper Delivered to South West Sydney Community Sector Conference, Bankstown, 26–27 November 1997.

Watts, R. *The Foundations of the National Welfare State*, Allen & Unwin, Sydney, 1987.

Weiss, L. 'Globalization and the Myth of the Powerless State', *New Left Review*, 225, September/October 1997, pp. 26.

Wellman, B. and Berkowitz, S. (eds) *Social Structures: A Network Approach*, Cambridge University Press, New York, 1988.

White, R. *Inventing Australia*, Allen & Unwin, Sydney, 1981.

Whitlam, E.G. *The Road to Reform: Labor in Government*, Chifley Memorial Lecture, Melbourne University ALP Club, 1975.

Whitlam, E.G. 'A Tribute to the Modest Member', Address to the Centre for Independent Studies, Bert Kelly Lecture Series, Sydney, 1997.

Williamson, R. and Ceretig, M. 'Salmon Free for all Left Stocks in Peril', *Globe and Mail*, 8 October 1994.

Wiseman, J. 'The Development and Outcomes of the Victorian Social Justice Strategy', in Costar, B. and Considine, M. (eds), *Trials in Power: Cain, Kirner and Victoria 1982–1992*, Melbourne University Press, Melbourne, 1992.

Wiseman, J. (ed.) *Alternatives to Globalisation: An Asia-Pacific Perspective*, Community Aid Abroad, Melbourne, 1997.

Woolcott, R. 'Advance Australia Where?', *Weekend Australian*, 25–26 January 1997, p. 28.

World Wildlife Fund (WWF) *State of the Climate*, WWF, London, 1997.

Yearley, S. *Sociology, Environmentalism, Globalisation*, Sage, London, 1996.

Yeatman, A. 'Multiculturalism, Globalisation and Rethinking the Social', *Australian and New Zealand Journal of Sociology*, 30, 3, 1994, pp. 247–53.

Yeatman, A. 'Women's Citizenship Claims, Labour Market Policy and Globalisation'. *Australian Journal of Political Science*, 27, 1992, pp. 449–61.

Yeatman, A. *Bureaucrats, Technocrats, Femocrats*, Allen & Unwin, Sydney, 1990.

Yetton, P., Davis, J. and Swan, P. *Going International: Export Myths and Strategic Realities*, Report to the Australian Manufacturing Council, Sydney, 1992.

Yoshiko Kurisaki. 'Globalization or regionalization? An Observation of Current PTO Activities', *Telecommunications Policy*, December 1993, pp. 699–706.

Zarsky, L. 'APEC and the Environment', Presentation to Conference on Taking Australia into Asia: Trade, Investment and Human Rights, Community Aid Abroad, 23 February 1996.

Zia Qureshi 'Globalisation: New Opportunities, Tough Challenges', *Finance and Development*, 33, March 1996, pp. 30–3.

Zimmerman, L. 'Globalisation: Can Australia Compete?, *Practising Manager*, October 1991, 11, 3, pp. 21–8.

Index